URBAN RAMBLES

*20 Glorious walks
through English cities*

Nicholas Rudd-Jones

Contents

Rus in Urbe

The importance of nature in Rome was seen as twofold: as a mark of civilisation and as a promoter of health and well-being. The Romans coined the phrase 'rus in urbe' to describe it.

The Romans were the first to recognise the benefits of rural features within a city; from the Campus Martius transformed into plush parkland by Emperor Augustus to the *'horti'* – urban villas within a park – created by wealthy citizens. Nero's palatial Domus Aurea incorporated the cultivated and the untamed simultaneously, housing a multitude of wild and domestic animals, vineyards and tilled lands, offset by the rural seclusion of woods and open ground.

'Rus in urbe' – the country in the city – has subsequently been used in Britain to refer to country features created in towns or cities. A thousand newspaper articles today use it as shorthand to describe a desirable new green feature that is proposed or that needs protection in a city. It has become the go-to phrase of green space cognoscenti. It was the phrase that inspired this book.

The invention of the London square

In Britain, the benefits of green spaces in towns were first recognised in the early seventeenth century, when a Commission on Buildings was established to oversee the development of Lincoln's Inn Fields, one of the first planned green spaces in the country.

The aim was to ensure that Lincoln's Inn Fields was set out with 'faire and goodlye walks, [which] would be a matter of great ornament to the Citie, pleasure and freshness for the health and recreation of the Inhabitants thereabout, and for the sight and delight of Embassadors and Strangers coming to our Court and Cittie'.

The desirability of 'rus in urbe' was soon taken up with enthusiasm by the British aristocracy as they began to create estates in London. St James's Square was enclosed in 1726, allowing residents 'to clean, repair, adorn and beautify the same, in a becoming and graceful manner'. Charles Bridgeman, the landscape gardener, was employed to create the 'illusion'. Many squares followed, providing the chance for a spot of tranquillity, fresh air and a reminder of the residents' country estates.

Left *Rus* is very nearly as much as *urbe* in London, green space accounting for 47 per cent of London's surface area

'I want the town to be impregnated with the beauty of the country, and the country with the intelligence and vivid life of the town' WILLIAM MORRIS

The pernicious effect of industrialisation

The square was an enclave usually only accessible to wealthy neighbours. As industrialisation took hold in the nineteenth century, so the gap between town and country grew greater, and the dividing lines became still more entrenched. Explosive population growth and squalid living conditions led to a crisis of the working class in cities.

It was not until the 1830s that things began to change with, among other welfare acts, the publication of the Report of the Select Commission on Public Walks, advocating the provision of public parks in cities as an important factor in improving urban living standards. By the end of the century, every city had at least one municipal park. And towards the end of the nineteenth century visionaries were starting to think about how altogether more pleasant cities could be created. William Morris, in *News from Nowhere* (1890), a utopian vision, has his observer wake, and finds himself in the London of the twenty-first century. This is what he imagines: 'The soap-works with their smoke-vomiting chimneys were gone; the engineer's works gone; the leadworks gone; and no sound of riveting and hammering came down the west wind ... I opened my eyes to the sunlight again and looked round me, and cried out among the whispering trees and odorous blossoms, "Trafalgar Square!"'

But the divide between town and country persisted, and perhaps grew even stronger in the inter-war years as aspirations grew and people became more frustrated by the political order. The political emphasis in this period was on housing – the Housing Act of 1919 pledged 500,000 'homes fit for heroes', within three years – and inevitably this was also the period of the rapid growth of the suburb as people strove to escape the confines of city squalor and start a new life with more space and amenities.

The immediate post-war years, 1945-50, were a time of immense social change. As well as the growing provision for health for everyone – the NHS was founded in 1947 – it was also a golden era for the outdoors, with the Act of Parliament to establish National Parks passed in 1949.

The Green Belt, encircling a dozen of our larger cities, also emerged out of this furnace of social revolution and remains intact to this day. There was a strong desire to avoid further urban sprawl, along the lines that was being witnessed in American cities; and to that end the Town & Country Planning Act was passed in 1947, allowing local authorities to include green belt proposals in their development plans. As the campaigning journalist Ian Nairn so memorably remarked in 1966: 'When the green belt came into force, the outward swell of building stopped dead ... there is a terrifying forty miles of solid brickwork behind those demure-looking semis two fields away. You feel as Canute might have on the beach, but unexpectedly successful.'

The Clean Air Act of 1956 made it much more pleasant to be outside in cities. In response to London's Great Smog of 1952, with fog so thick it killed more than 10,000 people and on occasion stopped trains, cars and public events, the government introduced a number of measures to reduce air pollution, especially by introducing 'smoke control areas' in which only smokeless fuels could be burnt.

But the need for rapid homebuilding to replace the war damage, the growth in traffic and its associated safety risks, and a planning doctrine which manifested the view that motorists and pedestrians should be segregated through the use of flyovers, clearways and gyratory systems, all dramatically reduced the pleasure and ease of walking through cities.

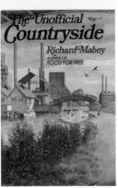

Far left *Traffic in Towns* advocated the separation of cars from walkers, with cars in the ascendancy

Left *The Unofficial Countryside* finally changed the perceptions of city versus country

Above London's dense smog made city walking very undesirable

The fight back begins

Ian Nairn began his famous fight back against this tide of traffic-justified despoliation in the Outrage issue of the *Architectural Review* in 1956, in which he attacked post-war planners' destruction of Britain. But it was not until the 1980s that cities began to emerge from these dead-end policies that so blighted their centres, making them most unwelcoming places to walk through.

The defining work of literature that changed perceptions of city versus country was Richard Mabey's *The Unofficial Countryside*, published in 1973. In it he writes: 'Our attitude to nature is a strangely contradictory blend of romanticism and gloom. We imagine it to 'belong' in those watercolour landscapes where most of us would also like to live. If we are looking for wildlife we turn automatically towards the official countryside, towards the great set-pieces of forests and moor. If the truth be told, the needs of the natural world are more prosaic than this. A crack in the pavement is all a plant needs to put down roots. Provided it is not actually contaminated, there is scarcely a nook or cranny anywhere which does not provide the right living conditions for some plant or creature. There are twice as many birds per acre in urban areas as there are in most of the countryside.'

City walking becomes cool . . .

Following hot on the heels of *The Unofficial Countryside* came a whole new genre of writing about walking through cities; most notably Ian Sinclair's *Lights Out for the Territory* (1997) and his walk around the M25 *London Orbital* (2002). This genre of writing is often labelled 'psychogeography', a way of exploring cities designed to jolt the walker into a new awareness of the urban landscape and popularised by Will Self in his newspaper column of the same name in the *Independent*.

But also, the 'mainstream' appreciation of walking in cities was becoming just as important. The Green London Way, formed in 1991, is a different way of looking at London: a walking route of over 110 miles encircling the capital, the first long-distance footpath around London and one of the very first entirely urban long-distance footpaths in the country. In the words of Bob Gilbert, its creator: 'What was once regarded as a rather cranky idea has now been enthusiastically embraced – including by some of those who rejected it at the time. It marks a change in attitude, an acceptance of a different sort of landscape, and a realisation of the richness that an urban exploration has to offer.'

But perhaps the most significant factor during this period was the switch in employment from manual to office work. Manufacturing collapsed in cities between the 1970s and the 1990s, which had two beneficial side-effects – the greater focus that became possible on the environment, and the regeneration of large open spaces that had previously been industrialised. A revolution in city planning finally took place.

The green and walkable city emerges

English cities are now going through a truly transformative phase, making them much more appealing places to walk through than ever before.

As a result, none of our cities looks anything like it did a generation ago in terms of visual and walker appeal. Take the South Bank in London, for example: it was a bleak zone that you passed through as quickly as possible to get to the National Theatre or to Waterloo station; now it is teeming with life and walkers. The docklands area in Liverpool is now full of visitors and night-time activity. Almost all English cities are finally casting off the shackles of the motor car and establishing shared outdoor living spaces that bring them to life and create a buzz of well-being and creativity.

National bodies have played an important role in this transition:

- The National Lottery has spent an astonishing £850 million on restoring parks and green spaces in cities; this has been matched by time and money from councils and community groups.
- The National Trust has announced a new strategy that focuses less on historic country houses and more on urban green spaces.

This shift in thinking has been underpinned by popular movements around the world:

- The 'Ciclovia' – car-free days in major cities, where the people reclaim the streets (Paris has one, and the Champs–Élysées is typically thronged with thrilled pedestrians).
- 'Critical Mass' gatherings of bicycle riders dense enough to occupy a piece of road to the exclusion of motorised vehicles.
- Urban spaces repurposed for leisure e.g. urban beaches, concert venues.
- Art installations along walking routes – fountains, water features, sculpture trails.
- Ambitious extension of car-free zones: Oslo will be car-free in the city centre from 2019.
- The creation of new 'green spaces' which become huge attractions, e.g. the High Line in New York.

And the health benefits have become much more valued:

- Recognition that green spaces are a crucial part of a healthy human habitat, in an age of obesity and increased mental stress.
- A growing appreciation of the calming and restorative powers of nature, especially trees, amid a city.

Most importantly, city planning attitudes have fundamentally changed:

- A key thrust of city planning nowadays is to re-connect cities: Linking Lincoln, Connecting Leicester etc.
- The post-war consensus, that traffic was the biggest challenge that a city faced and that it should be given priority over pedestrians, has been broken.
- 'Smarter' public transport is helping the cause – passes, alerts, on-call, free wifi, public bikes etc.
- More restrictions are being placed on cars – congestion charges, lower speed limits, car-free zones (and of course the driverless car is on the horizon, perhaps heralding the end of mass private car ownership).
- Policies to encourage the re-habitation of city centres in favour of the suburbs are creating locals who care about their environment.
- And councils are actively encouraging much more street life, by promoting festivals, street fairs etc.

But a note of caution: recent council funding cuts have meant that the upkeep of parks and green spaces has been drastically reduced in recent years, and the great work achieved in the last generation is in danger of going into reverse. We can all do our bit here in terms of campaigning and supporting our local 'Friends of the Park' groups that do so much to maintain the vitality and viability of green spaces.

The first half of the twenty-first century can be the time when cities are recreated as they were in the days of the first Greek and Roman cities – public spaces for citizens to share and enjoy. This book is intended as a contribution to that process.

Rus

A major feature of our urban rambles is that wherever possible we choose a route that maximises time spent in urban green spaces. But before we set out, let's pause a moment to find out more about their origins.

The traditional square

In the seventeenth century, open areas between terraces were created as part of a Royal mandate designed to enhance the rural character of the setting. James I created a special commission on the matter, which in 1615 affirmed his policy of transforming London into a 'truly magnificent city comparable to the Rome of the Emperor Augustus'.

But by the 1720s many of these open areas had become choked with rubbish and were the focus of crime and antisocial behaviour. Thomas Fairchild, who ran a nursery off Hoxton Square, wrote in *The City Gardener* (1722) about how to lay out London squares in a 'Rural Manner': 'I think some sort of wilderness-work will do much better, and divert the Gentry better than looking out of their Windows on an open Figure.'

In 1726 the St James's Square Enclosure Act was passed, granting a board of trustees the power to make a regular charge on residents to 'clean, repair, adorn and

beautify' the square. This was a turning point, the 'creation moment' of the aesthetic value of green spaces in English cities, and many other squares followed suit.

By the early nineteenth century, Hermann von Pückler-Muskau reflected on the image of the square we have become accustomed to seeing in costume dramas: 'Country and town in the same spot is a charming idea. Fancy yourself in an extensive quadrangular area surrounded by the finest houses, and in the midst of it beautiful plantations, with walks, shrubberies, and parterres of fragrant flowers.'

By the start of the twentieth century there were over 200 town squares in the capital, but most of them were enclosed and only accessible to the local residents who held a key. It took a war to open them up to the public: as part of the Second World War effort almost every square was stripped of its metal railings, which were melted down as scrap iron. Several squares also became part of the 'Dig for Victory' campaign and were turned into temporary allotments. Access today is much better than it was, but there are still many squares that are private. Squares outside the capital seem to do much better in this respect.

Left St James's Square was subject to one of the first city Enclosure Acts in 1726

Five finest traditional squares on our walks:
- Queen Square, Bath (1728)
- Queen Square, Bristol (1727)
- Queen Square (1710) and Park Square, Leeds (1710)
- Abercromby Square, Liverpool (1820s)

The lifestyle square

In recent years, the 'lifestyle square' has emerged, a re-interpretation and expansion of what the traditional square of old had to offer – a public space, a place to relax or enjoy an open-air performance, often with a food arcade and a modern 'urban edge' in the form of public art, water features (often) and large reflective silver balls (almost always). They are rather like the old 'pleasure gardens' of the seventeenth to the nineteenth centuries, two of which we pass through on our walks – Sydney Gardens in Bath and St Ann's Well Gardens in Brighton, both in their day full of exotic surprises.

Five finest lifestyle squares on our walks:
- Central Square, Brindleyplace, Birmingham (1995)
- Millennium Square, Bristol (2000)
- Leeds Millennium Square (2000) ③
- Granary Square (2014), London I
- Sheldon Square (2014), London IV

The royal park

London's Royal Parks are lands originally owned for the recreation of the Royal Family. They are part of the hereditary possessions of the Crown. Starting in 1845 with Regent's Park, they were opened to the public on a grace and favour basis. There are eight parks that cover almost 2,000 hectares (4,900 acres) of land in Greater London: Bushy Park, Green Park, Greenwich Park, Hyde Park, Kensington Gardens, Regent's Park, Richmond Park and St James's Park.

The municipal park

Derby Arboretum, opened in 1840, is generally accepted as Britain's first public park. It was the inspiration of a wealthy local textile manufacturer and philanthropist,

Joseph Strutt. In his words, 'As the sun has shone brightly on me through life, it would be ungrateful in me not to employ a portion of the fortune which I possess to offer the inhabitants of the town the opportunity of enjoying, with their families, *exercise*, and recreation in the fresh air, in public walks and grounds devoted to that purpose.' By the outbreak of the First World War, there were around 27,000 urban public parks in the UK, and they were highly valued by the population.

In both wars, but much more in the Second World War, they were used as a vital war resource, often combining many roles – an area for cultivation, air raid shelters, anti-aircraft guns and military installations. Inevitably this often left them in a dilapidated state, and post-war re-building efforts focussed on housing; the situation became worse in the 1960s and 1970s as park funding was cut back still further. This led to the closure of facilities such as cafés and toilets, a reduction in policing and management and the creation of banal, low-maintenance landscapes. It was really not until the mid-1990s that campaigning groups – notably the Open Spaces Society, the Garden History Society and the Victorian Society – started to change attitudes.

But the real game-changer was the Heritage Lottery Fund. So many of the parks that we walk through have been renovated and improved thanks to Lottery funds, usually with matched funds from councils and other bodies. This has truly enhanced the urban landscape and been a key factor in the much-enhanced city walking experience in the last decade or so. The challenge is now to maintain adequate funding to keep them in good order and secure, particularly in an era of renewed council cutbacks.

Five finest municipal parks on our walks:
- Victoria Park (1880s), Bristol
- Princes Park (1843) and Sefton Park (1872), Liverpool
- Victoria Park, London I (1845) ①
- Devonport Park (1850s), Plymouth

The campus

Campuses are designed to create peace and harmony around a seat of learning. The word originates with Augustus's Campus Martius (fields of Mars) and was first used in the eighteenth century to describe the grounds of Princeton University. In the twentieth century the term was adopted by the new post-war British universities like Leeds ②, and in many ways the campus became a more contemporary, open and inclusive version of the 'closed' collegiate court. Nature is implicitly felt to be a good environment for untrammelled thinking.

The botanic garden

The first botanic garden was founded in Oxford in 1621 with the mission 'to promote the furtherance of learning and to glorify nature'. Edinburgh followed in 1670, the Chelsea Physic Garden in 1673, Glasgow in 1705, Kew in 1753 and Cambridge in 1760. The high point for botanic gardens was the first half of the nineteenth century, when seventeen were founded across the country.

Whilst the early gardens were mostly linked to institutions and designed to provide living material for the study of botany, the Victorian gardens were usually privately funded – and, in addition to the botanical collections, they also included ornamental features designed for recreational use and pleasure. This shift to recreational use has been still greater in recent years with the need to generate funds, with events including music, art exhibitions, special botanical exhibitions, theatre and film.

Five finest botanic gardens on our walks:
- Botanical Gardens, Bath (1887)
- Cambridge University Botanic Garden (1831; original site 1760) ④
- University of Oxford Botanic Garden (1621)
- Sheffield Botanical Gardens (1836)
- Museum Gardens, York (1830s, now a park)

Allotments ⑤

Allotments existed for hundreds of years, with evidence pointing back to Anglo-Saxon times. But the system we recognise today has its roots in the nineteenth century, when land was given over to the labouring poor for the provision of food growing as compensation for loss of commoners' rights during the onset of enclosure. The General Enclosure Act of 1845 and later amendments attempted to provide better protection for the interests of small proprietors and the public. There is no set standard size, but the most common plot is ten rods, an old measurement equivalent to 302 square yards, judged to be of sufficient size to meet the needs of a family. Local authorities cannot sell off or convert allotments without ministerial consent.

The biggest spur to allotments in the twentieth century was undoubtedly wartime food shortages; their use to support the war effort was enshrined in the Defence of the Realm Act (DORA) in the First World War and the 'Dig for Victory' campaign in the Second, which encouraged full use of existing allotments and created many new ones, including temporary ones on playing fields and in parks.

Today allotments are very fashionable with the shift to organic produce and sustainability, and the advent of celebrity chefs who are happy to film in the scenic surrounds of an allotment. There are estimated to be 330,000 plots in the UK, with current demand for a further 90,000 plots. The National Allotment Society campaigns for the development and protection of allotments.

Cemeteries

The key spur to the creation of cemeteries was the Public Health Act of 1848 that sought to improve sanitary conditions and public health in Britain's rapidly expanding towns, including the ending of burials in town churches and chapels that were becoming dangerously over-full.

Cemeteries were established on the edge of towns away from heavily populated areas and were often municipally owned or run by their own corporations, and thus independent from churches and their churchyards.

Non-conformists were often the driving force behind the development of these early cemeteries as it meant that they could break free from the Church of England's grip over church burials.

One of the first, the Rosary Cemetery in Norwich, was opened in 1819 as a burial ground for all religious backgrounds. Similar private non-denominational cemeteries were established near industrialising towns with growing populations, such as Manchester (1821) and Liverpool (1825). The best known in London were the seven 'garden cemeteries', later dubbed the 'Magnificent Seven', which comprised Kensal Green, West Norwood, Highgate, Abney Park, Nunhead, Brompton and Tower Hamlets cemeteries.

The heyday of these cemeteries lasted until the death of Queen Victoria, after which there was a move away from funereal ostentation, shaken further by the vast casualties of the First World War. As people spent less on their burials and more people were cremated, so these great Victorian cemeteries began a slow but steady decline. According to Darren Beach, 'Many became badly neglected and developed into a bizarre form of urban forestry as they passed in and out of public, private and eventually council ownership. Several began to resemble overgrown gardens, with trees, ivy and shrubs allowed to run riot among the rows of headstones.'

But in many ways, this is the appeal of the urban cemetery, nature running wild, full of butterflies, insects and birds and a history story around every corner, often a non-conformist family that has done their bit in making the city more prosperous or worthy. You get a great sense of the sheer effort and belief of our Victorian ancestors. For me, urban cemeteries have been the biggest single discovery of urban rambling.

Five finest cemeteries on our walks:
- Rosary Cemetery, Norwich (1819)
- General Cemetery, Sheffield (1836)
- Arnos Vale Cemetery, Bristol (1837)
- Warstone Lane Cemetery, Birmingham (1847) (6)
- Smallcombe Cemetery, Bath (1856)

Churchyards

In the words of the Church of England, 'A churchyard is much more than a garden around a church. It is a burial ground, but also a place of quiet reflection and recreation, a habitat for rare plant and animal species, and the setting of the church building.' Taken together, churchyards make up a significant area of land that has survived almost untouched by intensive agriculture and urban development over the centuries.

Richard Mabey writes in *The Unofficial Countryside*, 'Churches and churchyards are double-strength sanctuaries for wildlife. They provide a refuge not just because of their mature trees and stonework, but because even the wiliest schoolboy nester would think twice before pinching jackdaw's eggs from under the sexton's nose. The age and continuity of use of churchyards also gives them a chance to build up stable communities of plants.'

Five finest churchyards on our walks:
- St Nicholas Rest Gardens, Brighton
- St Clement's Churchyard, Cambridge
- St Andrew's Churchyard and St Nicholas Church Gardens, Liverpool
- St Pancras Churchyard, London IV (7)
- St John's Gardens, Manchester

Riverbanks

Since the war years, rivers throughout the country have generally been much improved, both in terms of their cleanliness and their accessibility. Rivers in industrial cities used to be best avoided because they were busy, noisy and polluted places. Now all that sea-borne activity has vanished there has been a terrific opportunity to open them up to leisure.

The Thames is a great practical example. In 1957, the pollution levels had become so bad that the river was declared biologically dead. Fifty years on, the Thames has become a very different place. It teems with life: it has 125 species of fish, more than 400 species of invertebrates, seals, dolphins and even otters.

*'This Park belongs to the people of East London, if you harm it,
you harm them.'* BOW NEIGHBOURHOOD SIGNBOARD

Walking alongside waterways is a great way to get 'under the skin' of a city and understand it better; also, to imagine how it must have been in the past – after all, the river was there long before even one house had been built: it was one of the key reasons that the city grew there in the first place.

As interesting as the main rivers are the 'underground' rivers – the clues lie in the squiggle of the street, the exit culvert into the main river, the glimpsed torrent – this is the detective work that makes city walks so fascinating.

Five finest rivers on our walks:
- River Avon, Bath and Bristol
- River Thames, London II and III
- River Tyne, Newcastle
- River Cherwell, Oxford
- Porter Brook, Sheffield (open, then hidden)

Canal towpaths

The British canal system played a vital role in the Industrial Revolution at a time when long trains of packhorses were the only means of mass transit by road. Canal boats were quicker, could carry much larger volumes and were safer for fragile items. Canal mania took hold from the 1790s to the 1810s, but with the arrival of the railways from the 1830s onwards, the network fell into slow decline, ultimately leading to a complete re-think of their future role in the 1960s.

Fortunately, the Transport Act of 1968 was quick to recognise the value of the waterway network for leisure use. Combined with a vociferous and active campaigning group, this meant that much of the canal system has been successfully preserved – a jewel in the crown of Britain's industrial heritage.

On several occasions I have found that canals offer vital stretches of 'green access' through a city centre – especially in the cities that industrialised most rapidly and consequently have fewest green spaces.

Five finest canals and canal basins on our walks:
- Brayford Pool and Foss Dyke, Lincoln (AD 120)
- Kennett & Avon Canal, Bath (1810) **9**
- Worcester and Birmingham, Gas Street Basin, Grand Union Canal; Birmingham (1815)
- Leeds and Liverpool Canal, Leeds (1816)
- The Regent's Canal, London I & IV (1820) **8**

Nature reserves

Wherever possible, our walks incorporate the meadows, woodlands, heaths and moorlands which have been retained within these cities. In addition, nature reserves offer oases of tranquillity and natural life and are sometimes found in the most unlikely places.

City authorities have given a high priority to supporting nature reserves within their boundaries. Plymouth has ten, for example and Oxford manages over 900 acres of SSSIs (sites of special scientific interest). The London Wetlands Centre (40 hectares, 100 acres) is one of the biggest schemes in Europe.

Five finest nature reserves on our walks:
- Whitehawk Hill, Brighton
- Camley Street Natural Park, London IV **10**
- Burgess Field, Port Meadow, Oxford
- Devil's Point, Plymouth
- Porter Valley Nature Reserve, Sheffield

Urbe

What makes urban rambling so special compared to its country cousin is the opportunity to see so many fine buildings. Here are pointers to each architectural style, and some of the best examples you can see on our rambles. Unless otherwise stated, all quotes are from Pevsner's monumental Buildings of England.

Roman 43 BC–AD 450

Look out for arches, defensive walls, columns, pediments, monumental lettering

Top three on our walks:

- The Roman Baths, Bath (AD 60): the cornerstone of Bath's attraction for two millennia
- Temple of Mithras, London III (3rd century AD): under the swanky new Bloomberg building, alongside the hidden Walbrook river
- Mamucium Roman Fort, Manchester (AD 79): a vantage point for controlling the region

Anglo-Norman 1066–1190

Look out for castle-like solidity, carved columns, strapwork, arcading.

Opposite York cathedral was at the heart of the medieval city

Top three on our walks:

- The Round Church, Cambridge (1160): inspired by the rotunda in the church of the Holy Sepulchre in Jerusalem
- Rougemont Castle, Exeter (11th century): built by King William on an outcrop of volcanic red rock
- Tower of London, London II (from 1060): built as a statement of power and dominance

Gothic 1190–1485

Look out for rose windows, pointed Gothic arches, vaulting, tracery, gargoyles.

Top three on our walks:

- Bishop's Palace, Lincoln (late-12th century): controlled the vast wealth of the Diocese of Lincoln, which stretched from the Humber to the Thames
- Cow's Tower, Norwich (14th century): built to a height to enable it to fire onto the hillside opposite
- York Minster (completed 1472)

Tudor 1485–1558

Look out for perpendicular, timber-framed, battlemented parapets, Tudor arched.

Top three on our walks:

- King's Chapel, Cambridge (1515): a study in sheer perpendicular perfection ⑬
- The Merchant Adventurers' Hall, York (1530s): the largest timber-framed building in the UK still used for its original purpose
- Guildhall, Exeter (refaced 1590s): still in use today, this has been a courthouse, a prison, a woollen market hall and a council meeting place

Renaissance 1558–1702

Look out for domes, colonnades, pediments, fountains, rusticated stonework.

Top three on our walks:

- Clare College, Cambridge (1638 and 1715): from Gothic to classicism in one picture postcard building
- Trinity Great Court, Cambridge (1600s): Sir Isaac Newton among others looked out on this view
- Wren churches, London III (1670s–1710s); exquisite and perfectly proportioned

Georgian 1702–1837

Look out for symmetry, classic proportions, domes, sash windows, façades.

Top three on our walks:

- Royal Crescent, Bath (1770s): if you dream Georgian perfection, this will be the dream . . .
- Birmingham Town Hall (1834): they weren't going to toe the line with the burgeoning Gothic Revival
- Grey Street, Newcastle (1824–41): 'one of the finest streets in England'

Victorian 1837–1901

Look out for Gothic Revival, ostentation, elaboration, Eastern influences, new materials.

Top three on our walks:

- Houses of Parliament, London III (1840–60): wonderfully opulent, with just the small problem that it could cost £6 billion to fully restore
- Natural History Museum, Oxford (1860): A visionary techno-Gothic combination of medieval style and cutting edge materials ⑪
- General Infirmary, Leeds (1869): George Gilbert Scott's building incorporated ideas from Florence Nightingale ⑫

Railways

These walks are designed to fit with travel by train and there is plenty of magnificent built heritage to see.

- Liverpool Lime Street (1836): the oldest grand terminus station in the world
- Newcastle Central Station (1850): the earliest surviving covered roof
- St Pancras station (1868)
- York station (1877)
- Bristol Temple Meads station (1840 and 1870s): a glorious way to arrive

Edwardian 1901–1910

Look out for more restrained and less complex design, lighter stone, quality materials.

Top three on our walks:
- Port of Liverpool Building (1907): large dome, ornamental detail and many maritime references
- Grand Midland Hotel, Manchester (1903): highly individualistic Edwardian Baroque style. The Rolls-Royce company was founded over a lunch here . . .
- Central Arcade, Newcastle (1906): stunning faïence tiles and a famous independent music store

Arts and Crafts 1860s–1920s

Look out for traditional craftsmanship, asymmetry, historical or vernacular styles of decoration.

Top three on our walks:
- Birmingham School of Art (1885): the Pre-Raphaelite Brotherhood formed here
- Church of St Michael and All Angels, Brighton (1862 and 1893): the first time that the Pre-Raphaelite Brotherhood was let loose on a project, producing exceptional stained-glass windows
- Liverpool Anglican Cathedral (1904–78): stained glass, sculptures, fine furniture and woodwork (16)

Art Nouveau 1890s–1910s

Look out for sinuous lines and flowing organic shapes based on plant forms.

Top three on our walks:
- Edward Everard Printing Works, Bristol (1901); delightful Doulton tiles (15)
- The Philharmonic Hotel, Liverpool (1900): superb gates and sumptuous interior
- John Rylands Library, Manchester (1900): 'a cathedral filled with books'

Art Deco 1920s–1930s

Look out for bold designs, clear lines, vibrant colours and patterns.

Top three on our walks:
- Embassy Court, Brighton (1935): enclosed balconies and England's first penthouse suites made this a highly desirable address
- GWR Paddington Office, London IV (1935): many Art Deco features, including a row of shell-like protrusions
- City Hall, Norwich (1938): sleek bronze lions guard the entrance to the three massive bronze doors (14)

Arcades

The origins of the shopping arcade can be traced back to Paris, where they first started to appear in the late eighteenth century. The narrow streets without pavements, crowded with horse-traffic, must have made shopping hazardous. An arcade provided comfortable, stylish and safe shopping away from the dirt and clatter of the street. Arcades suited the British climate too.

Top three on our walks:
- Glass Arcade, St Nicholas Market, Bristol (1854): an early example of an arcade, linked to a Corn Exchange
- The Arcades, Leeds (1900): designed by a theatre architect who understand how to create dramatic effect with entrances and exits
- Royal Arcade, Norwich (1899): Art Nouveau style arrives in Norwich

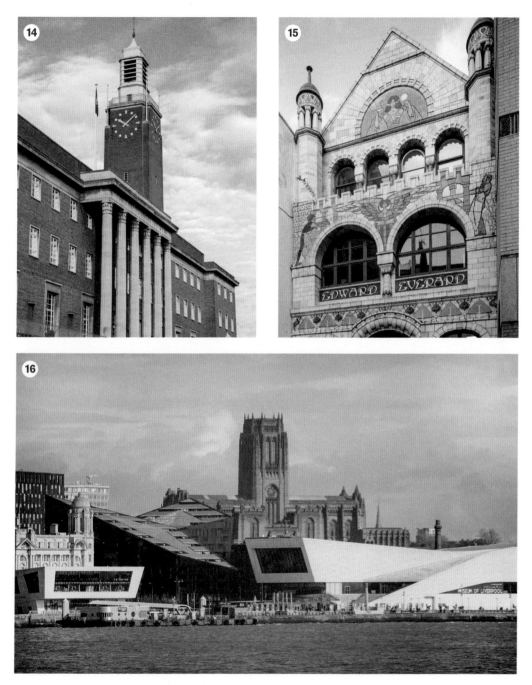

Modern 1920 onwards

Look out for 'less is more', straight lines, sheer planes
of glass, steel or concrete.

Top three on our walks:

- E.C. Stoner Building, Edward Boyle Library
  and other Leeds university buildings (1960s):
  post-war architectural design as influenced by Le
  Corbusier **(19)**
- St Catherine's College, Oxford (1962): every
  detail, from the cutlery to the landscaping, was
  worked through by the Danish architect Arne
  Jacobsen
- The British Library (1999), London IV: 'Is this a
  factory or is it a temple? A library needs to be a
  bit of both'

Streamline Moderne 1930s

Look out for a style that emphasises curving forms
(following on from Art Deco), with long horizontal lines
and occasional nautical elements.

Top three on our walks:

- Philharmonic Hall, Liverpool (1939): local violinist
  John Frederick Clarke, part of the RMS *Titanic*
  orchestra, has a memorial plaque
- The Battleship Building, London IV (1969): it won
  the Concrete Society's 'Building of the Year' in 1969,
  thus cementing its reputation . . .
- The Daily Express Building, Manchester (1939): one
  of Norman Foster's favourite buildings when he was
  growing up in the city

Brutalist 1950s–1970s

Look out for large scale, concrete (the name Brutalism
derives from 'Béton brut', French for concrete),
repeated modular elements, exposure of building's
function.

Top three on our walks:

- The Queen Elizabeth Law Courts, Liverpool
  (1970s): ribbed panels of reddish sandy concrete
  and a glass-sided walkway
- National Theatre, London III (1976): Sir John
  Betjeman was effusive in his praise and wrote
  to Lasdun stating that he 'gasped with delight at
  the cube of your theatre in the pale blue sky . . .
  it has that inevitable and finished look that great
  work does'
- Park Hill, Sheffield (1961): a Utopian vision of
  'streets in the sky', recently regenerated to acclaim

Postmodern

Look out for ornamental features around a modern shape
– portholes, cupolas, columns, humorous flourishes.

Top three on our walks:

- No. 1 Poultry, London III (1997): an ancient
  Egyptian tomb-like opening takes visitors into
  the heart of the building **(18)**
- TV-AM building, London IV (1982): egg cups
  straddle the roof-line of the country's first
  breakfast TV station
- Leeds Magistrate's Court (1994): one of the most
  successful buildings from the 'Leeds look' era

Twenty-first century

- Broadcasting Tower, Leeds (2009): student
  accommodation, using the same rusted metal
  material as the Angel of the North, to great effect
- Aquatics Centre, London II (2011): Zaha Hadid
  at her finest and most sinuous
- Manchester Civil Justice Centre (2007): named
  one of the 'Best British Buildings of the 21st
  century' **(17)**

CATHEDRAL CITIES

English cathedrals are one of the great architectural, cultural and historical glories of our country. Even today, they create a huge physical impression when you first set eyes upon them – imagine just how awe-inspiring they must have been in medieval times.

Cathedral cities became the focus of wealth and power, and were among the most important trading cities of their era. In the late fourteenth century, York was the second most populous city after London, Norwich was fifth and Lincoln sixth, with Exeter not far behind. This lasted until the Industrial Revolution, when they were quickly overtaken by the cities of Victorian industry that grew at more than double their rate. In recent years though, cathedral cities have enjoyed a renaissance as tourists have flocked to them and they have become desirable places to live.

SO, WHAT SHOULD YOU LOOK OUT FOR IN A CATHEDRAL CITY?

1. **Roman remains:** walls, baths, palaces may still be seen
2. **The cathedral at the heart of the city:** usually close to the castle and often alongside a monastery
3. **A cathedral close:** a tranquil green space within the hectic heart of the city
4. **Lanes and alleys around the cathedral:** this was never a planned space, it grew willy-nilly
5. **Historic pubs and coaching inns:** many of the country's oldest hostelries are close to cathedrals
6. **City walls remaining:** York – 95 per cent still exist; Exeter – 70 per cent
7. **Access to the sea via river:** you have to ship massive amounts of stone to build a cathedral

Exeter

Three things immediately strike us about Exeter: its elevated position on a steep ridge above the River Exe, making it a natural defensive site; its proximity to nature, with hills on the horizon in every direction and the sea close by; and its students who account for a quarter of the population during term time.

Exeter is one of those rare cities where you are always aware of the encircling countryside. From any good vantage point, you can see hills in every direction; the city doesn't seem to have sprawled in the way that many have, giving it more the character of a large market town. And in the city itself there are lots of green spaces, with the university proudly boasting that it has the highest tree per student ratio in the country.

Exeter is an ancient city, founded around AD 50 by the Romans who were attracted by the easily defensible higher ground of the ridge combined with direct access to the sea. It has remained economically and politically active ever since, with the foundation of the cathedral dating back to the eleventh century. The topography of the city is dictated by its position alongside the Exe, and its shape was little altered during the nineteenth century as, without a source of nearby coal, it was not able to develop a significant manufacturing base.

A big change to the built environment occurred, however, in 1942 when the Blitz destroyed a large area of the city centre. Pevsner reflected: 'The German bombers found Exeter primarily a medieval city; they

WALK DATA

- **DISTANCE:** 9.9 km (6.2 miles)
- **HEIGHT GAIN:** 115 metres
- **WALK TIME:** 2½ hours
- **START & FINISH:** Exeter St David's (EX4 4NT)
- **TERRAIN:** Pavements and tracks, some modest slopes

left it primarily a Georgian and early-Victorian city.' The Luftwaffe destroyed about half of Exeter's historic buildings and much of the commercial centre. Large areas of the city centre were rebuilt in the 1950s, but little attempt was made to preserve its ancient heritage. Damaged buildings were generally demolished rather than restored, and even the street plan was altered in an attempt to improve traffic circulation.

Because of Exeter's compactness, it is easy to get into the countryside in any direction. If you have a little more time, I recommend the Exeter Green Circle Walk, a 12-mile ramble that skirts around the green edge of the city, taking in many of the hills that we have looked out upon from our central vantage point.

THE WALK

Exeter St David's station (1840) was first designed by Isambard Kingdom Brunel, with several later extensions. If level crossings are your passion, you're in the right place. The one here is a six-track crossing, making it one of the widest in the UK; and, in a nice touch for walkers, we are let through on a different (and more frequent) flow than cars.

In the autumn of 1960, following very heavy rain, the Exe overflowed and flooded large areas of Exeter. The water rose as high as 2 metres above ground level in places and 2,500 properties were flooded. These floods led to the construction of new flood defences including three flood relief channels, one of which we are now walking alongside. Although clearly very necessary, they are not pretty, being empty concrete basins, vital for 0.1 per cent of the time when they are brimful of flood water, used occasionally by skateboarders, but rather an eyesore the rest of the time.

Exeter Quay had been in regular use since Roman times. During the thirteenth and fourteenth centuries, rival merchants built weirs across the river near Topsham to land cargoes further downstream but in the mid-sixteenth century John Trew built the first stretch of the Exeter Canal to enable delivery of cargo closer to the city. Exeter's wealth came from the woollen cloth trade which reached its peak in the mid-eighteenth century. Cloth produced in the area was finished around Cricklepit Mill and loaded onto ships at the quayside to be taken all over the world. In recent years, the quay has been redeveloped for leisure.

The Customs House (1681), on the east side of the river, was built next to the Watergate, placing it strategically for controlling the importing of goods and assessing them before they were transported into the city. H M Customs and Excise used it until 1989. Originally, the arches at the front were open, allowing goods to be stored out of the rain.

An estimated 70 per cent of Exeter's **Old City Wall** still survives, making it one of the most notable in the country. Originally built by the Romans, the wall was

WALK DATA

- **CITY POPULATION:** 117,773 (#66 in UK)
- **ORIGINS:** AD 50 (Roman)
- **CITY STATUS:** Since time immemorial
- **FAMOUS INHABITANTS:** W.G. Hoskins (*The Making of the English Landscape*), Tommy Cooper (comedian), Chris Martin (Coldplay), Charles Babbage (father of the computer)
- **NOTABLE BUILDERS:** Thomas Sharp (town planner), Vincent Harris (university masterplan)
- **SCREEN TIME:** *The Onedin Line* (the quay), *Broadchurch* (the university)
- **ICONIC CITYSCAPE:** Northernhay Gardens

repaired in Saxon times when the defences helped repel attacks from the Vikings. The next main phase of development occurred during Norman times. Throughout the Middle Ages, the wall was important in repelling sieges and rebellions. The last time that the wall helped defend the city was during the English Civil War.

We come off the wall at the cut through to Cathedral Close, which was made in 1753. In 1814, Mayor Burnet-Patch found the task of clambering down the wall and back up the other side of the opening rather onerous, so he had Exeter's first wrought-iron bridge erected to span the gap.

At this point, we take in a loop of the charming Georgian **Southernhay Gardens**. The main terraces of townhouses were built from 1789. Whilst originally they were owned by wealthy professionals, members of the gentry, retired army colonels and the like, now they are mostly offices for solicitors, accountants and estate agents.

Before the area was developed for smart housing, it had been many things, typical of a piece of land 'edging' the town walls: from as far back as the thirteenth century it was the scene of the annual Lammas Fair; the Protestant martyr Agnes Prest was burnt at the stake here in 1557; in the early seventeenth century the area became a pleasure gardens, until destroyed during the

EXETER

Exeter University

START

RIVER EXE

Bury Meadows

Northernhay Gardens

The Guildhall

Southernhay Gardens

Exeter Cathedral

The Customs House

EXETER QUAY

N
W · E
S

'The Beer stone is of an exquisite soft colour' SHELL GUIDE

English Civil War; and towards the end of that century it became a burial ground.

Heading back under the wrought-iron bridge and along Cathedral Close, we see **Exeter Cathedral** (1400) on our left. I like the old Shell Guide's rather evocative description of it: 'It's like entering the belly of a whale: pillars and roofs are grooved and vaulted like the thews and sinews of an anatomical drawing. The Beer stone is of an exquisite soft colour; grey and cream in the nave, pinker over the choir from the reflected colour of the glass.'

After the Blitz had destroyed 37 acres of central Exeter, the City Council was confronted with the task of re-building the city. In 1944, they created the Re-planning and Reconstruction Committee after a visit by W. Morrison, the Minister of Town and Country Planning. Thomas Sharp, an eminent town planner, was appointed, having already started work on a plan for Durham. His remit was to draw up an outline plan for the rebuilding of the city.

Like much development after the war, the actual results turned out to be a very mixed bag – a shortage of money and quality building materials, a pressure from traders to re-build quickly, continuing obeisance to the car, and a willingness to knock down historic buildings if they didn't fit in with the 'comprehensive' redevelopment plan or threatened to be costly to restore.

A walk along the High Street soon demonstrates this mix of good and bad. Let's concentrate on the good bits and ignore the bad. **The Guildhall** (fourteenth century)

has been the centre of civic government for the city for at least 600 years. It has functioned as a prison, a courthouse, a police station, a place for civic functions and celebrations, a city archive store, a woollen market hall, and as the meeting place for the City Chamber and Council. Pop in and have a quick look around.

Passing through an arched entrance, we enter the delightful **Northernhay Gardens** (3.5 hectares, 8.6 acres). This is reputed to be the oldest public open space in England, originally laid out in 1612 as a pleasure walk for Exeter residents. The site was quarried in Roman times for stone for the city walls. The gardens themselves incorporate a stretch of the Roman wall and the only length of Saxon town wall to be seen in England.

The early park was destroyed in the Civil War, in 1642, when large defensive ditches were dug outside the walls. Soon after the Restoration, in 1664, the city set about restoring the park, planting hundreds of young elms and laying out gravel paths. The gardens underwent a major re-landscaping in 1860, receiving a group of monuments to major Victorian figures in the city's history. We enjoy a great view from the gardens looking north towards the university.

William the Conqueror built **Rougemont Castle** (1068). The gatehouse, which is the only part of the castle remaining, is the oldest castle building standing in Britain. It crowned a strategic position on a hill of volcanic red rock, which gave the castle's occupants sight of all the city and beyond.

Above left The Guildhall has been the centre of civic government for at least 600 years

Above right Rougemont Castle is the oldest castle building standing in Britain

Below The city wall runs through the charming Northernhay Gardens

'The German bombers found Exeter primarily a medieval city; they left it primarily a Georgian and early-Victorian city' NIKOLAUS PEVSNER

Walking the length of Northernhay Street, we follow the line of the wall to our left, which can be seen up a little alley, Maddocks Row. And we spot the wall again on the far side of a car park; and then at the end of the street, we come face to face with the very solid-looking granite wall supporting the start of the **Iron Bridge** (1834).

Boards of Improvement Commissioners were ad hoc urban local organisations created in three hundred or so towns and cities during the eighteenth and nineteenth centuries by a private Act of Parliament. The powers of the boards varied, but typically included street paving, cleansing, lighting, providing watchmen or dealing with various public nuisances. They were to have a fundamental influence on development during the Victorian period and were the prototype for reformed municipal boroughs that eventually superseded them.

The Exeter Board of Improvement Commissioners was formed around 1810 to ensure a more rational approach to town planning in the city. In 1834, they commissioned the construction of the Iron Bridge over the steep-sided Longbrook Valley, immediately in front of the North Gate in order to eradicate the steepness of the slope, which had proved very treacherous for heavily-laden horse-drawn carts. As a result, we notice the incongruous placement of front doors on what would have originally been second floors in the houses of Lower North Street.

St David's Church (1900), which we go past next, was designed by William Douglas Caroe. John Betjeman described it as 'the finest example of Victorian church architecture in the south-west'. Caroe became known as 'a consummate master of building according to medieval precedent', in other words, he was something of an Arts and Crafts advocate.

Bury Meadow (1.5 hectares, 3.7 acres), opposite the church, was opened in 1846, on part of a site that had been used for cholera victims in the 1832 outbreak. And in the days after the Blitz, it was used for a field kitchen to feed women and children. Now, it is a pleasant green space, well used and popular with students from the nearby Exeter College.

The steep **Lower Hoopern Valley**, with the intriguingly named Taddiforde Brook running through it down to the Exe, is a natural divide between the city and the university. It really has the 'rus in urbe' feel about it. The site is designated as a County Wildlife Site and one of

Above The Italianate Reed Hall formed the nucleus of the university

Below Exeter does fun and funky cafés too

the City's Valley Parks, of which there are five altogether.

Exeter University was founded in 1855, has expanded steadily and is now consistently ranked in the Top 10 of universities in the National Student Survey. Streatham, which we are passing through, is the largest campus, and can make a strong case for being one of the most beautiful in the country, being set in the grounds of a former Victorian mansion, the Italianate Reed Hall.

In 1928 the architect Vincent Harris was appointed to develop a master plan for the new campus. Although the plan was never fully realised, he was responsible for several landmark buildings, including the Washington Singer Laboratories (1931), Roborough (1938), Hatherly (1950s) and the Mary Harris Memorial Chapel (1956). Sir Basil Spence, of Coventry Cathedral fame, was the architect of the modernist 1960s Physics Building; and more recent buildings of note include the New Library (1983), the Institute of Arab and Islamic Studies and Xfi, both from the 2000s.

The buildings all benefit from a fabulous setting, on a hillside with grandstand views over Exeter; and a mature tree stock of around 10,000 trees, including two arboretums, a cherry orchard and a wild conifer collection. This legacy dates back to the late nineteenth-century when the first specimen trees were planted in the grounds of Reed Hall.

Even better, there is a **Sculpture Walk** (a map can be downloaded) which features such distinguished artists as Barbara Hepworth, Paul Mount and Geoffrey Clark; some are in university buildings and others are in the grounds.

Having spent a lot of time admiring the university campus, we finally make it up onto the ridge behind, the highest part of our walk at 120 metres, and proceed west along Belvidere Road. To the north-west we have

fabulous views across the Duryard Valley, towards Dartmoor. Most of the land is in private ownership but there is access to the tranquil **Belvidere Meadows Local Nature Reserve** (8 hectares, 19.8 acres) through a kissing gate. And then we wind our way back through the campus to the station to complete a very satisfying walk.

PIT STOPS
- **TEA ON THE GREEN**, 2 Cathedral Close, EX1 1EZ. Traditional ambience, stellar location.
- **THE EXPLODING BAKERY**, Queen Street, EX4 3SB
- **QUAYSIDE COFFEE SHOP**, 85 Waterside, EX2 8GY

QUIRKY SHOPPING
- **GANDY SREET**, EX4 3LS. More of a passage than a street; a good mix of shops and eating places.
- **FORE SREET**, Old West Quarter, EX4 3AN

PLACES TO VISIT
- **EXETER CATHEDRAL** (EX1 1HS)
- **EXETER GUILDHALL** (EX4 3HP)
- **ROYAL ALBERT MEMORIAL MUSEUM AND ART GALLERY** (EX4 3RX)

WHEN TO VISIT
South West Food and Drink Festival, Northernhay Gardens (April), Lammas Fair and Cathedral Green Craft Fayre (July), City of Exeter Regatta (July, Exeter Quay), Northernhay Gardens Big Screen in the Park (Aug)

Lincoln

Lincoln is rich in history, one of Britain's most important medieval cities, but is often overlooked today. This walk takes you through every era from Roman to the modern day, with the glorious cathedral as its high point.

Lincoln is situated in a gap in the Lincoln Cliff, a major escarpment through which the River Witham flows. Consequently, the city is divided into very distinct parts, known locally as 'uphill' and 'downhill'.

The uphill area is the historical quarter, including Lincoln Cathedral, Lincoln Castle and the Medieval Bishop's Palace. The downhill area comprises the city centre and the suburbs to the south and south-west. The very accurately named street 'Steep Hill' connects the two. This divide gives Lincoln its distinctive character.

It is not difficult to understand why the Romans were drawn here. The gap through the Lincoln Cliff offered them a natural east–west route either by water or on foot. Roman engineers also saw the possibility of linking the River Witham to the River Trent by building a canal. That canal, the Foss Dyke, is remarkably still in use today; and through the ages, the links to Yorkshire and the Midlands via the Foss Dyke have brought trade and prosperity.

Even after the Romans left Britain in the early fifth century, the importance of the port remained, and William the Conqueror saw it as an important strategic outpost to his kingdom. The great and prosperous medieval city of Lincoln was built on the wealth, mostly in wool, that

WALK DATA

- **DISTANCE:** 9.6 km (6 miles)
- **HEIGHT GAIN:** 59 metres
- **WALK TIME:** 2½ hours
- **START & FINISH:** Brayford Pool (LN1 1YW); or from the station (LN5 7EQ)
- **TERRAIN:** A steep ascent up the 'Lincoln Edge'; otherwise, straightforward

traded up and down the River Witham. It was one of the most important cities in the country.

But as Britain industrialised, so Lincoln became something of a backwater, separated from the great routes north, the A1 and the East Coast rail line, which both pass to its west. Today it is perhaps one of the least visited cities and county capitals.

Its more recent renaissance has been helped significantly by the emergence of the University of Lincoln, which has grown to nearly 13,000 students in little over a decade and has made a marked difference to the city, adding a youthful buzz.

THE WALK

Brayford Pool is a natural lake formed from a widening of the River Witham. It was used as a port by the Romans, and has a long industrial heritage. Since the early 1990s, it has been the focus of Lincoln's urban regeneration. Although this has helped bring this area of the city back to life, it is occupied by a dispiriting array of chain bars and restaurants. There is one interesting structure amid it all; now housing the likes of Nando's and Prezzo, the original building was designed in 1959 as a sleek car showroom, featuring a reinforced concrete hyperbolic paraboloid shell roof (that's a mouthful). Its petrol pumps originally faced the water.

The south side of Brayford Pool is home to the thriving University of Lincoln. The architecture is striking, with several good new buildings (notably the Isaac Newton Building, the School of Architecture and much of the student accommodation) and the conversion of the old Engine Shed, which you will pass if you start at the station.

The **Foss Dyke**, which runs into Brayford Pool, connects the River Trent to the River Witham. It is the oldest canal in England still in use. Built around AD 120 by the Romans, it was renovated in the twelfth century during the reign of King Henry I and further improvements were made towards the end of the seventeenth century, including a navigable lock at Torksey at the River Trent, and warehousing and wharves at Brayford Pool.

We cut up to the expanse of **West Common** (100 hectares, 297 acres), which has been an open space since Roman times, when it was used as an area of agricultural production for the military. A race track was built here in 1773, but closed in the 1960s. The grandstand, the stables and the numbers board still survive, giving added character to this delightful green space, kept now as meadowland. During the First World War, the common was used to test aircraft assembled in the city's many industrial plants. The airfield had turf runways and a number of outbuildings,

WALK DATA

- **CITY POPULATION:** 93,541 (#69 in UK)
- **ORIGINS:** 1st century BC
- **CITY STATUS:** Since time immemorial
- **FAMOUS INHABITANTS:** George Boole (developer of Boolean logic), John Hurt (actor), Penelope Fitzgerald (novelist), William Byrd (composer)
- **SCREEN TIME:** *Possession* (University of Lincoln), *The Da Vinci Code* and *The Young Victoria* (Lincoln Cathedral)
- **ICONIC CITYSCAPES:** Looking up High Street to the cathedral; and the walls of Lincoln Castle

several of which are still evident as earthworks. Directly south of the grandstand there is an earthwork marking the location of a former training trench.

We make a very worthwhile detour, all of 50 metres, to **Ellis's Windmill**. Placed on the top of the hill to get the most wind, this evocative mill is located on Mill Road, so called due to the nine windmills that formerly faced west over the steep slopes of the Lincoln Edge. Ellis Mill is now the sole survivor of these mills and an excellent example of a small tower mill. The mill we see dates from 1798 but there has been a mill on this site from at least the seventeenth century; the mill was working until the 1940s and has since been restored.

Before we storm the castle, we pop into **The Lawn** (1820), a notable Greek Revival building that began life as a lunatic asylum, and where we find the **Joseph Banks Conservatory**, a tropical house themed with plants reminiscent of voyages the botanist took with Captain James Cook. Past the conservatory we discover the very tranquil walled **John Dawber Garden**.

Lincoln Castle (eleventh century) was constructed by William the Conqueror on the site of a pre-existing Roman fortress. The castle is unusual in that it has two moats, one of only two in the country. We walk around the immense Norman walls which provide

LINCOLN

West Common

THE FOSS DYKE

BRAYFORD POOL

START

Ellis's Windmill

John Dawber Garden

House on
High Bridge

Lincoln Castle

Lincoln Cathedral

Bishop's Palace

RIVER WITHAM

The Lincoln Arboretum

W
S   N
E

Above left Ellis's Windmill is the sole survivor of nine windmills that faced west atop the Lincoln Edge

Above right Lincoln Cathedral dominates the skyline

Below Steep Hill lives up to its name as you will discover!

'Few things in this Island are so breathlessly impressive as Lincoln Cathedral, nobly crowning its hill, seen from below.' J.B. PRIESTLEY

a magnificent view of the castle complex, together with panoramic views of the cathedral, the city and the surrounding countryside.

Another major reason we want to visit the castle is to gaze at one of the four surviving originals of the Magna Carta, sealed by King John in 1215. In many ways this was the beginning of rights for the individual, especially the right to timely justice. The Bishop of Lincoln had been one of the original signatories to the Magna Carta and consequently it was kept for hundreds of years at the cathedral before being transferred here.

Lincoln Cathedral is nearly a thousand years old and was reputedly the tallest building in the world for more than two centuries (1311–1549). John Ruskin, never shy in his opinions, declared: 'I have always held that the cathedral of Lincoln is out and out the most precious piece of architecture in the British Isles and roughly speaking worth any two other cathedrals we have.' Pevsner was also effusive, especially about its spectacular setting.

Standing in the shadow of Lincoln Cathedral, with sweeping views over the ancient city and the countryside beyond, the medieval **Bishops' Palace** (twelfth century) was once among the most important buildings in the country, being the administrative centre of the largest diocese in medieval England, stretching from the Humber to the Thames; its architecture reflected enormous power and wealth. The only bit surviving today is the undercrofted West Hall, which is an English Heritage site. We experience a fit of house envy admiring the **Cathedral Close** with its fine Georgian townhouses, each in a different hue.

The Lincoln Arboretum (9 hectares, 22 acres), a park to the east of the cathedral, was designed and laid out between 1870 and 1872 by well-known Victorian gardener Edward Milner, following the national trend for providing public parks for workers to relax in and enjoy the fresh air. Part of the deal was also to sell 1.2 hectares (3 acres) of the land for residential building purposes; we see these large Victorian houses on the northern side of the park. This practice of property speculation around the added amenity that a park view offered was a very common way of funding the many Victorian parks that sprang up across the country during this period.

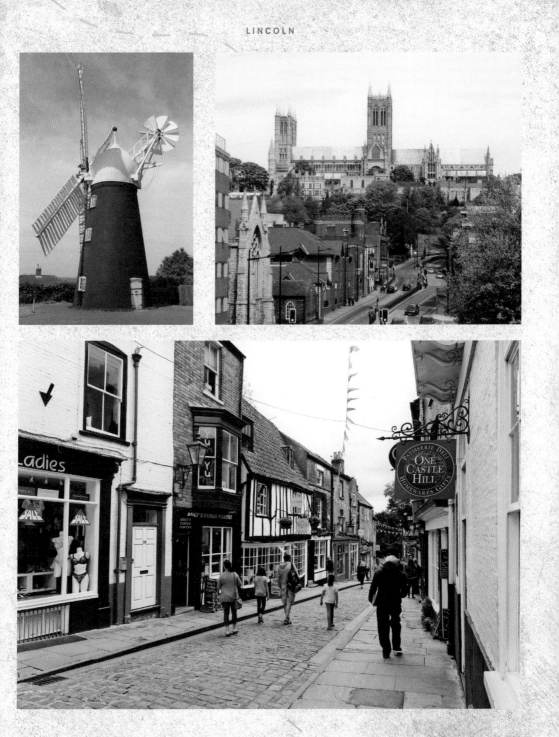

A bandstand was added in 1884, and during the 1890s the arboretum became a very popular music spot, frequently attracting over 40,000 people to concerts. After being badly neglected in the second half of the twentieth century, a major restoration project was carried out just after the turn of the millennium, and the park we see today gives enormous pleasure, with its well-tended gardens, lakes and bridges, children's maze and two fountain features.

Leaving the park, we walk down through terraced streets of small artisan houses to reach the **River Witham**. Looking across to the south bank, we notice the site of the famous Lincoln engineering company, Ruston & Hornsby, which in the 1960s was Europe's leading supplier of land-based gas turbines. It is a good example of Lincoln's strong engineering heritage, much of which sadly was swept away in the de-industrialisation of the 1980s. Happily, this plant still survives, now under the ownership of Siemens.

As our route nears its finish point we cross the High Street at the **House on High Bridge** (sixteenth century). This is one of only three bridges in England with shops on it, the others being Pulteney Bridge (which we cross in the Bath walk) and Frome Bridge in Somerset – of which this is the oldest, dating back to the twelfth century, making it possibly the oldest standing bridge in the country.

Lincoln is full of history and medieval buildings, and is probably the most unchanged city of any we have walked through; still dominated by its historic quarter and never really having had a massive population spurt in its history, nor having been significantly damaged by bombing in the Second World War, nor having attracted new town status.

And the council is to be applauded too. In its future plans for the city, encapsulated in the Linking Lincoln Masterplan of 2005, one of its primary aims is to 're-stitch the city centre to its wider context' – basically favouring the pedestrian over the car. Three cheers for that.

PIT STOPS

- **THE ICE CREAM PARLOUR**, 3 Bailgate, LN1 3AE. If you fancy a really good ice cream.
- **THE CLOISTER REFECTORY**, Lincoln Cathedral, LN2 1PX. For the perfect location and good local produce.
- **RISING CAFÉ**, 22 Newland LN2 1PX. A fun, lively café with great food.

QUIRKY SHOPPING

- **STEEP HILL AND THE STRAIT** provide a great selection of food and drink, exclusive and vintage clothing, old bookstores and other speciality shops.
- **BAILGATE**, by the cathedral, is another place for interesting independents.

PLACES TO VISIT

- **LINCOLN CASTLE**, LN1 3AA. Lots of fun, especially for kids. And, of course, the Magna Carta.
- **THE COLLECTION**, LN2 1LP. An award-winning archaeology museum and the region's premier art gallery, the Usher Gallery.
- **LINCOLN CATHEDRAL**, LN2 1PX. Take a look around one of Europe's finest Gothic buildings.

WHEN TO VISIT

Steampunk Festival (late Aug), Lincoln Christmas Market (early Dec)

Norwich

Norwich is one of our best preserved medieval cities, with something to delight around every corner and oodles of green space to roam around in.

Norwich has been a thriving town since the eighth century, and by the time of the Norman invasion was one of the largest cities in England. The Domesday Book states that it had approximately twenty-five churches and a population of between 5,000 and 10,000.

From the Civil War until the eighteenth century, it was second in size only to London, and was a major trading centre with a history of wool-based wealth and subsequently the cloth industry. The city established wide-ranging trading links with other parts of Europe, its markets stretching from Scandinavia to Spain, and the city housing a Hanseatic warehouse. The River Wensum was convenient export route to the River Yare and Great Yarmouth, which served as its port.

A city that stood on its own, with a proud tradition of dissenting and individual political thought, Norwich's geographical isolation was such that until the railway came in 1845 it was often quicker to travel to Amsterdam than to London.

In the later part of the nineteenth and twentieth centuries, the city was relatively successful at moving in to manufacturing, becoming well-known for footwear, transitioning throughout the 1980s and 1990s to a service-based economy. But its relative wealth declined as other cities had better access to raw materials and a large population.

Happily, it was one of the first cities to take conservation seriously, with the establishment of the Norwich Society in 1923. This has meant that despite having its fair share of multi-storey car parks, shopping centres and ring roads, it has retained both its historic core and green spaces.

The corporation has also been a leader in the creation of parks and green spaces. After the First World War it took advantage of government grants and constructed a series of parks as a means of alleviating unemployment. The city has won the 'Greenest City in the UK' award and also 'The Best Place to Work in'.

WALK DATA

- **DISTANCE:** 7.7 km (4.8 miles)
- **HEIGHT GAIN:** 35 metres
- **WALK TIME:** 2 hours
- **START & FINISH:** Norwich station (NR1 1EF)
- **TERRAIN:** The first stretch could be muddy

THE WALK

Norwich station (1886) makes for a grand arrival, built as it is in a grand French Renaissance style. In Simon Jenkins' words 'the ticket hall hints at Versailles ballroom'. Our feet want to take us into the centre straight away, but our green space instincts take us up the hill instead to the **Rosary Cemetery** (1819), the first non-denominational burial ground in the country, reflecting Norwich's important role in the history of non-conformism. The Presbyterian minister Thomas Drummond paid for the land out of his own savings, partly as a protest against the law which said that all Norwich citizens had to be buried according to the rites of the Church of England in their local parish graveyards.

Today the cemetery is a wonderfully overgrown labyrinth of trees, passageways and toppling gravestones and the steep slope it is situated on adds to its intrigue.

Next, we tramp through **Lion Wood** (9.2 hectares, 23 acres), about a third of which is ancient woodland, with the remainder dating back at least 200 years when the surrounding landscape was a mosaic of farmland and heath. Two steep-sided valleys carved into the woodland floor flow down from the north towards the River Yare in the south. It is a remnant of Thorpe Wood which was mentioned in the Domesday Book and was the hunting ground of the Bishops of Norwich, and before them the king.

We turn left down the hill at the **Britannia Barracks** (1887), a rather formidable building in the Queen Anne Revival style. The view of the city from **St James Hill** is spectacular and a useful way to gain our bearings.

To the north (a very worthwhile extra 2-km loop) is **Mousehold Heath** (81 hectares, 200 acres), a Local Nature Reserve and one of the few examples of heathland surviving the Victorian period in an urban area. This spot was the encampment of Robert Kett during the 1549 Peasants' Revolt against the enclosure of land which deprived them of a subsistence. They stormed the city but were eventually beaten by forces of the king. Mousehold Heath was famously painted by a number of the Norwich School artists including John Crome and

WALK DATA

- **CITY POPULATION:** 132,512 (#38 in UK)
- **ORIGINS:** 7th century AD
- **CITY STATUS:** Since time immemorial
- **FAMOUS INHABITANTS:** Robert Kett (leader of 1549 Peasants' Revolt), Lord Nelson (sea admiral), Delia Smith (celebrity chef), Philip Pullman (author), Cathy Dennis (singer songwriter)
- **NOTABLE BUILDERS:** Thomas Ivory (Assembly Rooms, Octagon Chapel), George Skipper (Norwich Union, Royal Arcade)
- **SCREEN TIME:** *Stardust* (Elm Hill), *Alan Partridge* TV series (train station, cathedral), *45 Years* (Gentleman's Walk)
- **ICONIC CITYSCAPES:** St James Hill (NR1 4LU), Norwich Castle

John Sell Cotman. Another artist, reflecting on its free access described it as 'the property of those who have the privilege of Norwich birth'.

Coming down off the hill we follow the **River Wensum** south along the line of the old city wall. Wensum means 'winding' in Old English, and you can see why – on the short stretch we take, it makes two ninety-degree turns. On the other bank is **Cow Tower** (fourteenth century), built to defend the north-eastern approach to the city. It stood apart from the main city walls, close to the river where its height would have allowed it to fire onto the higher ground that we have just come from. Next, we cross **Bishop Bridge** (1340), one of the oldest bridges in England. The **Jarrold Bridge** (2012), by contrast, has only been walked across for a handful of years, but is a structure of modern beauty, appearing to float over the river with little visible means of support.

We stroll along the **Norwich Quayside**, which would have been at the heart of the city's trade in medieval times, with warehouses and industrial activities.

Colegate is full of historic interest. **St Clement's** (fifteenth century) light and simple interior is pleasantly

NORWICH

City Hall

Royal Arcade

Norwich Castle

Elm Hill

St Andrew's & Blackfriar's Hall

Norwich Cathedral

Norwich Quayside

START

RIVER WENSUM

Cow Tower

Rosary Cemetery

Lion Wood

Mousehold Heath

W N S E

Above Bishop Bridge has provided access to the cathedral from the east for over 600 years

Below Norwich Quayside was at the heart of the city's medieval trade with Europe

'People say hello to each other, baristas remember your coffee order, you get to know all about interesting local projects.' LAUREN RAZAVI, NORWICH RESIDENT

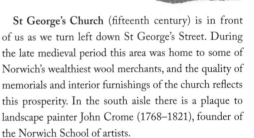

unpretentious. Sadly, it is a 'redundant' church, one of many in the city. This is perhaps inevitable given that fifty-eight parish churches have stood within the medieval city walls, most originally funded by wealthy wool merchants. Although twenty-seven of these buildings have been lost, either to the religious turmoil of the mid-sixteenth century or during the air raids of the Second World War, Norwich can still boast the greatest concentration of medieval city churches in Northern Europe.

On our right we peer up an alley to the **Old Meeting House** (1693). This is an active Congregationalist church, part of Norwich's long tradition of non-conformism. Many of the leading Dissenters of Norwich were Congregationalists, and they included among their numbers some of the wealthiest and most influential members of local society. Life was repressive for the Dissenters, but in 1689 the Act of Toleration finally made it legal for them to build their own place of worship.

A short way further on is the **Unitarian Octagon Chapel** (1756). Perfectly octagonal, so that no corners are distant from the pulpit, it pre-dates by 200 years the recent trend for 'congregation-friendly' spaces. John Wesley described it as 'the most elegant meeting house in Europe'.

St George's Church (fifteenth century) is in front of us as we turn left down St George's Street. During the late medieval period this area was home to some of Norwich's wealthiest wool merchants, and the quality of memorials and interior furnishings of the church reflects this prosperity. In the south aisle there is a plaque to landscape painter John Crome (1768–1821), founder of the Norwich School of artists.

Across St George's Bridge is the **Old Technical School** (1891), now part of the Norwich University of the Arts. Its original aim was to 'put people in the possession of such knowledge as would enable them to learn a trade'. It taught classes in carpentry, carving and cabinet making and drawing, while the Higher Grade School offered science and art classes. The history of Norwich University of the Arts dates back still further to 1845 when the Norwich School of Design was established to provide designers for local industries.

St Andrew's Hall and Blackfriars' Hall (fourteenth century) make up the most complete friary complex surviving in England. The centrepiece is St Andrew's Hall, gloriously constructed in local flint, a vernacular that we see on many buildings and churches on our walk.

Right Norwich Castle was built on the orders of William the Conqueror to defend this key city

'Either a city in an orchard or an orchard in a city, so equally are houses and trees blended in it.' THOMAS FULLER

St Andrew's Church (fifteenth century) is a working church and one of the largest in the city; its spire is a notable landmark. John Robinson became associate pastor here in the early seventeenth century: he was one of the founders of the Congregational Church and later became pastor to the Pilgrim Fathers before they sailed to the New World. Bridewell Alley is a quaint alley alongside the church, where you will find the the Bridewell Museum, which tells the story of the city's industries. Turning right at the top, we walk along Bedford Street and then the curiously named Lobster Lane – apparently there was once a pub of that name here.

We turn left up Lower Goat Street, part of the medieval structure of streets, very quaint and full of interesting independent shops. On our left is the **Guildhall** (fifteenth century), the largest surviving medieval civic building in the country outside London. It was the seat of city administration until 1938, when it was superseded by the Art Deco **City Hall** opposite, a building which I love but is not popular with everyone. Its detailing is especially good – the sleek bronze lions guarding the entrance to the three huge bronze doors; and inside, furniture, fine panelling and light fittings and other details all designed by the architects themselves and still intact. Special bricks were fired for the building, each one being two inches longer than usual to better reflect the proportions of the finished building.

We pass in front of the Guildhall through the charming **Memorial Gardens**, also part of the new City Hall scheme, with a war memorial by Sir Edwin Lutyens.

Below us is the **Market** with its multi-coloured awnings, founded in the latter part of the eleventh century and the largest open-air market in the country. Then we head left down through the churchyard of **St Peter Mancroft** (1455) onto Gentleman's Walk, a fashionable avenue in Georgian times, and through the splendid **Royal Arcade** (1899). According to Sir John Betjeman, 'George Skipper [the architect of the arcade] was to Norwich what Gaudi was to Barcelona'. Arcade shopping was very much in vogue at the time and this arcade brought the fashionable, exotic and continentally influenced architecture of Art Nouveau to Norwich for the first time.

On a sunny day, **Norwich Castle** (eleventh century) positively gleams on its mound, and we walk around the top, enjoying great views in all directions. It was founded in the aftermath of the Norman conquest when William

Left The delightful Elm
Hill is the most complete
medieval street in the city

the Conqueror ordered its construction because he wished to have a fortified place in this important city. Its current good condition is thanks to a very thorough Victorian restoration that kept broadly to the original design.

We then make our way back via Opie Street to Andrew's Plain, 'plain' being a local name for an irregularly-shaped town square, which leads into **Elm Hill**, the most complete medieval street in the city. Ten mayors have lived here, but a century ago it was almost derelict; thankfully, after much campaigning by the Norwich Society, the council saved it. Many wealthy merchants had their houses facing Elm Hill with their factories and workshops at the rear with access to the river for goods in and out.

We make a worthwhile little detour round **Tomblands** before heading in to the cathedral close. Tomblands sounds like the name of an old cemetery, but in fact derives from the Saxon word *tom*, meaning open space, and was originally the pre-Norman marketplace.

Heading through the **Erpingham Gate**, we look onto the west end of the cathedral (1145), with the spire behind looking curiously disconnected from it, perhaps because it is so high, the highest in fact in England other than Salisbury. It is the most complete Norman Cathedral in England, and the inside is a thing of splendour. The cloisters are also very extensive, and in the grassed centre there is a labyrinth.

The Cathedral Close is one of the largest in England and contains more than eighty listed buildings, some of which are still connected to the cathedral, but many of which are available to rent. It really does offer complete tranquillity in the centre of the city, and there's even a cathedral Herb Garden to enjoy.

Pulls Ferry (fifteenth century) was the route for the stone used to build Norwich Cathedral. The stone came from France up the rivers Yare and Wensum. A canal, built by the monks, used to run under the arch, where the Normans ferried the stone and building materials to be unloaded to the front of the construction. Then we head back along the **Riverside Walk** to complete our journey.

PIT STOPS

- **CAFÉ BRITANNIA**, Britannia Road, NR1 4LU. Social enterprise, with great views over Norwich.
- **STRANGERS COFFEE HOUSE**, 21 Pottergate, NR2 1DS. Top-quality coffees, roasted on site.
- **BRITON'S ARMS**, 9 Elm Hill, NR3 1HN. A 14th-century building and garden balcony.

QUIRKY SHOPPING

- **THE NORWICH LANES**, bounded by Andrew Street to the north and St Giles Street to the south
- **MAGDALEN STREET** (NR3 1 HU) for vintage and antiques

PLACES TO VISIT

- **NORWICH CASTLE MUSEUM AND ART GALLERY**, NR1 3JU. Many paintings from the Norwich School of Art.
- **THE BRIDEWELL MUSEUM**, NR2 1AQ. Tells the story of the city's industries.
- **STRANGER'S HALL**, NR2 4AL. A fascinating museum of domestic history.

WHEN TO VISIT

Norfolk & Norwich Arts Festival (May), Norwich City Ale Festival (May/June), Shakespeare Festival in the Cloisters (July)

York

York is the country's best preserved medieval city, and there is something of interest at every turn; the 'walk time' given would suppose you are not detained by anything – it will almost inevitably take two or three times as long!

York sits at the confluence of the rivers Ouse and Foss, at a strategically important point with access to the sea. It was founded by the Romans in 71 AD and later became a stronghold of William the Conqueror, who dammed the River Foss and built a castle here. In the Middle Ages, the city grew as a major wool trading centre and became the capital of the northern ecclesiastical province of the Church of England. In the nineteenth century, it emerged as a hub of the railway network and a confectionery colossus. In recent decades, the economy has shifted towards services, with tourism now accounting for over 10 per cent of employment.

The walls, the most intact set of city walls in the country, have always defined York, but have had their ups and downs. In medieval times, they were key to the defence of the city; in the nineteenth century they were regarded by the council as a barrier to economic growth; whilst in the twentieth they became an intrinsic part of York's popularity as a tourist destination. Above all, though, it is the walls that have helped protect what is undoubtedly England's finest and most complete medieval city.

WALK DATA

- **DISTANCE:** 6.4 km (4 miles); add 2.4 km (1.5 miles) for Millennium Bridge loop
- **HEIGHT GAIN:** 16 metres
- **WALK TIME:** 1¾ hours; or 2¼ hours with extra loop
- **START & FINISH:** York station (YO24 1AB)
- **TERRAIN:** All on pavement; lots of steps

We make much use of York's famous 'snickelways' on our walk. It sounds like an ancient word, but it was in fact coined by local author Mark Jones in his 1983 book *A Walk Around the Snickelways of York*. It's a portmanteau of the words 'snicket', meaning a passageway between walls; 'ginnel', a narrow passageway between or through buildings; and 'alleyway', a narrow street or lane. I especially like Mark's advice on 'shopsnickets': 'The rule is simply to behave as a normal prospective customer (which of course you are). It is foul play to enter a shopsnicket without an interest in its wares nor a means to purchase them.'

THE WALK

Coming out of **York station** (1877), the grand Royal York Hotel (1878) looms large in front of us. York is very much a railway town, and the railways saved York from stagnation in the nineteenth century. Crucially, York's own 'railway king', George Hudson, convinced George Stephenson to build the line through York rather than bypassing it on the way to Leeds.

Clambering up some steep steps, we arrive up on the walls and a great view opens up for us of York Minster and the distinctive York skyline of myriad roofs and chimneys.

Lendal Tower (1300), on the north side of the bridge, was originally part of the city's defences. In medieval times a great iron chain that was stored in the tower was pulled across the river to Barker Tower on the opposite bank. The chain was a barrier to boats on the river, protecting the city in times of trouble and enabling tolls to be charged for entry.

The **Museum Gardens** (4 hectares, 10 acres) are a charming spot to relax in. They were created in the 1830s as botanic gardens by landscape architect Sir John Murray Naysmith. In the summer, they are York office workers' outdoor lunch spot of choice. The gardens also contain several medieval buildings, most of them relating to St Mary's Abbey, founded in 1086.

The centrepiece of Exhibition Square is a statue of renowned York artist William Etty, gazing towards Bootham Bar. He is standing alongside a model of the bar by his feet, reflecting his long campaign to protect the walls and bars, which began when in 1800 the Corporation of York applied for an Act of Parliament to demolish them, regarding them as a major constraint to economic growth.

The campaign to save the walls and create a public path along them crystallised in 1825 with the founding of the Association for the Protection of Ancient Footpaths in the vicinity of York, a forerunner to the campaigning national Ramblers Group (of which I am a proud member). This group set about raising money and restoring sections of the wall.

By the 1830s the corporation had fortunately given up on its goal of total removal and instead decided

WALK DATA

- **CITY POPULATION:** 198,051 (#39 in UK)
- **ORIGINS:** AD 71 (Roman)
- **CITY STATUS:** Since time immemorial
- **FAMOUS INHABITANTS:** Guy Fawkes, Joseph Rowntree (chocolatier), Judi Dench (actress), W.H. Auden (poet), John Barry (composer), George Hudson (railwayman), Jocelyn Bell (scientist), William Etty (painter)
- **NOTABLE BUILDERS:** John Carr (Fairfax House, the Pikeing Well-House, York Crown Court)
- **SCREEN TIME:** *To Walk Invisible* (Micklegate)
- **ICONIC CITYSCAPES:** The walls, York Minster tower, Clifford's Tower

to dismantle the barbicans (which were especially constricting of traffic) but repair much of the wall. With the onset of mass visitors by rail from the 1840s onwards, the value of the walls as a tourist attraction become very apparent.

But we aren't quite ready to go up on the walls; first, we choose to explore some of the medieval city within. We pass through Bootham Bar and slip left along **Precentor's Court**, named after the individual in charge of music in a cathedral. As we approach the end of the lane, so we are granted an amazing view of the west end of the York Minster, soaring majestically above us. We have truly arrived in York!

There is no limit to the time you can spend exploring and enjoying the cathedral, but for us, that will be for another day. Instead, we turn left through the gate into the charming **Dean's Park** (0.8 hectares, 2 acres). Originally the site of the Roman legionary fortress of Eboracum, which numbered 6,000 men, Dean's Park is now a quiet spot with the Minster Library almost all that is left of the Archbishop's Palace. It was here that, in 1483, Richard III invested his son as Prince of Wales.

We pause on **College Green** and put our feet up for five minutes. It isn't quite as ancient as it appears and is

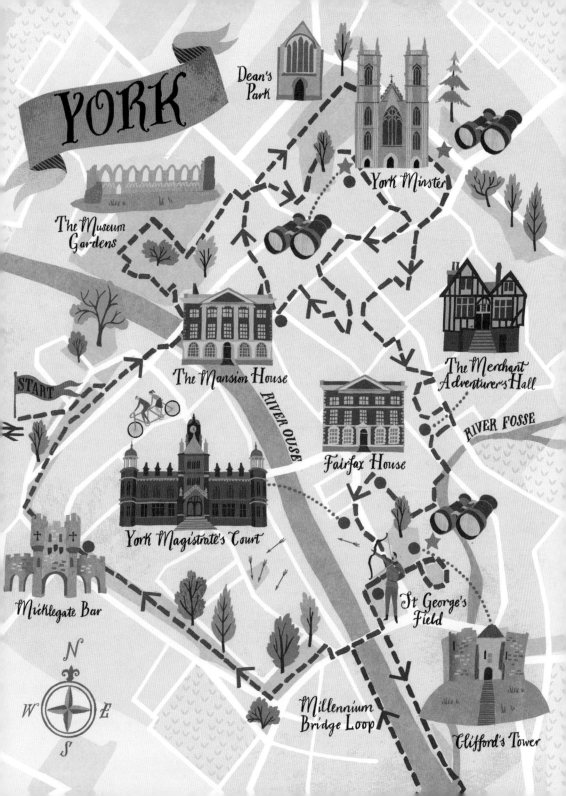

YORK

Dean's Park

York Minster

The Museum Gardens

START

The Mansion House

RIVER OUSE

York Magistrate's Court

Fairfax House

The Merchant Adventurer's Hall

RIVER FOSSE

Micklegate Bar

St George's Field

Millennium Bridge Loop

Clifford's Tower

N W E S

Above left The stone to build the Minster was dragged up Stonegate from the river

Above right The Mansion House is still the full-time residence of the Lord Mayor

Below If you're looking for a spot of tranquillity, Dean's Park is the perfect place

> *'The constriction of the walls has forced the tightest propinquity on York and brought about a spider's web of streets.'* GEORGE PACE

an interesting example of how green oases can be hewn out of the most unpromising of spots. Two houses and their gardens were removed on the north-east side to first create the green in the mid-nineteenth century; it was then extended further to its current size in 1955; and Deangate was finally closed to traffic in 1990, making it the tranquil spot we find today.

If the door built into the gate is hanging open, we can peer into the **Stoneyard Works Department**, which houses a team of eighty or so skilled craftspeople looking after the cathedral, including carvers, joiners, electricians, scaffolders and gardeners. If you think the cost of entering the cathedral is expensive, be assured that the money goes towards funding this vital army of artisans.

Stonegate, which we saunter down next, was the route that stone was dragged up from the river barges to build the Minster. It is estimated that 20,000 tons of it were needed for the central tower alone. It's easy to imagine that Stonegate has always been crowded and hard to navigate, first due to the mass transportations of stone, then in the twentieth century by vehicles, and since the route was pedestrianised in 1974 by hordes of tourists.

We couldn't really ignore the tiny opening to **Coffee Yard**, as it is marked by a Red Devil, the traditional symbol of a printer; it was in this alley, in the eighteenth century, that the eccentric writer and publisher Thomas Gent had his printing premises. Here we also find **Barley Hall**, a restored medieval house dating from about 1360, with a magnificent Great Hall.

There has been a Thursday market in **St Sampson's Square** since at least the fifteenth century – and the numerous alleyways in all directions are the short-cuts that people took to get to the market. Pop into the Roman Baths Pub for a quick drink; and then descend to the basement to see the well-preserved Roman Baths underneath.

Until the eighteenth century, most of **St Helen's Square** was the graveyard of the church. **The Mansion House** (1732), at the south side of the square, is one of York's signature buildings, and is still the full-time residence of the Lord Mayor.

Then we head west along Blake Street and for a moment think we have fallen asleep and woken up in Bath. To our left are the **York Assembly Rooms** (1730), built by Richard Boyle in a Palladian style with Egyptian influence. In their time, they were full of society balls and gatherings.

St Leonard's Place was built in the early 1800s by the City Corporation to emulate the grand crescents of Bath and London, and it soon became the hub of elite social life. The **York Theatre Royal** (1744) was given a new Victorian Gothic frontage in the 1880s. We admire the 'tree-canopy' structure of the modernist foyer (1967) by Patrick Gwynn. Three very distinct eras of architecture, the sum greater than the parts.

The **city walls** were first built by the Romans out of stone (you can see their work at the Multangular Tower), buried under an earth bank and topped with a palisade

Above left The Shambles derives from an Anglo-Saxon word for butchers' shop-front shelves

Above right The wall is a great vantage point

Below The top of Clifford's Tower gives you the best panoramic view of all

by the Vikings, rebuilt in stone in the thirteenth and fourteenth centuries, and then intermittently repaired until the nineteenth century when they were completely re-modelled to make them more accessible and appealing, with re-built battlements, extra mediaeval 'features' and walkways added. This stretch of the wall offers an unparalleled view of York Minster.

And so, to **Monk Bar**, the only bar with its original medieval wall and windows surviving on the city side and also the only one where we descend by steep, low-ceilinged internal stairs to get down to street level.

Behind the ancient houses of **Our Lady's Row**, through a charming eighteenth-century arch with wrought-iron gates, is **Holy Trinity**, dating mainly from the fifteenth century. Our first impression is of a quaint village church that has eloped to the bright lights of the city but doesn't want to be spotted. Walking into the interior is like stepping back into Georgian times. This is the only church in the city to have retained its box pews.

Now, **The Shambles** is York's most famous street, which means it is also its busiest (try and get there early or late) The name derives from 'shammel', an Anglo-Saxon word for the shelves which were a prominent feature of the open shop-fronts. And, yes, 'what a bloody shambles' originally referred to the mess at the end of the butchers' day.

At the bottom, but before The Pavement, we turn left into Whip Dog Lane which becomes **Whip-ma-whop-ma-gate**, York's shortest street. There are many different explanations offered for the origin of this name, but

maybe it's just a ninteenth-century outbreak of supercali-fragilisticexpialidocious-itis.

Next up is the atmospheric **Lady Peckett's Yard**, in which some of the houses date back to the sixteenth century. Coming into Fossgate, I love the **Electric Cinema** opposite, York's first purpose-built cinema, notable for its early fire-proof construction technology around the projection room, opened in 1911 and finally closed in 1951.

Then we turn right, through an arch with a brightly painted Merchant Adventurers' Coat of Arms above it, into one of the most important buildings in the medieval city, the **Merchant Adventurers' Hall** (1530). It's the largest timber-framed building in the UK still used for its original purpose.

There are two very notable Georgian buildings in Castlegate, both designed by the Yorkshire architect John Carr. One is **Castlegate House** (1759) and the other is **Fairfax House** (1755), which houses a fine collection of Georgian furniture.

Clifford Street is a must for fans of Victoriana (I am a fully paid-up member). The first building directly opposite is the **York Institute** (1885). And **York Magistrate's Court** is a fabulous piece of 1890s High Gothic, my favourite building of the walk so far.

We pass by **Clifford's Tower**, the keep of the medieval Norman castle (eleventh century), built on the orders of William the Conqueror to control and dominate the city; it's now the only part of the castle surviving.

Spread around the 'Eye of York' is a beautiful trio of eighteenth-century buildings. The earliest chronologically is the Male Debtors' Prison to the right of the (ugly) entrance to the Castle Museum, built in 1705. The next building is the Crown Courts on the right, built in 1777 by John Carr. Finally, the Female Prison on the left, built in 1780 in a similar style to the Crown Court.

And then we head south into **St George's Field** (0.7 hectares, 1.7 acres), passing the floodgate chart on our right, a reminder of just how much York has suffered from flooding through the ages. Charters dating back to the sixteenth century gave the citizens the right to hold pageants, play games, archery and dry linen here. But it was also the site of public hangings and ducking stool punishments.

New Walk, which begins on the south side of Skeldergate Bridge, is a tree-lined avenue created in the 1730s for promenading, an important part of the attempts made by the eighteenth-century City Corporation to raise York's status to that of a leading Georgian social centre. From here, we can't usually resist the option of the **Millennium Bridge** loop, which gives us an excellent extra blast of green space and the delightful 1920s **Rowntree Park** (10.1 hectares, 25 acres).

Now for the final part of our journey – we re-join the wall at Baile Hill and finally start to make relatively speedy progress as, although there are great views throughout, there are fewer buildings to admire.

Micklegate Bar (fourteenth century) was the traditional ceremonial gate for monarchs entering the city, who, in a tradition dating back to Richard II in 1389, touch the state sword when entering. Its symbolic value led to traitors' severed heads being displayed on the defences. Micklegate itself makes a pleasant excursion and there are numerous cafés and restaurants to enjoy there.

Our journey finishes with a grandstand view of York station and beneath us the two massive archways through the wall that allowed trains to enter the city to reach George Hudson's original station of 1841 on Station Rise just in front of the Grand Hotel.

PIT STOPS

- **PERKY PEACOCK CAFÉ**, North Street Postern Tower, Under Lendal Bridge, YO1 7DJ
- **BETTY'S STONEGATE**, 46 Stonegate, YO1 8AS. Cosy café and local institution.
- **GRAYS COURT**, Chapter House Street, YO1 7JH. Tea, and a garden down some steps off the walls close to York Minster . . . what's not to like about that?!

QUIRKY SHOPPING

York is a haven for independent shops – key streets for independents being The Shambles, Fossgate, Stonegate and Gillygate.

PLACES TO VISIT

For a full listing, visit York Tourist Board. Lesser-known attractions include:
- **MANSION HOUSE**, YO1 9QL. The Lord Mayor's residence
- **RICHARD III MUSEUM**, Fossgate, YO1 9XD
- **FAIRFAX HOUSE**, Castlegate, YO1 9RN. A fabulous Georgian townhouse designed by John Carr

WHEN TO VISIT

Jorvik Viking Festival (Feb), York's Chocolate Festival (March), Railfest (June), Festival of Food and Drink (Sept)

SEATS OF LEARNING

Spires and vistas offer the promise of a better life – the gaining of knowledge, cultural and social inspiration . . .

These old university towns have much in common. There is little evidence of industrialisation and there are myriad green spaces close to the centre. Water is key – the Isis and the Cherwell in Oxford, the Cam in Cambridge (and of course the punting tradition in both). The colleges dominate the topography of the centre, warping the 'natural expansion' of the town in a particular direction (north in Oxford, east in Cambridge) away from college land.

They tend to be politically engaged – campaigning groups and 'Friends' groups are especially vociferous – and to favour progressive politics (both cities voted Remain in 2016; in the 2017 General Election, two Labour MPs were elected, one Lib Dem and no Conservative). There is a thriving cultural scene with theatres and festivals, and world-famous libraries and museums. For all these reasons, they are very popular tourist destinations with the highest ratios of visitor nights to population of any of the cities we visit (Cambridge 4.1:1, Oxford 3.9:1); and they are also popular cities for young families to move to in search of the 'good life'.

Maybe because they are so similar, the two universities seem to go out of their way to do some things differently:

CAMBRIDGE	OXFORD
COURTS	QUADS
SUPERVISIONS	TUTORIALS
BEDDERS	SCOUTS
PUNTERS STAND ON THE END PLATFORM – THE 'CAMBRIDGE END'	PUNTERS STAND INSIDE THE BOAT AT THE OTHER END – THE 'OXFORD END'
Ph.D.	D.Phil.
COLLEGE STAIRCASES ASSIGNED LETTERS	COLLEGE STAIRCASES NUMBERED

Cambridge

This walk takes you past many of the classic university sites of the city, but also to places that you will never have seen before, even if you live here or studied here. In half a day you will feel like an insider!

Cambridge is a city still defined by academia. The most prominent (if plain) building remains Giles Gilbert Scott's 1930s University Library, only 157 feet in height but visible from miles around; for this is a very flat landscape, ideal for the cyclists you will encounter around every corner, often heading straight for you!

The dominance of the colleges in the landscape has meant a city grid that is skewed, with almost all of the nineteenth-century development taking place to the east of the city away from the colleges. The railway station was also relegated to the south-east edge of the city, apparently to discourage undergraduates from hopping on the train down to London and neglecting their studies.

However, the huge benefit of this tight collegiate land ownership has been the large green open spaces that have remained intact, along the Backs, the river to Grantchester and also the numerous sports fields.

The name 'the Backs' refers to the backs of the colleges. In the sixteenth century, the area consisted of pasture, gardens and orchards owned by the colleges, with wooden bridges across the Cam. Over time, the colleges planted avenues of trees and built sturdier bridges. In 1772, Capability Brown laid out a wilderness behind St John's College. This 'rus

WALK DATA

- **DISTANCE:** 12.8 km (8 miles). Reduce to 8.5 km by finishing at the railway station
- **HEIGHT GAIN:** None (it is the Fens after all!)
- **WALK TIME:** 3¼ hours
- **START & FINISH:** Grantchester Tea Rooms (CB3 9ND). Or, from the railway station (CB1 2JW), via Botanic Garden (entrance fee)
- **TERRAIN:** Can be muddy in places, and cows

in urbe' vision continues to this day, with sheep in front of King's, wild areas, specimen trees and vistas, making it one of the most picturesque spots in the country. Punting, which is an integral part of this rural idyll and looks like it has been around for ever, was surprisingly only introduced in 1903, when Jack Scudamore spotted the tourist potential.

The other very noticeable feature of Cambridge has been its pedestrian and cyclist-friendly policies. The city centre has been barred to traffic for many years and is consequently a delightful space to wander through, full of interesting shops and cafés.

THE WALK

We start our walk at the Grantchester Tea Rooms, which proudly makes the claim that 'more famous people have taken tea here than anywhere else in the world'. We peep into the Orchard on our way to the river, half expecting to see a group of academics in earnest conversation in old green deckchairs, with ancient bikes propped against the apple trees and a fair sprinkling of beards, sandals and eccentricities; and that is exactly what we do see.

If we had passed through a century or so ago, we might well have witnessed a very similar-looking gathering, the 'Grantchester Group', comprising Rupert Brooke, E.M. Forster, Virginia Woolf, Bertrand Russell, Augustus John, John Maynard Keynes and Ludwig Wittgenstein. They spent their days in animated discourse and enjoying the nature around them, 'in Arcadia', as Brooke described it.

This stretch along **Grantchester Meadows** (40 hectares, 99 acres) was also a favourite spot of Ted Hughes and Sylvia Plath, who would wander here together at unusual hours. She wrote: 'Got up at 4.30 a.m. this day with Ted and went for a long walk to Grantchester. I felt a peace and joy in the most beautiful world with animals and birds. We began mooing at a pasture of cows, and they all looked up, and as if hypnotised, began to follow us in a crowd of about twenty across the pasture to a wooden stile, staring fascinated. I stood on the stile and, in a resonant voice, recited all I knew of Chaucer's *Canterbury Tales* for about twenty minutes. I never had such an intelligent, fascinated audience.'

We skirt past Scudamore's Boat Hire, over Queen's Bridge and then head along the Backs to the finest view in Cambridge, King's Chapel and Clare College – gazing across the Cam and a meadow with sheep grazing in it. **King's College Chapel**, made famous the world over by its Christmas carols, dates back to the fifteenth century and is one of the finest, most graceful examples of late Perpendicular Gothic in the country.

Trinity Great Court (1600s) is the largest fully enclosed green space in the land. Sir Isaac Newton

WALK DATA

- **CITY POPULATION:** 122,725 (#49 in UK)
- **ORIGINS:** 1st century BC; University founded in 1209
- **CITY STATUS:** 1951
- **FAMOUS INHABITANTS:** John Maynard Keynes (economist), David Gilmour (Pink Floyd), Douglas Adams (writer), F.R. Leavis (literary critic), Richard Attenborough (film director)
- **NOTABLE BUILDERS:** Wren (Wren Library & Emmanuel Chapel), Giles Gilbert Scott (University Library), Philip Powell (Cripps Court)
- **SCREEN TIME:** *Chariots of Fire* (Trinity Great Court), *The Theory of Everything* (St John's), *Grantchester* TV series
- **ICONIC CITYSCAPES:** Tower of St Mary's in King's Parade, Varsity Restaurant roof terrace

had his rooms here, as did Lord Byron, who shared them with a pet bear. It is also famous for the Great Court Run, which involves attempting to run around the perimeter within the time that it takes the college clock to strike twelve. In 2007 Sam Dobin, a second-year undergraduate reading Economics, made it round within the sound of the final chime, although fierce debate still persists as to whether it was permissible to transgress from the flagstones onto the cobbles to moderate the sharpness of the corners.

A large fountain sits at the centre of Great Court. Until recently the fountain had its own water supply via a conduit from a spring a mile and a half to the west of the College (it might be fun to trace that route one day). Look up above the college gates and you will see a statue of the college's founder, Henry VIII. Some years ago, his sceptre was replaced with a chair leg as an undergraduate prank. When a bicycle pump was inserted in its place by a subsequent prankster, the authorities determined that the original prank took precedence, and reinstated the chair leg, which is what we see to this day.

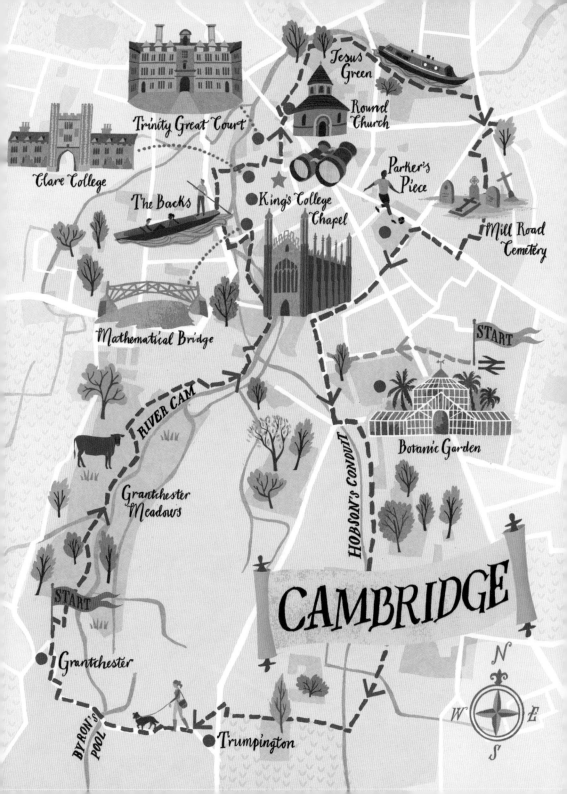

Trinity Great Court

Clare College

The Backs

King's College Chapel

Jesus Green

Round Church

Parker's Piece

Mill Road Cemetery

START

Botanic Garden

Mathematical Bridge

RIVER CAM

HOBSON'S CONDUIT

Grantchester Meadows

CAMBRIDGE

START

Grantchester

BYRON'S POOL

Trumpington

N
W   E
S

Above left Trinity Hall's modern Jerwood Library blends perfectly into the medieval buildings around it

Above right Jesus Green is a great place to escape the city centre bustle

Below King's College Chapel is one of the most graceful examples of late Perpendicular Gothic

'How could the wind be so strong, so far inland, that cyclists coming into the town in the late afternoon looked more like sailors in peril?'
PENELOPE FITZGERALD

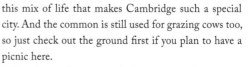

Heading to the top of Trinity Street we reach the **Round Church** (1160), one of the oldest buildings in Cambridge, and one of only four medieval round churches still in use in England, its shape inspired by the rotunda in the church of the Holy Sepulchre in Jerusalem.

As we stroll down the quaint, flower-bedecked Portugal Street, we spot a swirly yellow metal sculpture above the door of 19 Portugal Place. This was where Francis Crick, co-discoverer of DNA, lived in the 1950s; and the 'sculpture' represents a single helix, to commemorate his dwelling there.

We walk across **Jesus Green** (11 hectares, 27 acres) alongside the river. The dozen or so canal boats moored here hint at a different side to Cambridge – a more alternative and 'green' character that has long been alive in the city alongside the academia. Canal boats are the model of space efficiency – kitchen, bathroom, living and sleeping areas all within a 40-square-metre space. And on the roofs, bikes, firewood, herbs, flowers, vegetable plots, even a doghouse.

Midsummer Common (12 hectares, 30 acres) is host to Cambridge's plushest restaurant – the two-Michelin-starred Midsummer House, full of well-heeled regulars and hoi poloi on very special occasions. It is also home to the city's most multicultural fair, the Strawberry Fair, held every June, a mix of outlandish clothes, global food, exotic smells and eclectic music, organised 'by the people of Cambridge, for the people of Cambridge'. It's

this mix of life that makes Cambridge such a special city. And the common is still used for grazing cows too, so just check out the ground first if you plan to have a picnic here.

By the early years of the nineteenth century, overcrowded parish churchyards had become a serious problem in Cambridge, as they had in most UK cities, and a new burial ground outside the town was needed. **Mill Road Cemetery** was built in the 1840s when it was still agricultural land on the edge of the town.

One of the most influential designers of the period was John Claudius Loudon, who laid out Cambridge's nearby Histon Road Cemetery. He believed everyone should have access to green 'breathing spaces' within towns, and his vision was that well-planned and well-managed cemeteries, once full, could become the public gardens of the future. Which is pretty much how Mill Road Cemetery works today, in a slightly run-down but charming way: orange-tip butterflies flit from grave to grave and there is a profusion of wild flowers.

We eventually drag ourselves out of the cemetery along a delightful tree-lined avenue back into the bustle of the multi-ethnic Mill Road and thence to **Parker's Piece** (10 hectares, 25 acres). Now, although in many ways this prairie-like space looks unremarkable, it played a key role in our footballing history. In the early nineteenth century, village football teams would arrive brandishing rival rules to the game, which they each affixed to a nearby tree, and got down to sporting

'Cambridge was a joy. Tediously. People reading books in a posh place. It was my fantasy. I loved it. I miss it still.' ZADIE SMITH

business, usually involving large doses of roughness and certainly very little passing of the ball.

But over time, maybe as injuries and arguments mounted, so a common set of football rules emerged, emphasising skill above force, which forbade catching the ball and the 'hacking' that had up until then been the norm. These 'Cambridge Rules' eventually became the cornerstone of the 1863 Football Association Rules.

We move on now to the last part of our journey and the bit that most people will know least about. At the end of Lensfield Road, we come across **Hobson's Conduit**, marked by a Tudor Fountain that was originally in the Market Square but moved here in 1856. Thomas Hobson is well known in Cambridge for his conduit; but his claim to everlasting fame is the phrase 'Hobson's Choice', which of course means no real choice at all. He kept a stable of horses which he would hire out in strict rotation, the customer having to accept whichever horse he was offered, or none at all! Hence the phrase.

In 1610, Hobson helped finance the building of a conduit to convey fresh water to the centre of Cambridge from the springs in Nine Wells, near

Trumpington, no doubt for the benefit of his trusty steeds. It is still very much in evidence today; in 'runnels' alongside Trumpington Street, past the Fitzwilliam Museum; and in the southerly direction (which we are taking) pretty much in its original state, a wide and shallow stream.

The Botanic Garden of Cambridge University was founded in 1762 in the centre of the City, now the New Museums Site. It was conceived as a typical Renaissance physic garden, inspired by the Chelsea Physic Garden in London. It grew herbaceous plants used in the teaching of medical students at the University. Today's much larger **Botanic Garden** (16 hectares, 40 acres) was founded in 1846 by John Stevens Henslow, Professor of Botany at Cambridge. He laid out the garden to accommodate an extensive tree collection, and also started to develop ideas about variation and the nature of species that would be taken up by his famous student, Charles Darwin. The plant collections were so appealing to Victorian collectors that visitors were required to doff their hats on departure to prove that they weren't hiding away any rare cuttings.

South of the Botanic Garden, Hobson's Conduit becomes a much narrower stream, passing through the

Above left Trinity College's original gates in Garret Hostel Lane

Above right Hobson's Conduit meanders among the allotments

Below Clare College reflects every era of Georgian architecture

pretty **Empty Common Allotments**. There are forty-seven 'ten-rod' allotments for rent from the council. A rod is an old measurement dating back to Anglo-Saxon times; and ten rods (250 square metres, about the size of a doubles tennis court) is judged to be the area required to feed a large family.

The day we pass through there is plenty of activity. The allotment holders seem to be roughly split between the 'flat cap' brigade, perhaps escaping from household chores, growing mainly traditional root vegetables; and the younger 'urban farmer' brigade, in ethnic-style dress, intent on growing more challenging crops – herbs, salads, exotic vegetables, flowers – and a neatly arranged stack of rotting logs so that their kids can hunt for wildlife and learn about the countryside. After years of decline, allotments are back in fashion, at least in Cambridge. Fifty plots were added to this site in the last few years, and there are still nearly 300 people on the council's waiting list.

At the far end of the allotments, we take a detour through the tiny **Clare Woods**, supposedly a favoured habitat for bats – we feel we are deep in the countryside! Then alongside the Guided Busway, past the massive structure of Addenbrooke's Hospital. Founded in 1766, relocated here in the 1960s from its original Trumpington Street site (now the Business School), and progressively expanding to campus-style proportions, it is undoubtedly the biggest architectural structure that we will see today; a centre of medical excellence, but sadly a complete mishmash of nothing very particular in terms of architectural styles.

Finally, we cut through a residential part of Grantchester village, taking a detour to **Byron's Pool**, well worth it if you still have the energy left. These days it is a nature reserve; once it was the spot where Lord Byron regularly took a swim (we know not if the pet bear came too). We get back just in time for tea and a large slice of cake at the Orchard Tea Garden. Perfect.

PIT STOPS

- **GRANTCHESTER TEA ROOMS**, 43 Mill Way, Grantchester, CB3 9ND. Deckchairs in the orchard.
- **CAFÉ ON THE ROUND**, 16 Round Church Street, CB5 8AD. A great little 'indie'.
- **FITZBILLIES**, 51-52 Trumpington Street, CB2 1RG. An institution, especially famous for its Chelsea buns
- **CAMBRIDGE BOTANIC GARDEN CAFÉ**. Modern space, tranquil location. A favourite.

QUIRKY SHOPPING

Cambridge is full of independents, notably in Trinity Street, Green Street, Rose Crescent and the passages leading off King's Parade.

PLACES TO VISIT

- **THE COLLEGES**: Admission fees apply.
- **KETTLE'S YARD**, CB3 0AQ. A quirky, must-visit art gallery.
- **FITZWILLIAM MUSEUM**, CB2 1RB. Art and antiquities from all periods.
- **CAMBRIDGE UNIVERSITY BOTANIC GARDEN**, CB2 1JE. An oasis of nature and calm.

WHEN TO VISIT

Strawberry Fair on Midsummer Common (early June), Cambridge Folk Festival (late July), Mill Road Fair (early Dec)

Oxford

With two rivers as your path for much of the route, this walk takes you through the city's finest green spaces both tamed and untamed, past great architecture from many eras and a glorious view of the 'dreaming spires'.

Oxford is a city shaped by its rivers and colleges. The River Thames (Isis) to the west and south and the River Cherwell to the east define the old boundaries of the town, with the oldest buildings (mainly the colleges) to the south where the rivers join, and new housing stretching northwards through the centuries as the town expanded towards Summertown.

Oxford is consistently named among the world's top universities, and can claim many 'firsts':

- The first British university, dating back to the twelfth century
- The earliest botanic garden, opened in 1621
- The world's first university museum, the Ashmolean, founded in 1683

While Oxford developed a significant manufacturing base throughout the nineteenth and twentieth centuries (best known being the Cowley car plant), all the development was outside the core and you get no sense of it on this walk (unlike Manchester or Leeds, for example).

From the 1920s onwards, it became viewed as a city

WALK DATA

- **DISTANCE:** 9.8 km (6.1 miles)
- **HEIGHT GAIN:** 30 metres
- **WALK TIME:** 2½ hours
- **START & FINISH:** Oxford station (OX1 1HS)
- **TERRAIN:** Can be muddy on the meadows

of two halves, summed up in the saying that 'Oxford is the left bank of Cowley'.

The compactness of the central area has inevitably meant special traffic challenges. The city has perforce been an innovator, becoming the first in the country to establish a Park and Ride scheme in 1973 and still having one of the largest urban Park and Ride networks in the UK. It also has extensive bus and cycle lanes, which means that 17 per cent of people cycle to work (second only to Cambridge). As we discover, it's also an exceptionally agreeable city to walk around in, with more green spaces in the centre than just about anywhere else, and of course many stunning buildings to ogle at too.

THE WALK

Heading north out of the station, we soon come across the old track of the **Varsity Line**, dubbed 'the Brain Line', that linked Oxford with Cambridge until it was ripped up in a late-1960s post-Beeching purge.

Young mathematicians, linguists and off-the-wall thinkers would have trundled out of here very 'hush hush' during the Second World War on their way to 'Station X', the code breaking centre at Bletchley Park. Roy Jenkins, for example, who was an undergraduate at Balliol, went up to Bletchley in 1943 and was put to work cracking the Tunny codes. He subsequently became Chancellor of the university. There is much talk of the line being restored.

The Thames, as it runs through Oxford, is called the Isis; the reason is lost in the mists of time, but the Victorians insisted it was a distinct river until it met the River Thame at Dorchester-on-Thames and therefore merited its own Latin name. We follow the right bank up to the footbridge which takes us on to Port Meadow. It was under this bridge that the Reverend Charles Dodgson (better known as Lewis Carroll) rowed upstream one summer's day in 1862 with Alice and her two sisters. He began at their request to make up a story that later was expanded into *Alice's Adventures in Wonderland*.

Port Meadow (178 hectares, 440 acres) is the largest area of common land in Oxford. Since it was gifted to the Freemen of Oxford in the tenth century by Alfred the Great, by way of thanking them for helping defend his kingdom against the marauding Danes, it has been used for just about every purpose imaginable in its long unfurrowed existence; from grazing horses and cattle, to horseracing in the seventeenth and eighteenth centuries (low stone bridges laid over washes and ditches for this purpose still survive) to warfare (there are foundations of the fortifications from the Parliamentary siege of Oxford during the English Civil War here) to military encampments in both world wars; to 'make love not war' in the shape of free festivals and raves in the 1980s and 1990s (which the police tried to control with a specially re-enforced tractor that enabled them to navigate the boggy bits). Today it is used for leisure of all sorts –

WALK DATA

- **CITY POPULATION:** 150,245 (#45 in UK)
- **ORIGINS:** 8th century AD
- **CITY STATUS:** Granted in 1542 (the cathedral is Christ Church Chapel)
- **FAMOUS INHABITANTS:** A who's who of the British establishment including 52 Nobel Prize-winners, 27 prime ministers and 10 Poets Laureate
- **NOTABLE BUILDERS:** Christopher Wren (Sheldonian Theatre), Nicholas Hawksmoor (Radcliffe Camera), Arne Jacobsen (St Catherine's College), James Stirling (Florey Building)
- **SCREEN TIME:** *Inspector Morse* TV series, Harry Potter films (Christ Church, Oxford Botanic Garden)
- **ICONIC CITYSCAPES:** Top of South Park, Ashmolean Roof Terrace Restaurant (OX1 2PH)

walking, running, and, when the meadows are flooded and frozen over, skating.

And as if that weren't enough, there are several Bronze Age round barrows and an area of Iron Age settlement; plus, it is also a Site of Special Scientific Interest, with many species of birds and flowers. The fact that it has never been ploughed has made it a wildlife haven.

We soon find ourselves in **North Parade**, famously and somewhat incongruously situated to the south of South Parade. Apparently, during the Civil War when Charles I was besieged by Oliver Cromwell at Oxford, South Parade was the Roundhead southern front, whilst North Parade was the location of the Royalist northern front. Apocryphal or not, I like that story. Today the street is very far from a 'front line', replete with indie shops, trendy restaurants and an open food market.

From North Parade we cross into the heart of **North Oxford**, one of the country's finest Victorian residential areas, full of huge mansions with every imaginable High Victorian architectural twiddle: statement porches at the top of flights of steps, large bays, brick patterns, complicated rooflines, crenellations, plaques and crests

Left Butterfield's last masterpiece in brick, Keble College Chapel is pure Victoriana

'One almost expects the people to sing instead of speaking. It is all like an opera.' WILLIAM BUTLER YEATS

and many spires and larger-than-strictly-necessary chimneystacks. From the 1860s onwards, it was developed for the wealthy merchants of Oxford by St John's College, but today it is typically inhabited by successful academics and Londoners seeking more space and cultured living, as well as a smattering of student digs evidenced by the piles of bikes stacked outside some of the dwellings.

We are fascinated by **Park Town** (1850s), the first planned middle-class estate in the area, comprising seventy houses in total. Samuel Seckham, the architect, had a constricted space to work with, but ingeniously managed to create an estate that combined terraces and villas. Part of the scheme depended on sacrificing large back gardens for communal gardens and planting in the central area. Behind Park Town is the Dragon School, which numbers among its Old Dragons both the actor Emma Watson and Sir John Betjeman, a hero of preserving Victorian architecture. Maybe it was having regularly walked past such fine examples of Victoriana as a boy that made him such a passionate devotee.

The **University Parks** (30 hectares, 74 acres) feel pretty much like the heart of Oxford today, but used to be part of the fields to the north of the city. They were officially created in 1853, but the space was used for leisure long before that. Charles II is reputed to have walked his dog here. On the south-west of the park you can just see the splendid, polychromatic brick **Keble College Chapel** (1876) built by the great Victorian architect William Butterfield.

One of the objectives in laying out the Parks was the provision of facilities for team sport for members of the university, and this is still very much in evidence as we stroll through today. It is home to the Oxford University Cricket Club and a venue for first-class cricket matches. The sporting tradition has also seen a more recent novelty with the park becoming the home of the Oxford Quidditch league. Now Quidditch, as I'm sure you will recall, is the fictional game played in the Harry Potter books requiring impossible feats of aerobatics. Somehow, the enterprising students of Oxford have managed to create a 'ground' version of the game and codified it in the official Rulebook, the IQA, which was formally adopted in 2012; since which time there have been many inter-college, inter-university and even international games.

Provision of a bathing place alongside the river featured in the earliest discussions on the recreational use of the Parks. **Parson's Pleasure**, close to the rollerway that transports punts around the weir, was reserved for the use of male members of the university, and became a popular place for nude bathing. Similarly, **Dame's Delight** on the river bank opposite Mesopotamia Walk was reserved for ladies' bathing.

One anecdote has it that a number of dons were sunbathing nude at Parson's Pleasure when a female student floated by in a punt. All but one of the startled dons covered their genitals – Maurice Bowra placed a flannel over his head instead. When asked why he had done that, he replied haughtily, 'I don't know about you,

'There are few greater temptations on earth than to stay permanently at Oxford in meditation.' HILAIRE BELLOC

gentlemen, but in Oxford, I, at least, am known by my face'.

Mesopotamia is a narrow island, about half a mile long but not much wider than a tennis court, that lies between the upper and lower levels of the River Cherwell, just south of Parson's Pleasure. The name Mesopotamia in Greek means 'between the rivers' and originally referred to the area between the Tigris and Euphrates rivers in present-day Iraq.

We have the sensation at this point of being in deepest countryside – celandines and willows all around us, looking across the river and over a field of cut reeds in the sunshine, beyond which small figures of walkers and cyclists are moving peaceably to and fro. A living embodiment of the pastoral idyll.

In the distance to our right we can just see **St Catherine's College** (1962), the quintessence of cool modernism with a dash of Arts and Crafts. Every detail, from the cutlery and furniture to the landscaping, was worked through by the Danish architect Arne Jacobsen.

We climb the slope and cross into **South Park** (20 hectares, 50 acres) and one of the most iconic vistas of any city in Britain – the Jude the Obscure view, gazing over the spires of Oxford and dreaming of what might just be possible . . . We whoop down the hill in delight, through a space where many of the city's festivals, fairs and fireworks displays take place.

South Park only became a protected and public space fairly recently: the land was privately owned by the Morrell family of Headington Hill Hall until 1932, and was farmed. The Oxford Preservation Trust bought the land in 1932, and in 1959 gave it to the City of Oxford to be preserved as an open space for the benefit of the public.

When you think Oxford, you tend to think ancient buildings, but look out for the **Florey Building** (1960s) on the right along St Clement's. Designed by James Stirling as student accommodation for Queen's College, its unusual sculptural shape and bold use of bright red brick divided taste when it was built.

Heading back into the centre now, we cross **Magdalen Bridge**. The annual May Day celebration starts here at first light with the Magdalen College Choir singing the 'Hymnus Eucharisticus' from the top of the Magdalen Tower, a tradition that goes back over 500 years. Large crowds gather under the tower along

Above left Osney Power Station is a reminder of the city's industrial side

Above right Christ Church has glorious views over The Meadows

Below The Botanic Garden was an inspiration for *Alice's Adventures in Wonderland*

the High Street and on the bridge, many the worse for wear after all-night balls, incongruously attired for such an early hour in formal wear and tiaras.

The tradition of jumping off the bridge into the River Cherwell, which I also imagined to be steeped in tradition, apparently only began in the early 1980s. It was banned in 2005 after half the hundred or so jumpers required medical treatment due to the shallowness of the water.

Nearly as old as the May Day celebrations, The **University of Oxford Botanic Garden** (1.8 hectares, 4.4 acres) is the oldest botanic garden in the country and one of the oldest and most important scientific gardens in the world, dating back to 1621. It was founded as a physic garden growing plants for medicinal research. Lewis Carroll was a frequent visitor and it provided another source of inspiration for *Alice's Adventures in Wonderland*: the garden's water lily house can be seen in the background of Sir John Tenniel's illustration of the Queen's croquet-ground.

Finally, the *tour de force* of our walk, **Christ Church Meadows** (23 hectares, 57 acres). Roughly triangular in shape, it is bounded by the River Thames, the River Cherwell and **Christ Church College** (1525). On a summer's day it is flocked with people walking, picnicking, enjoying the river and (a few) even revising.

Being a big open space, people have also wanted to use the Meadows for getting places. James Sadler made the first ascent in a balloon by an Englishman from here in 1784. The balloon apparently rose to a height of around 3,600 feet and landed six miles away. More alarmingly, the Meadows were also earmarked for a relief road in the early 1960s. What became known as the Jellicoe Plan was unveiled in 1963 and consisted of a landscaped, sunken road through the middle of the meadow. Thankfully the plan eventually got kicked into the long grass. How our attitudes have changed; nowadays we are much more protective of our special green spaces.

From here we take the delightful river route (south and west side) past the city's first power station, the **Old Osney Power Station** (1892), back to the railway station, pausing to admire the **Saïd Business School** (2002).

PIT STOPS

- **THE JERICHO CAFÉ**, 112 Walton Street, OX2 6AJ. Quaint part of the city.
- **CAFÉ LOCO**, St Aldate's, OX1 1RA
- **THE HEAD OF THE RIVER PUB**, St Aldate's, OX1 4LB

QUIRKY SHOPPING

- **NORTH PARADE** (OX2 6LX) has indie shops, and a food market alternate Saturdays.
- **THE COVERED MARKET**, High Street, OX1 3DZ. Trading for over 200 years, not to be missed.
- **BROAD STREET** (OX1 3BQ) has Blackwell's bookshop and many smaller shops.

PLACES TO VISIT

- **THE ASHMOLEAN MUSEUM OF ART & ANTHROPOLOGY** (OX1 2PH). Established in 1683, it is Britain's oldest public museum.
- **THE PITT RIVERS MUSEUM** (OX1 3PP). A wonderful anthropological collection.

WHEN TO VISIT

Oxford Literary Festival (late March), Oxford Foodies Festival (late Aug), St Giles Fair (early Sept)

TRADING PORTS

Trading ports enjoy glorious topography. Think of the breathtaking view of Newcastle as you arrive over the gorge by train; or the natural arena of the hills around Plymouth Sound; or the breathtaking views along the Avon Gorge from the Clifton Suspension Bridge; or the panoramic views of Liverpool, the docks and the Mersey from the limestone ridge on which the two great cathedrals perch.

As we walk around these cities we are struck too by the character and individuality of the people. In Bristol, they have all taken to painting their houses in pastel colours, creating a rainbow of colour, supplemented by street art at every turn; in Liverpool we pass the Chinatown Gate, centre of the oldest Chinese community in Europe and thriving to this day with its distinctive culture, one of many different ethnic groups in the city; in Newcastle, we are hailed by a solicitous Geordie at every turn helping us to find the way; in Plymouth we reflect on longtime resident Beryl Cook's observations: 'I am constantly entertained by the activities going on around me. To see people enjoying themselves gives me the greatest pleasure, and the inspiration to paint.' Maritime folk are lively folk with lots of influences; they are most definitely not buttoned-up people.

SO, WHAT SHOULD YOU LOOK OUT FOR IN A TRADING PORT?

1. **Redeveloped dockyard areas:** from warehouses and dockers' pubs to galleries and organic cafés
2. **A taste for adventure:** John Cabot, Sir Frances Drake, the Pilgrim Fathers, America-bound emigrants
3. **Overseas cultural influences** – the Americas on the western ports and the Baltic on the north-eastern
4. **Fabulous Georgian quarters** enabled by eighteenth-century wealth – Clifton, Grainger Town, Canning, Devonport
5. **Evidence of wartime bombing** in re-drawn street patterns and bombed-out churches that survive as memorials to these terrible events.

Bristol
Arnos Vale & the Old Town

*The early English name for Bristol was 'Brycgstow', the place of the bridge,
and this walk explores that idea a little further – in all we encounter nineteen bridges!
Revealing a lot about the topography of Bristol and taking you through
big green spaces and major regeneration programmes.*

Above all, this walk is about the burgeoning growth and prosperity of Bristol – from the beginnings in the Old Town around Bristol Bridge, to the vast wealth of the merchant buccaneers epitomised by the Floating Harbour, to the economic development of the Victorian age – the train opening up communications with the rest of the country and the parks and cemeteries starting to serve a rapidly expanding population; and finally, in more recent years, to the massive new wave of regeneration emanating from the Temple Meads Development Plan.

In more practical terms, this is a walk about crossing three critical transport modes – water, rail and road – and the naturally hilly terrain either side of the Avon that gives Bristol such a distinctive and appealing character. Incredibly, we encounter nineteen bridges on our walk – crossing five, going under four, walking past seven and seeing a further three – something of a record for our urban rambles.

But there's one fly in the ointment. We love the rivers, we love the railways, we love the contours, but in the 1960s the road system threatened to irreversibly destroy the landscape we are planning to walk through. And it partly did – in the 'Tragedy of Totterdown' more than 500

WALK DATA

- **DISTANCE:** 9.9 km (6.2 miles)
- **HEIGHT GAIN:** 65 metres
- **WALK TIME:** 2½ hours
- **START & FINISH:** Bristol Temple Meads station (BS1 6EA)
- **TERRAIN:** Paths throughout, modest climb

houses were bulldozed in the 1960s to make way for the Outer Circuit Road designed to relieve traffic congestion. And it would have sliced straight through the middle of Victoria Park.

Green space often tends to be an easy victim for road 'improvers', as trees and blades of grass can't form protest groups. Thankfully, attitudes changed and in the 1970s the whole scheme was put on hold. Things really are better today. To celebrate Bristol being the 2015 Green Capital of Europe, the Bristol Greenway project was drawn up to connect all the City's Green spaces together with popular routes.

THE WALK

We begin our walk at **Bristol Temple Meads station**, built by Brunel in 1840. He designed it in a fifteenth century style, with flat arches and a hammer beam roof, fronted by offices in the Tudor style. This is the building we see on the right towards the bottom of Station Approach, called the Engine Shed, now a collaborative office space. The main station building is in the Victorian Gothic style and dates to the 1870s.

We soon reach an area of feverish building activity. This is the epicentre of the Temple Quarter Enterprise Zone, designed to drive local growth and create jobs. As Albert Road twists round to the east, so we get a great view south of the coloured houses of Totterdown on the slope on the other side of the River Avon. Bristol is famous for its rows of colourful houses, but no one is sure when and why the fashion started; it is a vernacular common to seaside towns.

We cross the **Sparke Evans Bridge**, painted yellow, which seems to be a favourite colour for Bristol bridges. We feel as if we are entering a stately home as we pass through the classically inspired entrance lodges of **Arnos Vale Cemetery** (18.2 hectares, 45 acres). It was opened in 1837 in response to the dangerous overcrowding of inner-city churchyards and was designed to be visually attractive in the style of a walled Greek necropolis, with neoclassical mortuary chapels set in a beautiful garden of trees and plants.

But in the twentieth century it fell into disrepair, and local groups began campaigning for its restoration. In 2003 it was featured on the BBC programme *Restoration* and subsequently received a £4.8 million Heritage Lottery Fund grant. The volunteers are doing a fabulous job keeping the place open, looked after, loved and visited, and we do our bit by having a cup of coffee and cake here.

The cemetery is also ecologically important, having morphed from medieval countryside to Georgian estate to Victorian cemetery to the present day with almost no use of chemical pesticides or insecticides, helping make it a rare urban haven for wildlife and plants. It forms a natural amphitheatre on the hillside, overlooking the city,

WALK DATA

- **CITY POPULATION:** 428,074 (#11 in UK)
- **ORIGINS:** 11th century
- **CITY STATUS:** Granted in 1542, when the Diocese of Bristol was founded
- **FAMOUS INHABITANTS:** William Watts (inventor), Billy Butlin (holiday camps), Samuel Plimsoll (social reformer), John Cabot (explorer), Woodes Rogers (sea captain)
- **LOCAL BUILDERS:** William Bruce Gingell (Bristol Byzantine style: General Hospital and Robinson's Oil Seed Mill), John Wood the Elder (St Nicholas Market)
- **SCREEN TIME:** *These Foolish Things* (King Street), *Starter for Ten* (Temple Meads and Floating Harbour), *The Duchess* (Bristol Old Vic); *Skins* (Somerset Square), *Sherlock* (Arnos Grove, Queen Square, King Street), *Being Human* (Redcliffe Caves, General Hospital)
- **ICONIC CITYSCAPES:** Perrett's Park, Redcliffe Parade

making it perhaps the most spectacular of all the urban cemeteries we visit.

We wend our way up the slope taking tiny paths here and there; at every turn there are gravestones or memorials commemorating Bristol citizens. You could while away many an afternoon imagining the lives of the worthies and not-so-worthies. Coming out at the top of the cemetery, it strikes us what a steep part of the city we are now in. Vale Street, a few hundred yards to our north, has reportedly the steepest street of houses in England. It feels a bit like San Francisco, especially the brightly painted dwellings and the relaxed vibe.

Crowndale Road is a good example of an excellent Greenway Route connecting Arnos Vale to Perrett's Park, lined as it is with trees and the houses having front gardens.

Perrett's Park (6.7 hectares, 16 acres) was laid out in 1929 on a steeply sloping site that forms a natural bowl. We marvel at the panoramic view from here – Ashton Court, the Clifton Suspension Bridge, both of Bristol's cathedrals and the Wills Memorial Building, we can spot them all!

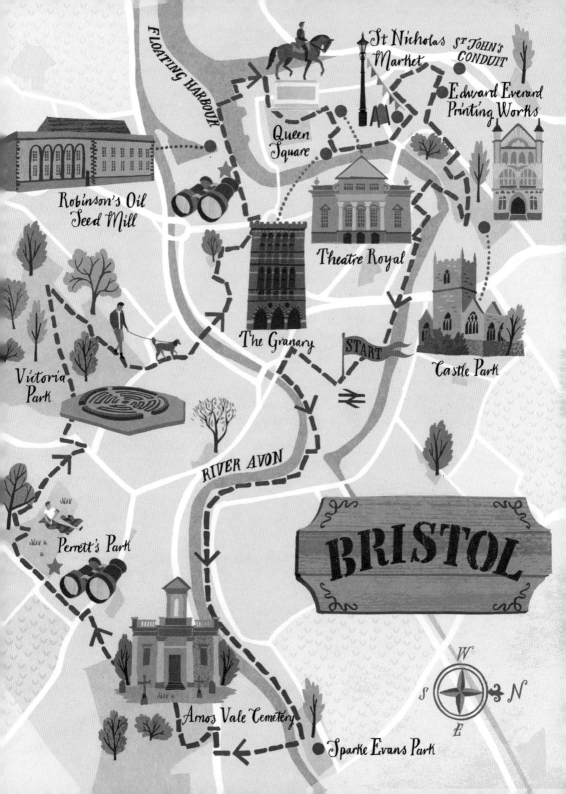

'If I had to show a foreigner one English city to give him a balanced idea of English architecture, I should take him to Bristol, which has developed in all directions, and where nearly everything has happened.' JOHN SUMMERSON

Strolling past the **Perrett's Park Allotments** reminds us of just how many allotments there are in Bristol and how committed the city is to self-sustainability. Take a look at the Bristol Food Network, which 'supports, informs and connects individuals, community projects, organisations and businesses who share a vision to transform Bristol into a sustainable food city'.

Next, we head into the ample and welcoming **Victoria Park** (20.8 hectares, 51.5 acres), established in the 1880s following the expansion of Bedminster as a residential and industrial area within Bristol. This was (and is) truly a 'people's park', designed from the start to be a 'green lung' for those people living locally who typically had no access to the countryside.

Langdon Street Bridge, more popularly called the Banana Bridge (you'll soon work out why) was erected in 1883 as a temporary bridge on the site where Bedminster Bridge now stands. It was then transported here on barges at high tide.

Redcliffe gets its name from the red sandstone atop of which it is built – the steep cliff face can clearly be seen at the Addercliff, below Redcliffe Parade. For centuries, this 'suburb' was home to many of Bristol's rich merchant

princes. But wartime bombing, slum clearance and road-widening damaged it greatly. Today a major regeneration programme is underway, and once again it is becoming a fashionable place to live.

Elizabeth I famously described **St Mary Redcliffe** (dating from the twelfth century) as 'the fairest, goodliest, and most famous parish church in England'. The church, in its prominent position alongside the harbour, was originally at the very centre of shipping and industry. The merchants of the Port of Bristol began and ended their voyages at the shrine of Our Lady of Redcliffe.

The views across the harbour from **Redcliffe Parade** take our breath away – we imagine waking up in one of these houses to that view – as merchant Thomas King, who traded palm oil, ivory and redwood, would have done in the 1800s. Many of his ships were built in the Sydenham Teast shipyards on Merchant's Wharf just to the west, so he would have been able to keep a close eye on them. And no doubt he popped in to **The Ostrich** (1745) on the quayside after work, one of only a handful of traditional dockside pubs left.

The General Hospital (1853), on the east side of Bathurst Basin, was built by W.G. Gingell to take care

Right The centre of Queen Square was previously the route of the Inner Ring Road!

of the casualties from the docks and the new factories, making a grand statement with its Italianate stonework and French Renaissance rooftops.

Then we cross **Bathurst Basin Footbridge** (late 1970s). Folks have been disparaging about this bridge ('It looks like one of those big tyre swings in an adventure playground'), but there's an explanation for that. The company that wanted to redevelop Bathurst Quay was required to put a footbridge in, but claimed it would make the overall scheme unviable. Then someone came up with the bright idea of using redundant steel dredging tubes from the harbour at about half the price quoted by the developer – and *voilà*, you have the bridge we see today and vital access along the quay.

Just to the left as we cross this bridge is the quaint Bathurst Parade and the very exotic **Robinson's Oil Seed Mill** (1875), also designed by W.B. Gingell in Gothic style. The façade of yellow brick is decorated in the Moorish manner with superb ornamentation and decorative ogee arches. Now we head round the waterfront along Merchant's Quay to the **Prince Street Swing Bridge** (1879), operated by water hydraulic power provided by the adjacent engine house and accumulator tower.

Then, skirting around the harbourside, we admire **Pero's Bridge** (1999), named in honour of Pero Jones, who came to live in Bristol as the slave of John Pinney. The most distinctive features of the bridge are the pair of horn-shaped sculptures which act as counterweights for the lifting section.

Queen Square (1727) is an outstanding example of urban regeneration. The site on which the square was built lay outside Bristol's city walls and was known as the Town Marsh. It was named in honour of Queen Anne and became the most sought-after place to live in Bristol; but as Clifton was developed from the end of the eighteenth century, it was supplanted as a prime location.

When Bristol was swept by violent riots in 1831, sparked when the House of Lords blocked the Reform Bill, nearly a hundred buildings in and around the square, including the mayoral Mansion House, Bishop's Palace and Custom House, were burned to the ground. Rebuilding took place over the next eighty years.

But worse was to come a century later. In 1937 the Inner Circuit Road was driven diagonally across the square, leading to a steady decline in the quality of the environment. Until 1999 that is, when the City Council made a successful Lottery grant application to restore the square to its glorious original form. Hurrah, what a victory!

On King Street is the classical **Theatre Royal** (1766), the oldest surviving theatre in England; and the famous Llandoger Trow pub of 1664. Tradition has it that Daniel Defoe met Alexander Selkirk here and was inspired by his tales to write *Robinson Crusoe*. King Street is a pleasure to walk along, described in the Pevsner guide as 'perhaps the most rewarding street in Bristol both for its gently curving composition and harmonious juxtaposition of 350 years of buildings'.

Above left The Granary is perhaps the finest example of the Bristol Byzantine style

Above right St Nicholas Market is a great spot for grazing

Below Graffiti art has been a major feature of the Bristol street scene since the 1980s

'Imagine a city where graffiti wasn't illegal, a city where everybody could draw whatever they liked. A city that felt like a party where everyone was invited.' BANKSY

Turning right into Charlotte Street and then left back into Little King Street, we go past the The Granary (1869), now Loch Fyne. It was a grain store, built by Ponton & Gough and to my mind at least is the very best example of the Bristol Byzantine style. So why is the stretch of water we are now walking alongside called the Welsh Back? Well, 'Back' because they were once literally the backs of merchants' houses from where goods were loaded directly onto ships; and 'Welsh' because vessels from Wales frequented this stretch of water. Simple really.

Bristol Bridge is the reason for Bristol being where it is. In the early days of the city, this was the best place to cross the river Avon and to bring ships conveniently on one tide. A settlement grew around the crossing from the early eleventh century.

The Old Town

As we clamber to the top of the St Nicholas Steps we find ourselves in the old town. The Glass Arcade running across All Saints' Lane is an early example of a shopping arcade. The Exchange (now St Nicholas Market) was built in 1743 by Bath architect John Wood the Elder. This became the place for trading. The clock has two minute hands, as Bristol worked to its own time, eleven minutes behind London time, at least until the advent of the railways.

Corn Street was the thriving hub of the old city; a twice-weekly corn market was held here from 1813 onwards. The writer Daniel Defoe, on a visit to the city, relates how the area became so thronged with ship owners, traders and merchants that they overflowed into the surrounding taverns and coffee houses. Perhaps not surprisingly, the street has many impressive nineteenth-century buildings and some good Art Deco too.

And then we head down a rather uninviting hole in the wall just a few yards after the Cosy Club – **Leonard Lane,** which follows the line of the old wall. In tabloid-speak, it has 'Britain's barmiest street markings' – there are double yellow markings down it, despite the fact that at several points you can easily touch both walls at the same time. It is also home to the Centrespace Gallery, a thriving community of artists and craftspeople in a former print works.

Look up in **Nelson Street** and you will see the street art for which it has become renowned. In 2011, its drab grey frontings and exposed brick exteriors were transformed

Left The ruins of St Peter's Church are now a memorial to those killed in the Bristol Blitz

into a vibrant exhibition of colour as part of the See No Evil festival.

Just a little way beyond our turning, we spot **St John's Conduit** in the old wall. The spring feeding it rises on Brandon Hill, and the system was constructed by the Carmelite Friars as a wooden conduit in the fourteenth century, providing one of the first public supplies of clean water. The water now travels under Park Street and eastwards through pipes, cisterns and tanks. During the aftermath of Second World War bombing raids, this tap was the only source of water available in the old city area.

Walking down Broad Street, we see on our left the old **Edward Everard Printing Works** (1901), which for a split second we take to be another piece of street art. In fact, it was built using Doulton ceramic tiles. There are many other buildings of interest in Broad Street.

Castle Park (4.1 hectares, 10 acres) was opened in 1978 and occupies the site that had contained Bristol's main pre-war shopping area, most of which was destroyed in the Bristol Blitz. The ruins of St Peter's Church are now a memorial to the civilians and auxiliary personnel killed in that event. Part-way round the park, the path crosses Castle Ditch, the remains of the moat that once surrounded **Bristol Castle**, the largest Norman castle in England, built in the eleventh century.

Spanning the Floating Harbour between Castle Park and Finzels Reach, **Castle Bridge** (2017) is the latest stage in the regeneration of Redcliffe. It seems to be *de rigeur* for urban bridges these days to have a kink in them and this one is no exception.

Finzels Reach is an impressive mixed-use development site on a former industrial site. Interesting buildings have been retained, including a sugar refinery (1846) and the old tramway generating station (1899).

Brutalist aficionados will love the now-listed 1968-built

Sheldon Bush lead shot tower on the far bank just after St Philip's Bridge, which has been converted into office accommodation.

And so, our walk finishes as we head through the 'back door' of Temple Meads station. Now, be honest, did you spot all nineteen bridges? (They are listed at urbanrambles.org if you want to check.)

PIT STOPS

- **KATE'S KITCHEN AT ARNOS VALE** is a must, helping to support this Arcadian wonder.
- **MRS BROWN'S CAFÉ**, Victoria Park, next to the park keeper's lodge
- **SMALL STREET ESPRESSO**, 23 Small Street, Old Town, BS1 1DW
- **EDNA'S KITCHEN**, Castle Park, specialises in Middle Eastern and Mediterranean food.

QUIRKY SHOPPING

- **ST NICHOLAS MARKET** (BS1 1JQ) has been voted one of the best indoor markets in the UK.

PLACES TO VISIT

- **ST MARY REDCLIFFE CHURCH**
- **REDCLIFFE CAVES** (limited opening times)
- **M SHED**, Wapping Road, BS1 4RN, for a spot of culture and Banksy.

WHEN TO VISIT

Bristol Food Connections Festival (early May), Get Growing Garden Trail (June), Picnic in the Park, Perrett's Park (Aug), Victoria Park, Art on the Hill Arts Trail (Oct)

Liverpool

This walk takes you from the Georgian elegance of the ridge through the bustle of the city to the drama of Liverpool's old docks, with amazing views and architecture throughout.

Liverpool was founded in 1207, but remained a tiny settlement for several centuries, only numbering about 500 people until the first commercial wet dock was built in 1715, which quickly supplanted Chester as the region's principal port.

By the start of the nineteenth century, a huge volume of trade was passing through, and the construction of major buildings reflected this wealth. The population expanded rapidly, growing nearly ninefold by the end of the century; and the city was described as 'the New York of Europe'.

During the Second World War, the city suffered a Blitz second only to London's, killing 2,500 people and causing damage to almost half the homes. A massive re-building programme took place, also designed to eliminate slum dwellings, but much of the historic fabric of the city was destroyed in the process.

In the 1960s, Liverpool became famous the world over for its cultural scene, and the emergence of the 'Merseybeat' Sound that became synonymous with the Beatles and fellow Liverpudlian rock bands. Alan Ginsberg famously declared the city 'at the present moment the centre of the consciousness of the human universe'. That creativity has shaped the city to this day.

WALK DATA

- **DISTANCE:** City loop – 7.6 km (4.7 miles); Parks loop – 7.7 km (4.8 miles)
- **HEIGHT GAIN:** 45 metres
- **WALK TIME:** City loop – 2 hours; Parks loop – 2 hours
- **START & FINISH:** City loop – Lime St station (L1 1JD); Parks loop – Hope Street and Canning Street (L1 9DZ)
- **TERRAIN:** Mainly pavements.

From the mid-1970s, Liverpool's docks and traditional manufacturing industries went into steep decline. A huge and well thought through regeneration programme was undertaken, leading to the triumph of UNESCO World Heritage status.

Ian Nairn captures the landscape of the city brilliantly: 'The Mersey runs north–south, and the docks stretch along it for seven miles, from Seaforth to Dingle. A mile inland, and parallel is a limestone ridge peppered with landmarks – the two cathedrals, the university, the football grounds at Goodison Park and Anfield. The centre is humane and convenient to walk in, but never loses its scale.'

THE WALK

Do try and arrive in Liverpool by train: for its history – opened in 1830, making it the oldest commercial train service in the world; for its beauty – two graceful Victorian engine sheds; and for its sense of place – being a terminus, it gives you the feeling of arriving on the edge of the land mass with a great view west over the city towards the estuary, anchoring you immediately in its maritime history.

The first bit of green space we come to is the **Roscoe Memorial Gardens** on our right, hemmed in on all sides by tall buildings. This was formerly the burial ground of the old Renshaw Street Unitarian Chapel, which stood where the central hall is now located. William Roscoe worshipped at the chapel and is buried here. He was one of the country's leading slave abolitionists and an educationalist.

During the Great Irish Famine of the mid-nineteenth century the Catholic population of Liverpool increased dramatically. About half a million Irish fled to England to escape the famine; many embarked from Liverpool to travel to North America, whilst others remained in the city. The Catholic population remained substantial in the twentieth century, and in 1967 the new **Catholic Cathedral** was consecrated.

It quickly became an iconic and generally loved landmark, and attracted affectionate nicknames including 'Paddy's Wigwam', 'the Pope's Launching Pad' and 'the Mersey Funnel'; as soon as we set eyes upon it we understand why. Upbeat and awe-inspiring at the same time.

We descend the steps behind the cathedral to the university, walking through an archway into the quadrangle of the gloriously neo-Gothic **Victoria Hall** (1892), designed by Alfred Waterhouse, built from a distinctive red pressed brick with terracotta decorative dressings. This building was the inspiration for the term 'red brick' university, used to refer to a group of six civic British universities founded in the major industrial cities of England in the nineteenth and early twentieth centuries – the others being Manchester, Birmingham, Leeds, Sheffield and Bristol.

WALK DATA

- **CITY POPULATION:** 465,656 (#6 in the UK)
- **ORIGINS:** 1207
- **CITY STATUS:** 1880
- **FAMOUS LIVERPUDLIANS:** The Beatles (music), William Gladstone (Prime Minister), Cilla Black (singer), Jimmy Tarbuck (comedian), George Stubbs (artist), Samuel Cunard (ship owner)
- **LOCAL BUILDERS:** Jesse Hartley (the docks), Alfred Waterhouse (Royal Infirmary, Prudential Assurance), Thomas Shelmerdine (Central Fire Station, St John's Gardens), Herbert Rowse (Mersey Tunnel, Philharmonic Hall), Graeme Shankland (town planner)
- **SCREEN TIME:** *Bullion Boys* (the docks), *The 51st State* (Anfield), *Nowhere Boy* (Hope Street); *Boys from the Blackstuff*, *The Liver Birds* TV series
- **ICONIC CITYSCAPES:** Liverpool Anglican Cathedral Tower

Abercromby Square dates from the early nineteenth century and for a time became the most desirable place to live in Liverpool. More recently, **Hope Street** was voted the 'Best Street in the UK' by the Academy of Urbanism. It has a great feeling about it, culture, pubs, a good hotel, interesting buildings, sculptures, historic spots, Beatlemania, a bit of everything.

Looking down Mount Street we spy the **Liverpool Institute** (1837), originally the Mechanics' Institution, subsequently the Liverpool Institute High School for Boys Grammar School – alumni include Paul McCartney and George Harrison. It closed in the 1980s and now houses the Liverpool Institute for Performing Arts, set up by Sir Paul McCartney and Mark Featherstone-Witty.

The **Liverpool School of Art and Design** (1883) was the hub of avant-garde activity in the late 1960s. A community of artists, poets, writers and intellectuals gathered in the pubs, clubs and at each other's houses in the area surrounding the art school. *The Mersey Sound*, an anthology of poems by Roger McGough, Brian Patten

Left It's easy to see from above why the Catholic Cathedral was given the nickname 'Paddy's wigwam'

'A good place to wash your hair, Liverpool – good, soft water.' JOHN LENNON

and Adrian Henri was first published in 1967. Breezy, unaffected and playful, it sold over half a million copies.

Parks loop

This extra loop takes you through the Georgian Quarter, and Princes Park and Sefton Park – two of the finest parks in the country.

Percy Street is the most distinguished street, dating from the 1830s. **St Bride** (1830), on the east side, is the finest surviving neoclassical church in the city, temple-like in appearance with its monumental portico of six Ionic columns across the west end.

From this classic Georgian architecture, we are hurled into the Mediterranean, first by way of the **Greek Orthodox Church of St Nicholas** (1870) built in the Neo-Byzantine style. The church was dedicated to St Nicholas, the patron saint to all seamen, as the money for the building was raised by the Greek ship owners who were based here.

A little further down is the **Princes Road Synagogue** (1874), according to Pevsner 'one of the finest examples of Orientalism in British synagogue architecture'. The style combines Gothic and Moorish elements, and reflects the status and wealth of the Jewish community in Liverpool at the time.

The roads overlooking the parks were the places to build your large villa if you were a magnate or merchant, close to green spaces and away from the grime of the city. Princes Road, 'a wide Victorian boulevard' was completed in 1846, that rare thing in a British city, a planned route. Princes Park was a pleasant stroll away, and a tram subsequently ran along its length. This became the 'Park Lane of Liverpool', the place to see and be seen.

Princes Park (45 hectares, 110 acres) was originally a private development, the creation of Richard Vaughan Yates, an iron merchant (I guess he won the contract for the park railings . . .), surrounded by grand Georgian-style housing. The park was designed by Joseph Paxton, the first major park he created. With its serpentine lake and a circular carriage drive, the park set a style which was to be widely emulated in Victorian urban development, most notably by Paxton on a larger scale at Birkenhead Park, which in its turn became a model for New York's Central Park.

Sefton Park (95 hectares, 235 acres) was once within the boundaries of the 2,300-acre Royal Deer Park of

Above The Anglican
Cathedral was the life work
of Sir Giles Gilbert Scott

Below St James's Garden,
a former quarry and then
a graveyard, is today a
delightful green space

*'Liverpool has always made me brave, choice-wise. It was never a city
that criticised anyone for taking a chance.'* DAVID MORRISSEY

Toxteth. The land was purchased by the council in 1867 and, as with Prince's Park, plots of land around the perimeter were sold for housing which helped to fund the layout of the park. It was opened in 1872 by Prince Arthur who dedicated it 'for the health and enjoyment of the townspeople'. The impressive Sefton Park Palm House (1896) has recently been refurbished.

We enter **St James's Garden** (4 hectares, 10 acres) through a rather fine low rusticated arch as if we are entering a catacomb. In the eighteenth century, the site had been a stone quarry supplying much of the material for the city's fine stone buildings, and was converted into a cemetery in 1829.

Back to the City loop

The Oratory (1829), the former mortuary chapel, is situated on high ground on the north-west corner of the cemetery. Designed by John Foster, it is in the form of a miniature Greek Doric temple, described as 'one of the purest monuments of the Greek Revival in England' and in such sharp contrast to the massive cathedral alongside it.

The Pevsner guide sums up the **Anglican Cathedral** (1904–78) best: 'Liverpool Cathedral, the life work of

Sir Giles Gilbert Scott, represents the final flowering of the Gothic Revival as a vital, creative movement, and is one of the great buildings of the twentieth century.' Going to the top of the tower is an experience not to be missed – it helps you immediately 'get' the topography of Merseyside. You can soak in all the different landmarks and topographies, and see where the Welsh, the Irish and all the many different overseas nationalities disembarked to settle in this melting pot of a city.

Then we stroll along **Rodney Street**, sometimes called 'the Harley Street of the North'. No. 62 (1793) was the birthplace in 1809 of William Gladstone, Prime Minister. Dr William Henry Duncan (1805–63), born at No. 54, was Liverpool's first Medical Officer of Health. He was one of the celebrated trio of pioneering officers appointed under the Liverpool Sanitary Act 1846, which became the precedent for later national legislation; the other two being James Newlands, Borough Engineer, and Thomas Fresh, Inspector of Nuisances (the title rather boringly changing to Sanitary Inspector in 1855, and more boringly still to Public Health Inspector in 1956).

The churchyard of the **Scottish Presbyterian Church of Saint Andrew** (1824) is not like any old churchyard,

Above left The Museum of Liverpool adds Modernism to seafront classicism of the Three Graces

Above right The Port of Liverpool building was built at the height of Liverpool's maritime wealth

Below The Albert Dock was the first non-combustible warehouse system in the world

'It is a world city, far more so than London or Manchester. Comparisons always end up overseas – Dublin, or Boston, or Hamburg.' IAN NAIRN

with serried ranks of gravestones, some slightly larger than others to denote greater fame or deeper pockets. Here one stands out way above all others, an imposing 15-foot pyramid-shaped tombstone, which looks rather like what you might imagine a nuclear bunker for Egyptians to look like. This is the grave of William MacKenzie, interred in 1851. The story goes that MacKenzie, an Anglo-Scottish civil engineer, was a keen gambler and left instructions that he should be entombed above ground within the pyramid, sitting upright at a card table and clutching a winning hand of cards.

Next, we head past **St Luke's Church** (1832), often referred to as 'the bombed-out church' because it was largely destroyed during the Liverpool Blitz of 1941, the ruins standing as a memorial to those who were lost in the war. Then, we boldly go down Bold Street, part of an area called the **Rope Works**, the name derived from the craft of rope-making for sailing ships that dominated the area until the nineteenth century.

Bluecoat Chambers (1717) is probably Liverpool's oldest building, built as a charity school. Now it is an arts centre, and home to over thirty creative industries including artists, graphic designers, small arts organisations, craftspeople and retailers.

Deep breath. Now we are about to enter one of the most amazing bits of industrial history you will ever experience. Herman Melville the American author, in Liverpool on his first seafaring voyage in 1839, marvelled at Liverpool's docks and compared them with the Great

Wall of China and the Pyramids of the Pharaohs.

The **Albert Dock** (1846) is one of the great monuments of nineteenth-century engineering. Pevsner says of it: 'For sheer punch there is little in the early commercial architecture of Europe to emulate it.' Designed by Jesse Hartley and Philip Hardwick, it was the first structure in Britain to be built from cast iron, brick and stone, with no structural wood, making it the first non-combustible warehouse system in the world.

Heading north along the waterfront, the **Museum of Liverpool** (2001) cuts across the skyline. Its Modernist style was always likely to be chewed over since this is such a sensitive site. I personally like it and it sits just fine among its more famous neighbours.

The southernmost building of the famous pier head trio of the Three Graces is the **Port of Liverpool Building** (1907), in the Edwardian Baroque style and notable for its large dome. The **Cunard Building** (1917) is designed in a mix of Italian Renaissance and Greek Revival style. Finally, the **Royal Liver Building** (1911) is one of the most recognisable landmarks in the city and is home to two fabled Liver Birds that watch over the city and the sea. Legend has it that were these two birds to fly away, then the city would cease to exist. So far so good.

The **Church of Our Lady and St Nicholas** is the Anglican parish church of Liverpool. There has been a church on this site since the thirteenth century, rebuilt several times. The churchyard was laid out in 1891 as a very pleasant public garden.

Above left The Town Hall is that unusual thing in Liverpool, an early Georgian building

Above right Every city had to have one – a statue of Queen Victoria

Below Looking up St John's Gardens to St George's Hall

We head up Water Street and soon on our left we see the **Oriel Chambers** (1864), the world's first building featuring a metal framed glass curtain wall. It was frowned on by the critics of the day, but Pevsner called it 'one of the most remarkable buildings of its date in Europe'. It directly influenced the modernist Chicago School of Architecture and the first skyscrapers.

The **Town Hall** (1754) is that relatively unusual thing in Liverpool: an early Georgian building, 'one of the finest surviving eighteenth-century town halls', built to a design by John Wood the Elder (of Bath fame) and replacing an earlier town hall nearby.

During the eighteenth-century, **Castle Street** was known as the Fleet Street of Liverpool because of the many newspaper offices located here. There are many buildings of note in this street – cast your eyes up and get your hands on a copy of the Pevsner guide if you crave more details. Sir James Picton said that 'The history of Castle Street is the history of Liverpool' and this fine street remains the identifiable centre of the city.

We emerge on Derby Square, originally the site of Liverpool Castle. The **Victoria Monument** was unveiled in 1906 by Princess Louise, Queen Victoria's daughter. A competent sculptor herself, she is reported to have said, 'Surely mama never looked like that.' I guess she should know . . .

St John's Gardens stand in a former area of heathland. The land slopes upwards to the east and was exposed to the westerly winds, making it a perfect site for windmills and washing lines. In 1749 the city's first General Infirmary was built here, followed by the Seaman's Hospital, a dispensary and a lunatic asylum. There was also a church and a cemetery. At the beginning of the twentieth century the site was re-landscaped and opened in 1904 as St John's Gardens.

Last, but definitely not least, **St George's Hall** (1854), one of Liverpool's finest buildings. Queen Victoria said it was 'worthy of ancient Athens'. Pevsner declared it to be 'one of the finest neo-Grecian buildings in the world'.

And finally, exhausted no doubt, you will find yourself back at the station, exhilarated, amazed, wanting more. Maybe add another day to your trip!

PIT STOPS

- **THE QUARTER**, 7 Falkner Street, L8 7PU. Great neighbourhood spot.
- **BOLD STREET CAFÉ**, 89 Bold Street, L1 4HF. Uber stylish
- **GELATO ICE CREAM PARLOUR**, 41 Lark Ln, L17 8UW. Useful stopping point on a hot day.

QUIRKY SHOPPING

- **BOLD STREET** (L1 4DJ)
- **LARK LANE** (L17 8UU)

PLACES TO VISIT

- **LIVERPOOL CATHEDRAL** – the Tower Experience
- **MERSEYSIDE MARITIME MUSEUM**, Albert Dock, L3 4AQ
- **TATE LIVERPOOL**, Albert Dock, L3 4BB
- **WALKER ART GALLERY**, L3 8EL. Impressive 20th-century art.

WHEN TO VISIT

International Music Festival, Sefton Park (July); International Beatleweek (Aug); Food & Drink Festival, Sefton Park (Sept); Liverpool Biennial, Contemporary Art (Summer 2018, 2020)

Newcastle

Newcastle grabs you by the throat and never lets you go, with all the ingredients of a great urban ramble – epic location, great buildings, loads of attitude.

Newcastle has a dramatic geographical setting; arriving by train is perhaps the most exhilarating arrival of any British city, perched atop the Tyne Gorge waiting for a station platform, and hoping one doesn't free up too quickly before you have had a chance to soak in the views in both directions and the city glistening on the north bank.

Newcastle developed around the Roman settlement of Pons Aelius. It grew as an important centre for the wool trade in the fourteenth century and later became a major coal mining region. The port developed in the sixteenth century, becoming one of the world's largest shipbuilding and ship-repairing centres, and a powerhouse of the Industrial Revolution.

In several parts, Newcastle retains a medieval street layout. Stairs from the riverside to higher parts of the city centre and the Castle Keep remain largely intact. Many buildings in Close, Sandhill and Quayside date back to the fifteenth century.

As the city became wealthier, so it needed to expand, and the obvious spot was the plateau behind the castle. This is where Richard Grainger set to work in the 1820s, with a plan for a new town that ingeniously and almost imperceptibly linked with the old arteries of the town.

WALK DATA

- **DISTANCE:** 7 km (4.4 miles)
- **HEIGHT GAIN:** 66 metres
- **WALK TIME:** 1¾ hours
- **START & FINISH:** Newcastle Central Station (NE1 5DL)
- **TERRAIN:** Steep ascent from the quayside; all on pavements

In the 1960s, the complete redevelopment of the city was spearheaded by the infamous T. Dan Smith, city mayor, who envisaged Newcastle as a 'Brasilia of the North'. The legacy of that architectural period is still very apparent: inner-city trunk roads, the metro, overhead walkways, the Eldon shopping precinct hard up against Georgian elegance.

More recently, the regenerated Quayside shows the city's determination to rebuild itself after the de-industrialisation of the 1980s. Terry Farrell developed a masterplan that was to transform the quayside into one of the country's most successful urban regeneration projects, creating a buzzing area of culture, pubs and restaurants.

THE WALK

Newcastle Central station (1850) is one of the great monuments of the early railway age. Opened by Queen Victoria, it was designed by John Dobson; and the train shed was the first of the great multi-span arched sheds.

We are soon reminded that we are in pioneering railway territory by a large bronze statue of **George Stephenson**, now somewhat inappropriately marooned on a traffic island. His famous locomotive Rocket was built in Newcastle in 1829, supervised by his son Robert at their factory in South Street (two minutes from here).

The Cathedral Church of St Nicholas's fifteenth-century lantern tower dominates the skyline. It served as a useful navigation point for ships in the Tyne for over 500 years. Formerly Newcastle's major parish church, St Nicholas was given Cathedral status in 1882, in recognition of Newcastle becoming a City.

The Castle Keep dates back to 1080. The well is nearly 100 feet deep, pretty much the height of the cliff on which the castle sits guarding the gorge; whilst the climb to the roof is well worth it for the views of the River Tyne and its famous bridges.

Described on completion as the most perfect specimen of Doric architecture in the North of England, the **Moot Hall** (1811) has columned porticos at the front and rear. In Ian Nairn's words, 'The Greek Doric portico of the Moot Hall has a monumental force that almost pushes you back across the road.'

Just to the right of the Moot Hall is one of the most famous chares (stairs) that goes down to Sandhill by the quay – **Dog Leap Stairs**. In 1772 Baron Eldon, later Lord Chancellor of England, eloped with Bessie Surtees, the daughter of a local merchant who lived in Sandhill. Local folklore suggests they made their escape on horseback up these stairs. I really pity the horse!

Designed by Robert Stephenson, the **High Level Bridge** (1849) was the solution to a complex problem: that of spanning 400 metres of river valley, 156 metres of which is across water. It was the world's first dual-decked rail and road bridge. Its fadedness and dripping patches are part of its charm today, taking us back in time as well

WALK DATA

- **CITY POPULATION:** 279,092 (#8 in UK)
- **ORIGINS:** 2nd century AD
- **CITY STATUS:** Granted 1882
- **FAMOUS INHABITANTS:** Peter Higgs (physicist), Sting (musician), Catherine Cookson (author), Ludwig Wittgenstein (philosopher), Alan Shearer (footballer), Rowan Atkinson (comedian)
- **LOCAL BUILDERS:** John Dobson (Newcastle Central station), Richard Grainger (Grey Street), Thomas Oliver (Leazes Terrace), T. Dan Smith (Civic Centre), Terry Farrell (Newcastle Quayside)
- **SCREEN TIME:** *Get Carter* (High Bridge), *Purely Belter* (Newcastle United); *Our Friends in the North*, *When the Boat Comes In* TV series
- **ICONIC CITYSCAPES:** Castle Keep, the High Level Bridge, Sage Gateshead

as across the gorge. Famously, it was the scene of the red Jaguar car chase in the film *Get Carter*.

We feel we are creeping up unawares on **Sage Gateshead** (2004), approaching it from the land side. The design itself divides opinion, but it seems to me its setting allows it to be 'big' without necessarily being obtrusive; and its acoustically smart form – each auditorium is a separate enclosure, sheltered beneath a roof that is 'shrink-wrapped' around the building – is more than justified by its rating as a top concert hall.

The Baltic Mill (1950s) was built as a flour mill, but was triumphantly re-opened in 2002 as an art space. Next, we cross the **Millennium Bridge**, which has very quickly stolen the crown of 'iconic Newcastle view' from the Tyne Bridge. On the far side, there is a list of when the gate will be 'tilted' to allow boats through. If you don't have the good fortune to pass at a time that it's opening, take a look on YouTube; you will be amazed.

The Quayside is full of interest. The area was once an industrial zone and busy commercial dockside, and also hosted a regular street market. In recent years, as the

Above left The Baltic Mill – transformed from flour mill to art gallery

Above right The elegant Edwardian Central Arcade has delightful faïence tiles

Below The Tyne Bridge was built to the same design as the Sydney Harbour Bridge

'The medieval town struggled up from the quayside, producing dozens of sets of steps or "chares" which produce a kind of topographical ecstasy as you go up and down, perpetually seeing the same objects in a different way.' IAN NAIRN

docks became run-down, so the area has been extensively redeveloped.

On our right we pass the Postmodernist **Law Courts** (1990), one of the first new buildings in the quayside redevelopment programme; now, despite the fact I generally hate Postmodernist buildings, I rather like this one, especially the red-brick 'tower' on the right side that feels very appropriate for this location.

Make sure to look up King Street, up a flight of steps to **All Saints' Church** (1786), according to Ian Nairn 'one of the best of its date in Britain', one of very few oval churches. It was de-consecrated in the early 1960s, and sadly, after flooding a few years back is now on the 'at risk' register. Fingers crossed.

The great **Tyne Bridge** looms ever closer into view. Completed in 1928, it was designed by Mott, Hay and Anderson, to the same broad design as their Sydney Harbour Bridge, which was being built around the same time. The 'experience' of the bridge is at its most intense as we go under it, with the roar of traffic on the roadway a hundred feet above, the base of the parabolic steel arch powerfully conjoined with the Cornish granite out of which the massive rectangular towers are constructed;

and all across the steelwork, myriad rivets, over three-quarters of a million in total, giving the structure a Lego-like appearance.

On the other side, we come to the **Guildhall**, once the heart of Newcastle's government. It housed the council chamber, whose powerful members were drawn from the various trade guilds in the town. They were responsible for regulating each of the trades, rights, rules, apprenticeships and the quality of produce.

The iconic **Swing Bridge** was opened in 1876. It stands on the site of the old Tyne Bridges of 1270 and 1781, and probably of the Roman Pons Aelius, replacing the old Georgian Bridge which had hampered larger vessels from moving upriver.

We cut up the west end of the Guildhall, from where we have a great view of the mediaeval **Bessie Surtees House**, dating back to the sixteenth century. Ian Nairn wrote of this part of the city: '[It is like] ... a city within a city, with the exchange and some famous half-timbered buildings that seemed to have skipped straight across the Baltic – Lübeck seems nearer than London.'

Then we swing around to the right and up the hill, this time under the railway viaduct carrying the line to

Right The Civic Centre is in a modern style with clear Nordic influences

Edinburgh; and doubling up as an 'entry gate' to Grainger Town, one of the most complete pieces of town planning in the UK, comparable to Edinburgh New Town or Bath Pulteney. Pevsner described Grey Street, which we pass along, as 'one of the finest streets in England'. Just a shame that nowadays there are so many chain restaurants here with their bland signage.

We stumble across the **Central Arcade** (1906), an elegant Edwardian shopping arcade, with delightful faïence tiles. And here we discover the perfect antidote to all those chains – one of the country's largest and most famous independent music shops, JG Windows, which has been trading in the arcade since 1908! Dire Straits' Mark Knopfler recounts how as a boy growing up in Blyth he would visit Newcastle to look longingly through the windows at his dream instrument – an expensive Fiesta Red Fender Stratocaster, just like Hank Marvin's.

Grey's Statue is in front of us as we emerge from the arcade. Grey is a man we should be grateful to for two reasons. First, of course, the eponymous Earl Grey tea; but perhaps more importantly, he was the politician who steered the 1832 Great Reform Bill through the House of Commons. The Act granted seats in the House of Commons to large cities such as Newcastle that had sprung up during the Industrial Revolution and removed seats from the 'rotten boroughs'.

Next up is one of my personal favourites in Newcastle, the **Civic Centre** (1967). The Nordic influence is clear, with walls of Norwegian Otta slate offset by the rich

walnut and marble of the interiors, and the aged copper finishings of the exterior. Designed by the city architect, George Kenyon, it was formally opened by HM King Olav V of Norway, who was also awarded the Honorary Freedom of Newcastle to mark the historic, cultural and economic links the city enjoys with the people of Norway. Among other things, it entitled him to let his cattle graze on public land in the city (there is no record that he ever took up this generous offer).

The Hancock Building has been re-configured by Terry Farrell to link with a group of other buildings that together create the Great North Museum. We stroll through it to the modern Devonshire Building. Completed in 2004, it is home to Newcastle University's Institute of Research on Environment and Sustainability. In keeping with its function, the building was designed with state-of-the-art systems that enable it to be environmentally sustainable.

Heading down **Lover's Lane,** a key walking route for Newcastle University, we bump into dozens of animated students; trying to stay calm and composed whilst taking in all the sights and sounds and new experiences. Ah, that wonderful in-between world called university, where on one hand you need to take responsibility, and on the other, you need to be a little bit reckless.

Leazes Park (29 hectares, 72 acres) has a history going back to the thirteenth century when King John gave the land to townsmen of Newcastle to be used for grazing their cattle (Leazes meaning 'meadowlands').

In 1857, Newcastle Council was presented with a

Above left Leazes Park is a great place to come and relax in front of the lakeside view

Above right The Chinese Arch frames St James' Park football ground

Below The town walls were built during the thirteenth and fourteenth centuries to repel Scottish invaders

'I intend to be at St James' Park as long as my brain, heart and legs all work … simultaneously.' BOBBY ROBSON

petition, signed by nearly 3,000 of the 'working men of Newcastle upon Tyne and its vicinity' that they should be granted ready access to some open ground for the 'purpose of health and recreation'. The 'people's park' was opened in 1873; and shortly afterwards an ornamental bandstand was added, which proved to be extremely popular, drawing large crowds on a Sunday to enjoy the free musical entertainment.

One of the great virtues of Leazes Park is its proximity to the centre of Newcastle, with a hospital, university buildings and the football pitch surrounding it, making it a popular place for lunch breakers, young families, students and visitors alike.

Leazes Terrace (1830) is another fine piece of work from the prolific team of Richard Grainger and Thomas Oliver. The extreme juxtaposition with the St James' Park stands is the first thing we notice, but for some reason, it is exhilarating rather than being an eyesore.

St James' Park has been the home ground of Newcastle United since 1892. Throughout its history, the desire for expansion has caused conflict with local residents and the local council. This led to proposals to move at least twice in the late 1960s, and a controversial 1995 proposed

move to the park we have just walked through, which fortunately was defeated by the Friends of the Park. The rather squashed location has led to the distinctive lopsided appearance of the present-day stadium as the development of the east side of the ground was restricted due to the effect it would have had on the terrace. The roar along this road is an experience not to be missed on a match day and having a stadium right in the centre of the city is very exhilarating, somehow much more so than a characterless (albeit larger) edge-of-town location.

Newcastle's Chinatown is a fairly recent invention, with Stowell Street at its heart – the first Chinese business only moved here in the late 1970s, but now the street is entirely made up of Chinese restaurants and shops. At its north end, looking towards the football ground, is the **Chinese Arch**, built in 2004 by Shanghai craftsmen, adding a dash of colour to the scene.

The town walls were constructed during the thirteenth and fourteenth centuries to repel Scottish invaders. When completed, they were about 3 km long, comprising six main gateways and seventeen towers, as well as several smaller turrets and postern gates. In Eneas Mackenzie's famous description: 'the strength and magnificens of the

waulling of this town far passeth al the waulles of the cities of England, and most of the townes of Europe.'

We admire the **Morden Tower** in Back Stowell Street, built in about 1290. Since the early 1960s, Connie Pickard has been its custodian and has made it a key fixture of Newcastle's alternative cultural life. Many memorable music and poetry events have taken place here. Basil Bunting, for example, gave the first reading of his long poem *Briggflatts* here in 1965; and notable others include Allen Ginsberg, Ted Hughes, Seamus Heaney, Tom Raworth and Carol Ann Duffy.

The **Blackfriars Monastery** (thirteenth century) was dissolved by Henry VIII and the land sold to merchants. It was then leased to nine of the town's craft guilds, to be used as their headquarters. The guilds' meeting houses in Blackfriars were well used until the nineteenth century, which probably explains why the building has survived, unlike the other Orders that had monasteries in the city.

Finally, we reach the somewhat garish **International Centre for Life** (2000), a science village where scientists, clinicians, educationalists and businesspeople work to promote the advancement of the life sciences. Another example of the innovative spirit of Newcastle. We were most struck by the bit of the development that wasn't new, the 1840s John Dobson-designed **Market Keeper's House** complete with clock tower. This spot had been a thriving cattle market in the nineteenth century, handling 10,000 animals a week. The opening of nearby Central Station in 1850 gave the market a boost as animals could be cheaply transported by rail.

A final treat for you if you love a bit of Gothic Revival. As we trudge back to the station we see the spire of the **Church of St Mary's** (1844). Designed by the Augustus Pugin (Houses of Parliament), the church became the Roman Catholic cathedral for the northern district in 1850,

a key piece of the restoration of the Catholic hierarchy – about 300 years after the nearby Blackfriars monastery had been dissolved, thus proving that everything really does come full circle in the end, including our walk!

PIT STOPS

- **BALTIC KITCHEN**, the Baltic Centre for Contemporary Art, NE8 3BA. Great views.
- **LONG PLAY CAFÉ**, 48–52 Quayside, NE1 3JF. Coffee and vinyl shop, where there is a collection of over 2,000 LPs and 1,000 45s to purchase.
- **QUILLIAM BROTHERS TEAHOUSE**, Claremont Road, NE1 7RD

QUIRKY SHOPPING

- **CENTRAL ARCADE** (NE1 6EG), the famous JG Windows music shop, and other shops.
- **GRAINGER MARKET** (NE1 5JQ, end of Market Street) houses over 100 very varied indie shops.

PLACES TO VISIT

- **CASTLE KEEP**, NE1 1RQ. Climb the 99 steps to the top for a great view.
- **THE BALTIC CENTRE FOR CONTEMPORARY ARTS**, NE8 3BA
- **LAING ART GALLERY**, New Bridge Street, NE1 8AG. British oil paintings and watercolours.

WHEN TO VISIT

Exhibition of the North (summer 2018), Hoppings Funfair on Town Moor (June), Chinatown, Stowell Street (Chinese New Year), Newcastle Community Green Festival, Leazes Park (June), Exhibition Park Mela (Aug)

Plymouth

Plymouth more than lives up to its moniker of 'Britain's Ocean City', with estuaries, sea views, steep hills, naval defences and dockyards creating a walk of immense variety and interest.

Plymouth is defined by its ocean setting, situated between the rivers Plym and Tamar in a beautiful natural harbour. The port and quaysides have always been at the centre of its livelihood – as a port for wool and tin in the Middle Ages; as a base for the British Navy during the period of the Empire; and, more recently, as a place to live and visit, with regenerated dockyards offering stylish apartment living and the café life, epitomised by the brilliantly restored Royal William Yard.

On closer inspection, the City of Plymouth is really three towns – Plymouth, Devonport and East Stonehouse – added together to achieve city status, which required a minimum population of 300,000 – a status that was duly achieved in 1928.

Plymouth was profoundly altered by bombing in the Second World War, which destroyed the town centre and displaced many inhabitants. Out of the rubble emerged Britain's first 'planned' town centre in an existing historic core, masterminded by Sir Patrick Abercrombie, the most eminent town planner of his day. Based on the Beaux Arts 'City Beautiful' style, the plan proposed the almost complete removal of the old city

WALK DATA

- **DISTANCE:** 9.1 km (5.7 miles); or 11.8 km (7.4 miles) with Devonport loop
- **HEIGHT GAIN:** 33 metres
- **WALK TIME:** 2½ hours; or 3½ hours with Devonport loop
- **START & FINISH:** Plymouth station (PL4 6AB)
- **TERRAIN:** Straightforward, all on pavements

centre with the formation of a grand north–south axis, connecting the railway station to the Hoe, the route we take.

Abercrombie was driven by a vision of a city with which it is hard to disagree: 'The city should be the focal point for the diffused rays of the many separate beams of life; it should be the centre of learning, of entertainment and of the market.' He felt that the Industrial Revolution had turned cities into 'something more like a labour pool for the large industrial works – soulless and meaningless.' English Heritage has described the result as one of the finest examples of post-war architecture in the UK.

THE WALK

Armada Way is a pleasant pedestrian route to the Hoe, with a water feature flowing down the hill towards the sundial, bordered by grassy areas with shrubs, flower beds and a generous sprinkling of benches. The Piazza, halfway down, was the scene of great celebrations when local lad Tom Daley returned to Plymouth as world diving champion. Everything in Plymouth seems to have a connection with water.

The most interesting stretch of the Way is the Civic Centre and the **Great Square** alongside it, which is on the National Register of Parks and Gardens, one of the few twentieth-century gardens listed. Its aim was to evoke 'dignity and frivolity' in equal measure and to be 'a civic amenity to be enjoyed by townspeople at all times'.

The **Civic Centre** (1962) embodies, in the words of English Heritage, 'the hopes and aspirations of a newly confident City Council and serves as a striking testimony to the spirit which guided the reconstruction'. Inevitably it garners mixed reviews, but it is very much of its time and, in my view at least, is a minor gem. Its days as a civic centre, though, are over – Urban Splash is in the process of redeveloping it for mixed use.

The **Guildhall** (1874) was constructed in a French Gothic style and reflected the burgeoning civic pride in Plymouth at the time. Most of the complex was destroyed in the Blitz, however about a third, including the tower, was remodelled in the 1950s by H.J.W. Stirling. The result is a rather curious Italianate-look, which nonetheless I like.

The **Royal Parade** is the main commercial east-west axis of the new city centre plan, and many of the department stores and building societies are located along here. We pass the House of Fraser (1949) and then Pearl Assurance House (1952) a little further along. They set the parameters for the style of the 'new town' buildings – slim, elegant windows with metal frames painted white; shopfronts with fixed projecting canopies perforated with glass lens lights; and white Portland stone façades rooted in classical ideals.

St Andrew's Church was built in the fifteenth century,

WALK DATA

- **CITY POPULATION:** 256,589 (#30 in the UK)
- **ORIGINS:** AD 700
- **CITY STATUS:** Achieved in 1928 through merging with Devonport and East Stonehouse
- **FAMOUS INHABITANTS:** Sir Francis Drake (navigator), Sir Joshua Reynolds (painter), Beryl Cook (painter), Michael Foot (politician), Sharron Davies (swimmer), Tom Daley (diver), Angela Rippon (journalist)
- **LOCAL BUILDERS:** Sir John Rennie the Younger (Royal William Yard), Sir Patrick Abercrombie and Paton Watson (1944 Plan for Plymouth), H.J.W. Stirling (City Architect, 1950s)
- **SCREEN TIME:** *Tomorrow Never Dies* (Devonport Naval Base); *Hornblower* TV movies
- **ICONIC CITYSCAPES:** Smeaton's Tower, Blockhouse Park

with its origins dating back still further. Sir George Gilbert Scott carried out a restoration in the 1870s, but the church was burnt out and left a roofless shell as a result of the Blitz. It became famous as 'the Garden Church' after the war where, for six years, thousands worshipped at the open-air services, until it was finally restored. A board bearing the inscription '*RESURGAM*' ('I will rise again') appeared over the north door after the destruction and is still there today.

The **Plymouth Synagogue** (1762), the white building to our right as we head down Catherine Street, is the oldest surviving synagogue built by Ashkenazi Jews in the English-speaking world. An unobtrusive location was chosen to avoid provoking the destructive riots that non-Anglican houses of worship often provoked in the eighteenth century. Nothing on the exterior distinguishes the building from the meeting houses of non-conformist Protestants.

The **Baptist Church** (1958) that we reach next replaced a church that had also been destroyed in the Blitz. It was designed by Louis de Soissons, the architect and planner

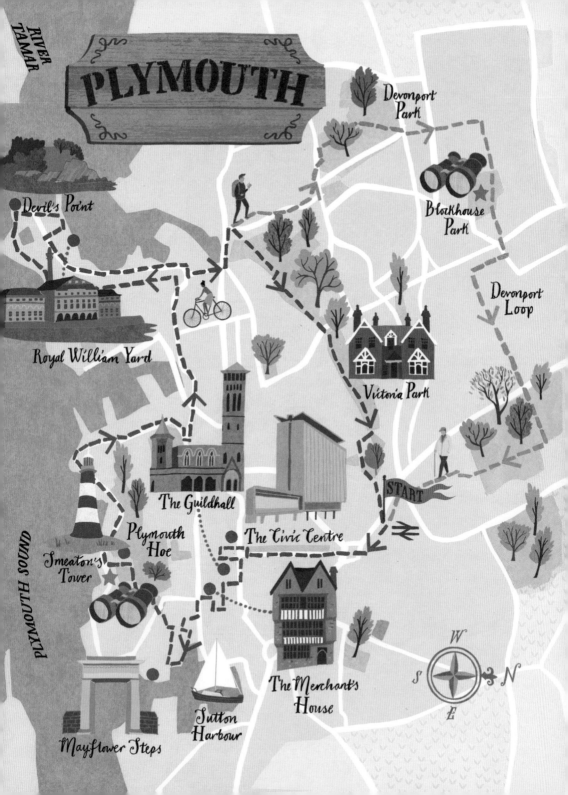

Right The Guildhall was remodelled after the Blitz and now has a rather Italianate look

'We have time enough to finish the game and beat the Spaniards too'.
SIR FRANCIS DRAKE, PLAYING BOWLS ON THE HOE

of Welwyn Garden City. Many interesting features include a decorated copper tower, a cobbled quadrangle, limed oak pews and pulpit, 'tulip' light fittings and a huge mural behind the altar. Legend has it that the forebears of this congregation 'kindly entertained and courteously used' the Pilgrim Fathers in 1620 prior to their departure from the Barbican on the Mayflower.

We slip through the car park just to the north of the church, then left up Finewell Street past the **Prysten House,** a Grade I listed fifteenth-century merchant's house, now a restaurant. **The Merchants' House** in St Andrew's Street also dates back to the fifteenth century. Its first recorded owner was William Parker, an Elizabethan privateer and merchant and Mayor of Plymouth.

The Old Custom House (1586) on the Parade is now the rather quaint 'Book Cupboard'. It too started life as a merchant's house. The subsequent, grander Customs House, built in 1820, is on the other side of the Parade. As we stroll along Sutton Quay, we look up at the old warehouses lining it – where cargoes like sugar and pearls from South America and spices from the East Indies were unloaded in the days when Plymouth was a thriving port.

Sutton Harbour is where it all began. In about AD 700 Anglo-Saxon settlers sailed here, making their first settlement on its shore. In the sixteenth century, it was used as the base for the fleet that gathered to face the Spanish Armada. In 1620 the Pilgrim Fathers sailed to America from the Mayflower Steps at the western end of the harbour.

Today this whole area is known as the Barbican. A barbican is a fortified entrance, in this case referring to the waterside gateway of Plymouth's long-gone medieval castle that stood on Lambhay Hill. But the street patterns still persist – a pattern that Drake, Hawkins and Raleigh would recognise, boasting the largest concentration of cobbled streets in England, with over 100 listed buildings, many dating back to Tudor and Jacobean times. What a sharp contrast to the 'new town' we have just come from.

The Old Fish Market (1896) (now the Edinburgh Woollen Mill) was a purpose-built harbour-side fish market. We mistake it at first for an old railway station, which is perhaps not surprising considering that the architect was principally a railway building designer.

New Street, as is often the way, turns out to be one of the city's oldest streets and has several listed

Above left Boats are never far away in Plymouth

Above right Smeaton's Tower was the model for a whole generation of British lighthouses

Below Devil's Point is a marine site of international importance today

'For twenty years I have had the good fortune to live, work and play in Plymouth. Going shopping, walking the dogs, sitting about in pubs, I am constantly entertained. To see people enjoying themselves gives me the greatest pleasure, and the inspiration to paint.' BERYL COOK

buildings (Nos 17, 18, 34 and 36, and the Elizabethan House Museum at No. 32) all of which were originally merchants' houses. We pause for a few moments in the delightful **Elizabethan Gardens** at No. 34.

Plymouth Hoe is the beating heart of Plymouth, with its stunning views of one of the most perfect natural harbours in the world. It's a place where people have always gathered, from the music of the Edwardian era to the morale-boosting dances that Nancy Astor organised here during the dark days of the Second World War, to the city's live band nights today. One of the most famous gatherings of all was in 1967 when Sir Francis Chichester returned to Plymouth after completing the first single-handed clipper route circumnavigation of the world and was greeted by an estimated crowd of a million spectators.

A charming feature of the Hoe is that there is a lighthouse plonked in the middle of it, called **Smeaton's Tower**. It was originally built in 1759 on the Eddystone Reef, a treacherous group of rocks that lie some fourteen miles south-west of Plymouth, but was taken down in the early 1880s when it was discovered that the sea was undermining the rock it was built on.

Smeaton originally modelled the shape of his lighthouse on that of an oak tree, and his robust tower set the pattern for a new era of lighthouse construction that led to similar structures up and down the coast of Britain. The lighthouse was depicted on the British penny for many years.

As we come into the Stonehouse area, we begin to spot plaques set in the pavement commemorating the Sherlock Holmes stories: 'They were the footprints of a gigantic hound' and such-like. In 1882, Arthur Conan Doyle worked as a newly qualified physician here and lived at the northern end of Durnford Street.

At the southern end, the street takes a wiggle and suddenly we are looking out to sea from **Devil's Point**. It is a truly spectacular view, the 'magic moment' of our walk. This is the point where for centuries family and friends have waved goodbye to or welcomed home their loved ones. It is a notable nature site, boasting unusual plant species on the low limestone cliffs and coastal grassland; and is also a marine site of international importance due to its wealth of marine and coastal wildlife.

We greatly appreciate the stairway linking Devil's Point with Royal William Yard, filling a gap in the South West Coast Path, and tying together for the first time two of the greatest jewels in Plymouth's crown, one natural and one built.

Designed by Sir John Rennie, the **Royal William Yard** (1831) is steeped in history. It was originally a Victualling Yard for the Royal Navy – and, as we explore, we discover an old bakery, a slaughterhouse, a spirits' store, a brewhouse, a food store, clothing stores and much else besides. It's the largest collection of Grade 1-listed military buildings anywhere in Europe. The Yard was decommissioned in 1992 and subsequently converted to an up-market mixed development by Urban Splash, who *The Times* have described as 'being in a class of its own when it comes to rescuing the great industrial landmarks of the past'. It's a stunning conversion, keeping many original features alongside a distinctly modern vibe.

As we head north from Royal William Yard, so we cross the **Stonehouse Creek**. Its lower reaches (on our right) were filled in from the 1960s onwards and now form a recreation and sports ground. The upper reaches of the creek, now Victoria Park, were formerly known as the Deadlake; that area was filled in way back in the 1890s.

On the south side of the creek was the Royal Naval Hospital, no longer in existence; and on the north side, the **Stoke Military Hospital** (1791), now the Devonport High School for Boys, complete with landing quays so that patients could be brought by water. Stoke is an important early hospital design – four original square ward blocks segregating patients, linked by an arcaded and vaulted walk at the front. The construction workforce was made up of Napoleonic prisoners of war who were housed in prison ships in the estuary.

Victoria Park (6 hectares, 14.8 acres) was originally designed to be completed for Queen Victoria's Diamond

Jubilee celebrations in 1897, and named in her honour, but wasn't completed until 1905, by which time she was no more. The former park keeper's lodge is in the centre of the park and is now a café. Three underground shelters were constructed in it to protect the population during the Blitz.

We finish off with a sharp contrast that typifies the old and new Plymouth – a cobbled street (Staddon Terrace Lane) at the end of which we peer straight over the Gyratory System in all its dismal glory.

Devonport Park, Blockhouse Park and Central Park loop

This route adds 2.7 km (1.7 miles) to your walk, but pays back handsomely in terms of great views in many directions, and a chance to explore Devonport a bit.

From around 1757, what is now **Devonport Park** (13 hectares, 33 acres) served as the 'glacis' – a part of the Devonport 'Dock Line' defences. These were open fields, kept free of development and providing no cover for an enemy. By the 1850s the 'Dock Lines' had little military value and Devonport was keen to respond to the national public park movement. Devonport Park was open by 1858 'for the purpose of healthful recreation by the public'.

Blockhouse Park is one of the highest points in the city (70 m) offering spectacular views of Dartmoor, Plymouth Sound and over the River Tamar to Bodmin Moor. The Mount Pleasant Redoubt sits at the highest point of the park, built in the Napoleonic era.

The route then comes back via **Central Park** (21 hectares, 52 acres), created in 1931. This loop finishes by coming back in under the railway line.

PIT STOPS

- **QUAY 33**, 33 Southside Street, PL1 2LE, has a great view.
- **BOSTON TEA PARTY**, 82 Vauxhall Street, PL4 0EX. A characterful indie chain.
- **COLUMN BAKEHOUSE**, the Factory Cooperage, Royal William Yard, PL1 3QQ. Plymouth's only social enterprise bakery.
- **THE PARK PAVILION CAFÉ**, the Lodge Victoria Park, PL1 5NQ.

QUIRKY SHOPPING

- **THE PLYMOUTH CITY MARKET**, Cornwall Street, PL1 1PS, sells a vast array of things, including fresh fish of course.
- **THE BARBICAN** area is full of gift shops and art galleries, including work of local artist Beryl Cook
- **27 NEW STREET**, PL1 2NB, one of the largest collection of antique traders in the south

PLACES TO VISIT

- **THE BARBICAN:** the Mayflower Steps, the spot from where the Pilgrim Fathers set sail for America.
- **THE LIDO**, just below the Hoe, is an Art Deco 1930s splendour.
- **THE NATIONAL MARINE AQUARIUM** (PL4 0DX) is the UK's largest aquarium.

WHEN TO VISIT

British Firework Championships (Aug), Plymouth Seafood Festival (Sept)

DESIGNED FOR PLEASURE

Cities designed for pleasure offer a more light-hearted way of life, new social interactions, a recharging of the batteries; they offer a change from the same old, same old . . . a place to start over, to discover yourself . . .

'Whatever your flavour, you'll find it in Brighton', says the Lonely Planet guide. In *Northanger Abbey*, Jane Austen observes: 'They arrived in Bath. Catherine was all eager delight; her eyes were here, there, everywhere. She was come to be happy, and she felt happy already.'

Bath and Brighton are our very own Las Vegases; both exploding in population from tiny bases, Bath growing twelvefold in the eighteenth century and Brighton seventeenfold in the nineteenth, faster than any other English cities. Their growth was fuelled by Georgian building booms, as intense in their way as the expansion of Las Vegas since the 1960s.

SO, WHAT SHOULD YOU LOOK OUT FOR IN A CITY DESIGNED FOR PLEASURE?

1. A 'creation myth' – in both cases, spa waters with special properties.
2. A 'master of ceremonies' to create social cachet for the place – Beau Nash in Bath, the Prince Regent in Brighton.
3. **Promenades** designed for social interaction – the Esplanade in Brighton, the paths, squares and parks of Bath.
4. **Pleasure gardens** – Sydney Gardens in Bath, St Ann's Well Gardens in Brighton; and, of course, the piers.
5. Many **places of entertainment** – theatres, vaudeville, racecourses, festivals.
6. **Gorgeous Georgian areas**, driven by the 'building aristocracy' – the Woods in Bath, the Wilds in Brighton.
7. **Railway stations** that arrive in great curving sweeps. After all, visitors have always been the *raison d'être* of the pleasure cities.

Bath

Bath is unlike any other British city, all planned perfection around a single glorious era of leisure and intrigue, with none of the 'edginess' usually associated with the urban scene.

Bath has a striking setting in a 'hollow of the hills', with the River Avon running through its heart. From many vantage points on the surrounding hills you get excellent panoramas across the city; and from many points within the city you can look straight out along a street and up into the countryside; always a great joy in a smaller city, a glimpse of the country beyond the urban landscape. Almost all the open land on slopes around the city is specially protected to retain the mixture of woodland and meadows, and this contributes greatly to Bath's immense charm. And the city is small-scale: you can walk out of the city from Bath Abbey to Bathwick Meadows in little more than fifteen minutes.

The city's fame was assured by a unique natural asset – very hot water bubbling up from the ground as geothermal springs. The Romans built baths and a temple here. In the seventeenth century, claims were made for the curative properties of water from these springs, and Bath became famous as a spa town in the Georgian era.

Unlike so many British cities, Bath is emphatically not a Victorian-inspired or Victorian-looking city. Whilst Bath only doubled in size during the nineteenth century, neighbouring Bristol grew fivefold and became

WALK DATA

- **DISTANCE:** 9.5 km (5.9 miles)
- **HEIGHT GAIN:** 90 metres
- **WALK TIME:** 2½ hours
- **START & FINISH:** Bath Spa station (BA1 1SU)
- **TERRAIN:** Mainly pavements, but Bathwick Fields can be muddy

the dominant economic force in the region, whilst Bath's fashionability faded.

In 1987, the recognition of Bath's glorious architectural heritage was confirmed when UNESCO awarded the whole city World Heritage status – one of only two cities in the world to be designated in its entirety, the other being Venice.

Today, tourism and professional services underpin the city's employment. More than one million visitors stay and there are four million visits each year. It has become a fashionable 'lifestyle haven' for publishers, software programmers, lawyers and accountants.

THE WALK

We alight at the delightful **Bath Spa station** (1840), designed by Brunel; but setting out on our walk we find ourselves having to skirt around the rather unedifying neo-Georgian shopping centre before reaching the undiluted Georgian joy of the city.

The Bath of our imagination soon becomes a reality as we reach South Parade, Duke Street, North Parade and Pierrepont Street. Almost all the houses on these streets, dating back to the 1740s, are Grade I listed.

The **Roman Baths** date back to AD 60 when the Romans constructed a temple to Sulis on the site, and the bathing complex was gradually built up over the next 300 years. The Baths themselves are now below the current street level and the spring is housed in eighteenth-century buildings. **Bath Abbey** was a former Benedictine monastery, founded in the seventh century, reconstructed in the twelfth century and subject to major restoration by Sir George Gilbert Scott in the 1860s. The abbey is one of the best examples of Perpendicular Gothic architecture in the region, with a particularly fine vault ceiling.

The **Grand Pump Room**, built by Thomas Baldwin, was the centre of Bath's social scene at the start of the nineteenth century. In Jane Austen's words, 'Every creature in Bath was to be seen in the room at different periods of the fashionable hours.' On arrival in the city, you were expected to write your name, address and the length of your stay in 'the Register'. Everything 'Society' needed to know about you could be gleaned from these inputs, an early version of Facebook.

Queen Square is the first element in 'the most important architectural sequence in Bath', which includes the Circus and the Royal Crescent. It was the first speculative development by the architect John Wood the Elder, who later lived in a house on the south side of the square, apparently with the best view (builders always seem to wangle the best houses).

He understood that polite society enjoyed parading, and in order to do that he provided wide streets, with raised pavements, and a thoughtfully designed central

WALK DATA

- **CITY POPULATION:** 88,859 (#80 in UK)
- **ORIGINS:** AD 60 (Roman)
- **CITY STATUS:** Royal Charter granted by Elizabeth I in 1590
- **FAMOUS INHABITANTS:** Thomas Gainsborough (painter), Beau Nash (master of ceremonies), Bill Bailey (comedian), Ken Loach (film director), Mary Berry (chef), William Pitt (Prime Minister), Jane Austen (novelist), Thomas Robert Malthus (economist), Roger Bannister (athlete)
- **NOTABLE BUILDERS:** John Wood the Elder (Queen Square, South Parade, the Circus), John Wood the Younger (Royal Crescent, Bath Assembly Rooms), Thomas Baldwin (Pump Room, Laura Place)
- **SCREEN TIME:** *Les Misérables* (Pulteney Bridge), *The Duchess* (The Assembly Rooms), *Vanity Fair* (Great Pulteney Street); *Inspector Morse* TV series
- **ICONIC CITYSCAPES:** Bath Abbey Tower, Lansdown Crescent, Bathwick Fields, Beechen Cliff

garden in Queen Square. From the square, we take the **Gravel Walk**; this is the secluded, gently rising walk that Captain Wentworth and Anne Elliot take in *Persuasion* when they are finally reconciled. And it's not too fanciful to say it has a peace and auspiciousness about it that promotes calm and harmony.

The **Royal Crescent** (1774) takes our breath away, the acme of architectural beauty, with its ha-ha wall emphasising its 'rus in urbe' ambitions. It has the 'definitive' Georgian crescent feel about it and does it better than anywhere else. But all is not what it seems; whilst Wood designed the great curved façade of what appear to be about thirty houses, with Ionic columns on a rusticated ground floor, that was the extent of his input. Each purchaser then bought a certain length of the façade, and employed their own architect to build a house to their own specifications behind it. A perfect way to combine overall uniformity with individual flexibility.

Above left The obelisk in Queen Square was erected by Beau Nash in honour of Frederick, Prince of Wales

Above right Royal Victoria Park has many secluded spots to relax in

Below The Royal Crescent encircles a beautiful open green space

'Bath is the worst of all places for getting any work done'.

WILLIAM WILBERFORCE

Royal Victoria Park (23 hectares, 57 acres) is a beautiful expanse of green parkland. Originally an arboretum, the park dates back to 1829 and is named after Queen Victoria, who officially opened it in 1830 at the age of eleven. During her visit, it is said that a local resident commented on the thickness of her ankles. The observation was duly reported to the princess, causing her to shun the city for the duration of her reign. The only time she passed through again was by train from Bristol to London, when she reportedly kept the blinds in her carriage firmly drawn. Bath didn't quite give up on Victoria, though. The three-sided Obelisk of the Victoria Majority Monument was erected in 1837 to honour the princess's eighteenth birthday.

The Botanical Gardens were formed in the north-west area of the park in 1887. They contain a fine collection of plants that thrive on limestone, the same strata that are so amenable to the hot springs.

Jane Austen may have taken this very same sneaky route that we take up Park Street to avoid the throngs, as she loved walking to relax and have time on her own (notably to Lansdown, the route we are taking). She writes about her Bath walks often in her letters: 'The pleasure of walking and breathing fresh air is enough for me, and in fine weather, I am out more than half my time.'

We are so pleased with our little 'snicket' up the hill as it comes out in front of the stupendous **Lansdown Crescent**, laid out in the late 1780s by John Palmer. The

sheep spending part of the year in the field beneath the crescent belong to farmer Douglas Creed from Kelston. He began using the field in the early 1990s, so is very familiar with the practicalities of the site. He prefers to mate his sheep relatively late so that lambs are born after the worst of the winter is over. He also needs to wait until the lambs are of sufficient size not to be able to squeeze through the railings into Lansdown Crescent and face danger from passing traffic.

Cutting across east we reach the steep **Hedgemead Park** (2 hectares, 5 acres). Unusually for a park, it came about by an accident rather than years of community petitioning, when in 1889 the houses below Camden Crescent collapsed due to a landslide. The layout of the paths and terrain were engineered to prevent the possibility of future landslides.

The Circus (1768) consists of three long, curved terraces designed to form a circular space intended for civic functions and games. The inspiration was the Colosseum in Rome and, like the Colosseum, the three façades have a different order of architecture on each floor: Doric on the ground level, Ionic on the middle floor, and finishing with Corinthian on the upper floor, the style of the building thus becoming progressively more ornate as it rises.

The Assembly Rooms (1769) formed the hub of fashionable Georgian society in the city, the venue being described as 'the most noble and elegant of any in the kingdom'. People would gather in the rooms in

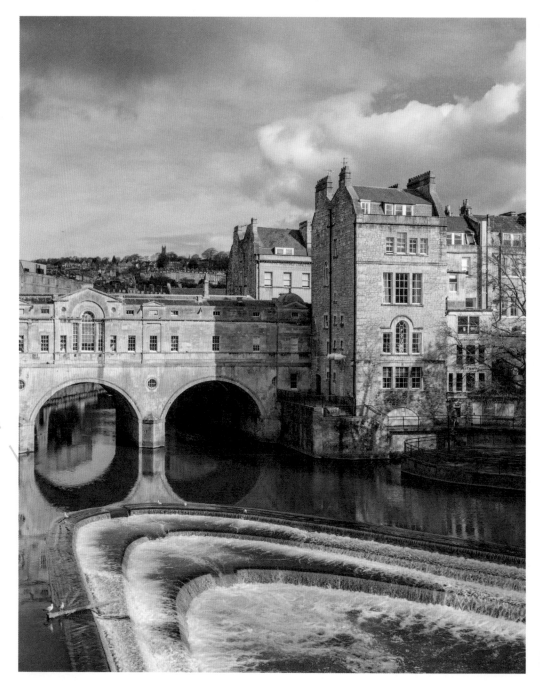

the evening for balls and other public functions, or simply to play cards. Mothers and chaperones bringing their daughters to Bath for the social season, hoping to marry them off to a suitable husband, would take their charge to such events where one might meet all the eligible men currently in the city.

The Corridor (1825) is one of the oldest shopping malls in the country. Customers were originally serenaded in galleries overhead, which are still there, a step up from piped muzak! It has perhaps seen better days shopping-wise but makes an interesting cut-through, coming out in front of the **Guildhall**, built in the 1770s by Thomas Baldwin.

Parade Gardens (1 hectare, 2.5 acres) is worth visiting for the views across the river and especially the view upstream to Pulteney Bridge. The bandstand is in that rarely found Bath architectural style, the not-Georgian. It dates back to 1925, replacing an earlier nineteenth-century version. The large building overlooking the Parade Gardens from Grand Parade is **The Empire**, built in 1898 as a hotel. The interesting rooftop, depicting cottages, a townhouse, a manor house with Dutch-style gable and a castle is said to have represented the different classes of Victorian customer who were all welcome to use the hotel!

Pulteney Bridge (1774) is one of the defining landmarks of Bath, built to connect the city to the new Georgian town of Bathwick. Designed by Robert Adam in Palladian style, it is exceptional in having shops built across its full span on both sides. **Laura Place** is named after Henrietta Laura Pulteney, whose father owned the Bathwick Estate, which comprises four streets joined on the diagonals of Laura Place. Pevsner describes it as 'one of the most impressive of all Neoclassical urban set pieces in Britain'.

Then we head left and up through **Henrietta Park** (2.8 hectares, 7 acres), laid out to celebrate the Diamond Jubilee of Queen Victoria of 1897 (it seems they didn't give up on her). We relax for a while in the Garden of Remembrance, a particularly tranquil spot.

Sydney Gardens (4 hectares, 9.9 acres) was created in the 1790s as a commercial pleasure grounds, in the tradition of the Vauxhall Pleasure Gardens. The Sydney Hotel, now the Holburne Museum, was built in 1796 as a casino and gateway to the gardens. It was entered through archways that took you first into a foyer and then through gauze curtains decorated with Apollo strumming his lyre, into a landscape of pure pleasure. Musicians played on the terrace above so that the visitor entered a magical scene of supper boxes, entertainments, masques, follies and numerous places of assignation. The gardens themselves included a labyrinth, grotto, sham castle and an artificial rural scene with moving figures powered by a clockwork mechanism. As Jane Austen remarked: 'It would be very pleasant to be near Sidney Gardens! – we might go into the Labyrinth every day.'

The Kennet and Avon Canal passes through the gardens via two short tunnels and under two cast-iron footbridges dating from 1800. There is also an iron footbridge over the railway which was designed by Brunel and built in 1840. **Cleveland House** is one of the treasures of the canal. Built by the Duke of Cleveland as the headquarters for the canal company, it was built half on land and half over the canal, and had a magnificent two-storey boardroom over the canal, with a trap-door in the tunnel roof that was used to pass paperwork between clerks above and bargees below.

Canals provide a nature corridor through cities. David Goode, in *Nature in Towns and Cities*, writes

about this particular stretch: 'The lock gates are colonised by a tangle of water-loving plants including gypsywort, skullcap, pendulous sedge and wild angelica, with a profusion of liverworts covering the woodwork at the lower levels. One heron, oblivious to passers-by, has learnt to wait patiently by the lock gates where it catches small fish carried through the leaky gates.'

The National Trust acquired **Bathwick Fields** (9.3 hectares, 23.7 acres) in 1984 with funds raised by the council and local people keen to see this meadowland preserved. From the top field, we marvel at a truly iconic view across Bath, from Beechen Cliff on our left to Lansdown Hill on our right, taking in views that have defined Bath since Georgian times.

The **Smallcombe Cemetery** (1.9 hectares, 4.7 acres), just south of Bathwick Fields, was opened in 1856. Population expansion had seen the Parish of Bathwick overwhelmed by demands for burials outside the city. At only £3, a 'decent burial' was affordable to most so artisans as well as aristocrats are buried here. Smallcombe remains the semi-wild, tranquil garden described when it opened as 'secluded and even picturesque, a beautiful spot, commanding a fine view of the city' and today is lovingly looked after by the Smallcombe Garden Cemetery Conservation Group.

For the final stretch, we return to the delights of the canal. **Pumphouse Chimney** was built in an ornate style as the wealthy residents on Bathwick Hill did not want to overlook an industrial-style chimney (how very Bath . . .). And then back over **Halfpenny** (Widcombe) Bridge. An earlier, wooden version of this footbridge had collapsed, tumbling dozens of people into the river. It was re-built in metal in the late 1870s and charged a halfpenny toll to recoup the building costs, hence its name. But don't worry, you won't need a halfpenny these days, and the structure looks robust. You will soon be delivered back safely to Bath Spa where our journey began.

PIT STOPS
- **COLONNA & SMALLS**, 6 Chapel Row, BA1 1HN. If you like hip minimalist, this is for you.
- **PARADE GARDENS CAFÉ**, Grand Parade, BA2 4DF
- **GARDEN CAFÉ**, Holburne Museum, Great Pulteney Street, BA2 4DB. Great garden location, modern building, recommended.

QUIRKY SHOPPING
Bath is a shoppers' paradise with hundreds of independently owned stores. Among the key areas are: Milsom Street (BA1 1DG), Green Street (BA1 2JY), Walcot Street (BA1 5BG), Farmers' Market at Green Park station (BA1 1JB).

PLACES TO VISIT
- **ROMAN BATHS**, Stall Street, BA1 1LZ
- **THERMAE BATH SPA**, The Hetling Pump Room, Hot Bath Street, BA1 1SJ. You can bathe in the natural springs, and there is a fabulous view from the rooftop swimming pool.
- **HOLBURNE MUSEUM**, Great Pulteney Street, BA2 4DB. Gainsborough and Stubbs paintings.

WHEN TO VISIT
Christmas Market (early Dec), Bath Literature Festival (early March), Bath International Music Festival (May/June)

Brighton

This walk is a revelation - lots of green space, a bracing walk along the seafront, myriad intriguing lanes and buzzing city life.

The mainstay of Brighton's economy for the first 700 years of its existence was fishing. Open land called the Hempshares, the site of the present Lanes, provided hemp for ropes; sails were made from flax grown in Hove; and boats were kept on the open land which became Old Steine. By the late sixteenth century Brighton's eighty-boat fleet was the largest in southern England and employed 400 men.

But it was not until the early eighteenth century, with the population still only standing at 2,000, that the town began to grow in ambition. The contemporary fad for drinking and bathing in seawater as a cure for illnesses was encouraged by Dr Richard Russell who sent many patients to 'take the cure' in the sea at Brighton, published a popular treatise on the subject and moved to the town soon afterwards to cash in on the fashion.

From 1780, development of the Georgian terraces got underway, and the town was transformed from the 'Cinderella' of a fishing village (at that time called Brighthelmston) into the 'fairy princess' of a fashionable resort, with a name simplification to Brighton for good measure. The growth of the town was further spurred on by the patronage of the Prince Regent (later George IV)

WALK DATA

- **DISTANCE:** 11.2 km (7 miles)
- **HEIGHT GAIN:** 120 metres
- **WALK TIME:** 2¾ hrs
- **START & FINISH:** Brighton station (BN1 3XP)
- **TERRAIN:** Steep climb to Whitehawk Hill

after his first visit in 1783. He spent much of his leisure time in the town and constructed the Royal Pavilion as a place for escape and indulgence.

Another spur to growth was the arrival of the London and Brighton Railway in 1841, which brought the town within reach of day-trippers from London. Today Brighton attracts over 8.5 million visitors annually and its tourism industry employs 20,000 people. But the city is also part of the digital economy – over 500 new media businesses have been founded in Brighton in the last decade.

N.B.: Brighton has about 400 restaurants, apparently more per head than anywhere else in the UK. This might well slow down your walk!

THE WALK

We emerge from our train into the beautiful engine shed of **Brighton station** (1841) in high spirits. The train to the coast from London has been a revelation, groups of friends spread across the seats chatting nineteen to the dozen, romantic couples of all ages and persuasions, parents with their young children, all with one thing in common – they are coming down to Brighton to have fun, as of course are we, tucked quietly into the corner of the carriage as all good urban ramblers should be.

Our route takes us up a steep slope and then along Camden Terrace, a narrow twitten (Sussex dialect for 'passage'), emerging at **St Nicholas's Church** (fourteenth century), a lovely little green spot. Situated on high ground, it is the oldest surviving building in Brighton, albeit much modified by Victorian improvers.

The first extension to the churchyard was built in 1824, across Church Street to the north. This has been converted into a playground. But the most significant change came in 1841 when land to the west of Dyke Road was acquired and used to form a much larger burial ground, containing a series of vaults. We take a quick detour through it. Then we head along Vine Place, our second twitten of the day, which gives access to the tiny one-storey cottages that were the original mill-workers' cottages to Clifton Windmill. This windmill has gone but the miller's house, Rose Cottage, is still here.

On our right, as we walk along Victoria Road, the **Church of St Michael and All Angels** (1862 and 1893) looms large, built to serve the affluent local community. According to its Grade I listing, 'the architectural quality of both buildings and of their fittings, and the range and quality of the stained glass, make this a building of outstanding importance'. Most notably, the Pre-Raphaelite Brotherhood was closely involved with the decoration of the interior.

We positively drool as we peer down Montpelier Terrace at the beautiful 1840s stucco-clad terraced houses and villas, all beautifully maintained. The architectural partnership of Amon Wilds, his son Amon Henry Wilds and Charles Busby – the most important architects in

WALK DATA

- **CITY POPULATION:** 171,311 (#15 in UK)
- **ORIGINS:** 5th century AD (Anglo-Saxon)
- **CITY STATUS:** Brighton and Hove granted city status in 1997 (474,485 combined population)
- **FAMOUS INHABITANTS:** Sir Winston Churchill (politician), Nigel Kennedy (violinist), Max Miller (comedian), John Osborne (playwright), Dame Anita Roddick (the Body Shop), Paul Scofield (actor)
- **NOTABLE BUILDERS:** Amon Henry Wilds (Regency estates), Ken Fines (Borough Planning Officer, 1970s)
- **SCREEN TIME:** *Brighton Rock*, *Oh! What a Lovely War* (old West Pier), *Quadrophenia* (seafront), *Mona Lisa* (Palace Pier)
- **ICONIC CITYSCAPES:** i360 on Brighton beachfront, Whitehawk Hill

Regency-era Brighton and Hove – were the driving force behind almost the entire Montpelier development, building nearly 4,000 new houses in the Regency style, quite some achievement.

The ultimate showpiece in these parts is **Montpelier Crescent** (1840s), envisaged to have a sight of the South Downs; but within ten years, the downland vista had been obscured by the construction of Vernon Terrace opposite. Never mind. There are still many things to enjoy about the crescent, not least the generous green space out in front.

Next, we come to the quaint **St Ann's Well Gardens** (5.3 hectares, 13 acres), the spot where Brighton's status as a health spa was born. It was Dr Richard Russell who first made St Ann's Well famous by sending some of his clients to drink the water from a spring here. The Chalybeate (iron) spring became known as one of the finest natural springs in the whole of Europe. However, the distance of the spa from the centre of Brighton, competition from other facilities, and a slow decline in the flow of the spring led to the spa's declining popularity, and it eventually closed.

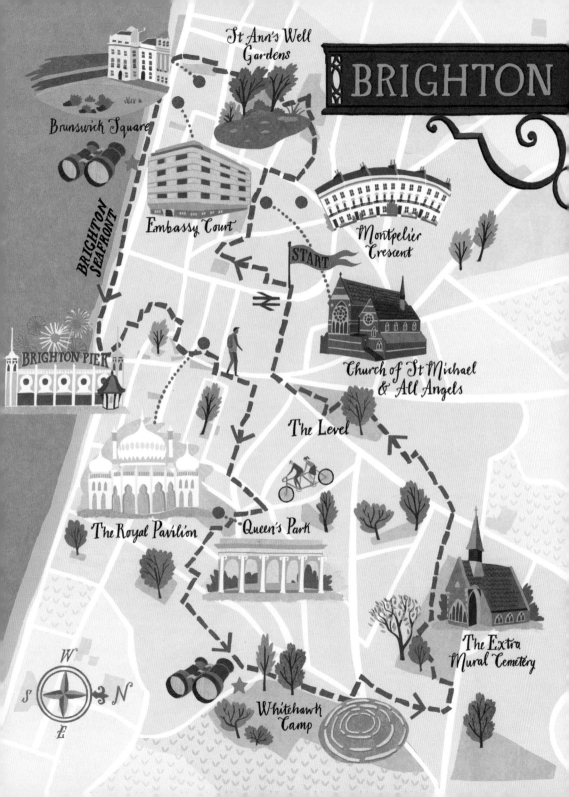

Above Brunswick Square has Regency architecture on three sides – and on the fourth side the sea!

Below The Orient comes to Brighton in the exotic shapes of the Brighton Pavilion

'Brighton comprises every possibility of earthly happiness.' JANE AUSTEN

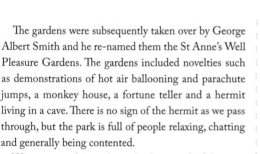

The gardens were subsequently taken over by George Albert Smith and he re-named them the St Anne's Well Pleasure Gardens. The gardens included novelties such as demonstrations of hot air ballooning and parachute jumps, a monkey house, a fortune teller and a hermit living in a cave. There is no sign of the hermit as we pass through, but the park is full of people relaxing, chatting and generally being contented.

We saunter down through the wonderful green expanse of **Brunswick Square** – what more could you wish for than a beautiful garden to relax in, three sides of perfect Regency architecture, and on the fourth side the sea!

Embassy Court (1935) is an eleven-storey block of luxury Art Deco Modernist apartments, which were originally let to wealthy residents, including Max Miller and Terence Rattigan. Features such as enclosed balconies and England's first penthouse suites made the building one of the most desirable and sought-after addresses in the country. The Modernist layout provided for levels of comfort and amenity that were exceptional for their day, including under-floor central heating, constant hot water, built-in electric fires and fitted kitchens with integral cookers and fridges. These were almost unheard-of innovations at the time.

Now we are on the true 'tourist' part of the trail, poking into the shops of West Pier Arches Creative Quarter, peering up as we pass the i360 observation tower (highly recommended for an all-round bird's eye view), taking a step back in history at the Brighton Fishing Museum.

Brighton's first pier was the Old Chain Pier (1823), used as a landing stage for cross-Channel passenger ships. Realising its commercial value, the owners began charging an entry fee of 2d and set up kiosks selling souvenirs as well as entertainment stalls. The Chain Pier was struck by many storms and eventually replaced by the **Brighton Marine Palace & Pier** (1899), which is what we see today, bustling in every corner with energy and pleasure.

Old Steine Gardens (1 hectare, 2.5 acres) was originally a natural drainage point, where the Wellesbourne River (now underground) met the sea. Local fishermen stored their boats and dried their nets here. In the late nineteenth century, as part of ongoing 'improvements', the area was drained and enclosed, and visitors began to use the Steine to promenade.

Right Looking along the colourful Hendon Street towards Whitehawk Hill

'The beautiful thing about Brighton is that you can buy your lover a pair of knickers at Victoria Station and have them off again at the Grand Hotel in less than two hours'. KEITH WATERHOUSE

The **Royal Pavilion** (1787–1822) is a former royal residence. It was built in three stages, as a seaside retreat for George, Prince of Wales, who became the Prince Regent in 1811. The designer John Nash redesigned and greatly extended the Pavilion, and it is his work that can be seen today. The palace has an Indo-Islamic appearance on the outside, whilst the fanciful interior design is influenced by both Chinese and Indian fashion.

The seaside town had become fashionable through the residence of George's uncle, Prince Henry, Duke of Cumberland, whose tastes for cuisine, gaming, the theatre and fast living the young prince shared. And rather conveniently, his physician advised him that the sea water would be beneficial for his gout. The Royal Pavilion became his playground.

Next, we snake up **Victoria Gardens** (2 hectares, 4.9 acres), heading north along the line of the old river, at the bottom of a valley, steeper to the east than the west. We clamber up a steep flight of steps to Richmond Heights, which affords views back to the centre of the city.

We are heading for **Queen's Park** (6.5 hectares, 16.1 acres), opened to the public in 1890. In the 1830s, Thomas Attree had acquired land to build a residential park surrounded by detached villas, inspired by Regent's Park in London. Whilst the park itself materialised, with access by subscription, very little of the development did, other than an Italianate villa, which no longer exists. All that is left today, at the top of Tower Road, is the 'Pepper Pot' (1830), but no-one seems quite sure what it was originally for.

From the park, we take the exit immediately to the right of the tennis courts and head down Evelyn Terrace and then Bute Street, at the end of which we take some steps up to Whitehawk Hill. The hill is an ancient habitat designated a Local Nature Reserve, with areas of species-rich chalk grassland. From the top, we gaze down over the city and the sea, and can just make out the Isle of Wight, more than 65 km west.

The very first settlement in the Brighton area was here at **Whitehawk Camp**, directly opposite today's racecourse stands, dating back to the Neolithic period. Archaeologists have found numerous burial mounds, tools and bones, suggesting it was a place of some importance.

Brighton Racecourse staged its first race in 1783; and according to legend, George IV, when still Prince Regent, invented hurdle racing nearby whilst out riding with aristocratic friends. They found some sheep pens which they proceeded to jump for a bit of fun. The racecourse was home for a while to top-class racing and was attended by fashionable society, but it drifted out of fashion when the prince and his friends lost interest. The course began to thrive again, however, with the arrival of the railway, which enabled London punters to have a day out at the races by the seaside.

Taking the tunnel under the racecourse, we come out into the patchwork-quilt landscape of **Tenantry Down Allotments**. The land was purchased by the council in the 1880s and has been used for allotments ever since.

Above left Book yourself tickets on the i360 for incomparable panoramas

Above right St Peter's Church is a Charles Barry creation

Below The North Laines have a cornucopia of indie shops

The **Extra Mural Cemetery** (1851) occupies one of the most delightful spots in the whole of Brighton: a sheltered, gently sloping, well-wooded area of downland between two much steeper hills. As early as 1880, its potential as a green space as well as a burial ground was recognised when J.G. Bishop published a walking guide called *Strolls in the Brighton Extra Mural Cemetery*. What he first discovered, we experience too – the cemetery is a delight to walk through – headstones, more elaborate and ornate tombs and a Gothic Revival chapel, all within a leafy landscape of studied neglect.

Now we're on the final leg of our journey. The **Level** (6.4 hectares, 15.7 acres) used to be open grassland, with two streams, the Wellesbourne and the Springbourne, converging here. Cricket was played here from the mid-eighteenth century, until 1822 when the space was formally laid out. It has recently been extensively restored, with a skatepark and children's play area.

We stop at the **Open Market**, just to the west of The Level, reached through a multicoloured and inviting archway, for a snack and a drink. The original market, which had been on The Level itself, dates back to the 1880s when barrow boys began selling fruit and vegetables.

St Peter's Church (1828), by Sir Charles Barry, is a fine example of the pre-Victorian Gothic Revival style. It was the parish church of Brighton from 1873 to 2007 and is sometimes unofficially referred to as 'Brighton's Cathedral'.

Finally, we head up Trafalgar Street to the **North Laines**, with the quaint mid-nineteenth-century Pelham Square on our left. 'Laine' is a Sussex dialect term for an open tract of land at the base of the Downs.

Ken Fines was Borough Planning Officer for Brighton in the 1970s. He is credited with having saved the North Laines area from extensive redevelopment that could have seen existing buildings being replaced by new high-rise buildings, a flyover and a large car park. An early pioneer for interesting, walkable, independent space in cities, I take my hat off to him. Today it is buzzing and full of indies, cafés and bars.

PIT STOPS

- **THE GARDEN CAFÉ**, St Anne's Gardens (BN3 1RP) is a very welcoming spot.
- **PAVILION GARDEN CAFÉ** (BN1 1UG) is a great location on a sunny day. A bit of a Brighton institution.
- **THE OPEN MARKET** (BN1 4GE) by the Level has several good indie cafes.

QUIRKY SHOPPING

- **THE NORTH LAINES** has a huge mix of interesting indies and unusual stuff.
- **THE OPEN MARKET** (BN1 4GE) is especially strong on jewellery and knitwear.

PLACES TO VISIT

- **BRIGHTON FISHING MUSEUM** (on the beach): beautifully preserved boats and fascinating histories.
- **BRIGHTON PAVILION**
- **BRITISH AIRWAYS i360**, a 162-metre observation tower on the seafront

WHEN TO VISIT

The Brighton Arts Festival & Fringe (May), St Ann's Well Gardens Festival (late May); Brighton Summer Pride (Aug); Brunswick Festival (mid-Aug)

VICTORIAN INDUSTRY

Britain was the first country in the world to industrialise and our four featured cities were at the heart of this revolution.

Breakneck industrialisation led to a population explosion in these cities – growing sixfold over the nineteenth century – with chaotic urbanisation, few green spaces, little civic structure and extremes of wealth and squalor. The Report on the Sanitary Condition of the Labouring Population of Great Britain (1842) pointed out that a typical country farmer lived twice as long (forty-one years) as a city shopkeeper (twenty years).

But from about this time a group of reformers begun to emerge, philanthropists and politicians who wanted to improve the lot of the city dweller through better sanitation and the provision of open spaces (or a city's 'green lungs' as they were already being referred to, a term coined by William Pitt the Elder).

These men (the likes of Chamberlain in Birmingham, Baines in Leeds, Roebuck in Sheffield and Engels in Manchester) 'did not argue on the defensive', according to historian Asa Briggs. 'They persistently carried the attack into the countryside, comparing contemptuously the passive with the active, the idlers with the workers, the landlords with the businessmen, the voluntary initiative of the city with the "torpor" and "monotony" of the village, and urban freedom with rustic "feudalism".'

Non-conformism played a huge role in helping to transform cities. Non-conformists were behind many of the institutional initiatives of the nineteenth century – schools, libraries, parks and cemeteries. Furthermore, they were instrumental in campaigning for social and political reform that has subsequently formed the bedrock of modern civil liberties. You will see many fruits of their endeavours on our walks.

Today these cities are full of vitality and remain at the forefront of education and new service-based industries.

Birmingham

Birmingham was the epitome of the great city brought low by post-war planning that favoured the car and the shopping centre. The good news is that in the last decade Birmingham has managed to reverse many of its worst mistakes and a new, more walkable city is emerging from the rubble.

Birmingham's early history is that of a remote and marginal area. It lay on the upland Birmingham Plateau and within the densely wooded and sparsely populated Forest of Arden. A medium-sized market town during the medieval period, it only began to gain commercial significance in the sixteenth century with the manufacture of iron goods.

Its key drawback was that it had no navigable river, and it wasn't until the canals arrived that economic growth could take off. Within forty years the city was at the hub of the country's canal networks and at the forefront of worldwide advances in science, technology and economic development. By 1791 it was being hailed as 'the first manufacturing town in the world'. It had a distinctive economic profile, with thousands of small workshops practising a wide variety of specialised and highly skilled trades, encouraging exceptional levels of creativity and innovation.

The city also rose to national political prominence in the campaign for political reform, with Thomas Attwood and the Birmingham Political Union bringing the country to the brink of civil war during the Days of May that preceded the passing of the 1832 Great Reform Act. The Union's meetings on Newhall Hill were the largest political assemblies Britain had ever seen.

WALK DATA

- **DISTANCE:** 11.7 km (7.3 miles)
- **HEIGHT GAIN:** 30 metres
- **WALK TIME:** 3 hrs
- **START & FINISH:** Birmingham New Street station (B5 4AH)
- **TERRAIN:** Straightforward, all on pavements or gravel paths

The process of rebuilding after the bomb damage of the Second World War was led by the pragmatic Sir Herbert Manzoni, the City Engineer. His priorities were rehousing, civic redevelopment and sorting out traffic congestion. What he oversaw was to have a profound effect on the image of Birmingham in subsequent decades, with the mix of concrete ring roads, shopping centres and tower blocks giving the city its 'concrete jungle' tag.

By the 1980s the council and its planners finally realised that all was not well; and they set about improving the 'liveability' of the city, making it more appealing and 'connected' once again.

THE WALK

From the moment we step off the train, encapsulated by a gleaming new station full of light and space, we appreciate that Birmingham has been transformed. So very different from the grim 1960s warren of the old New Street station, deserved winner of the ugliest building in Britain award back in the day.

And the landmark **Rotunda** (1965) is a triumph of 1960s architecture brushed up for the twenty-first century. Listed Grade II, it has recently had the Urban Splash treatment, being converted from an office block into luxury apartments. And it's a bit of a rarity in Birmingham, a building that has been re-purposed rather than knocked down and started from scratch.

As we approach the Bullring, we realise that things are really not the same at all – where I recall only a decade ago acres of concrete, impersonality and dull chains, now there are delightful walking spaces, punctuated by trees, statues, steps and water features; and then suddenly, on our left, the visual raucousness of the **Selfridges** (2003) 'bubble wrap' building.

Walking past St Martin's, we reach the bustling **Birmingham Market** area. There have been markets here since the Middle Ages, and we feel sure that the liveliness of the traders and the breadth of food and non-food products today is as strong as it always was. A real joy of a market.

We walk under Holloway Circus past the rather incongruously situated Chinese pagoda. Wing Yip gave this pagoda to Birmingham as a gesture of thanks to the city for providing him with a home. He had arrived by boat from Hong Kong in 1959 at the age of nineteen with just £10 in his pocket. He opened a grocery store in Birmingham and, from these small beginnings, built a food empire that now supplies more than 2,000 Chinese restaurants around the country. Brummies, whether born and bred or incomers, seem to share a strong work ethic.

The **Singers Hill Synagogue** (1856) has played an important part in the lives of the Jewish community in Birmingham. There has been a Jewish community here since the thirteenth century.

WALK DATA

- **CITY POPULATION:** 1,073,045 (#3 in the UK)
- **ORIGINS:** 7th century AD (Anglo-Saxon)
- **CITY STATUS:** 1889
- **FAMOUS INHABITANTS:** Edward Burne-Jones (Pre-Raphaelite painter), Joseph Chamberlain (politician), Tony Hancock (comedian), Enoch Powell (politician), Malala Yousafzai (Pakistani activist), James Watt (inventor), Alec Issigonis (designer of the Mini)
- **NOTABLE BUILDERS:** Sir Herbert Manzoni (City Engineer 1935–63), John Madin (1960s buildings, many now demolished)
- **SCREEN TIME:** *Brassed Off* (Town Hall), *She Who Brings Gifts*, *Take Me High* (Gas Street Basin); *Line of Duty* TV series
- **ICONIC CITYSCAPES:** 25th floor of the Cube (bar), Skyline Viewpoint in Birmingham Library

The **Mailbox** is a good example of the building and rebuilding that has taken place in Birmingham over the decades. When it opened in 1970 as the Royal Mail sorting office, it was the largest mechanised sorting office in the country. Canalside wharves were demolished to make way for it and an underground tunnel connected it to New Street station. The building re-opened in 2000 as an upmarket development of offices, shops and restaurants.

The 25-storey **Cube** (2010), which we come to next, was designed by Birmingham-born Ken Shuttleworth, who co-designed London's Gherkin building: 'The cladding for me tries to reflect the heavy industries of Birmingham which I remember as a kid, the metal plate works and the car plants – and the inside is very crystalline, all glass; that to me is like the jewellery side of Birmingham, the light bulbs and delicate stuff – it tries to reflect the essence of Birmingham in the building itself.'

And now we reach the part of the canal where the vast majority of people who walk alongside the water are to be found, along the half-mile or so around **Gas Street**

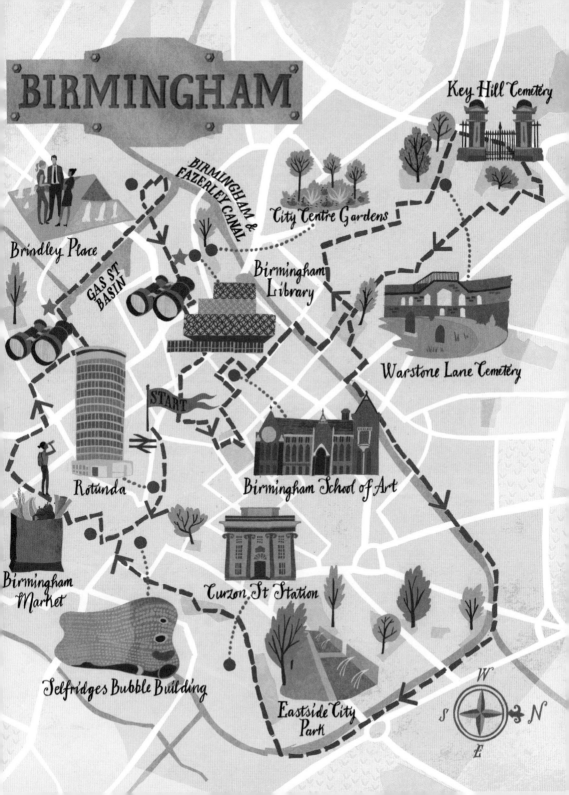

Above left The Rotunda
is a triumph of 1960s
architecture brushed up for
the twenty-first century

Above right The Cathedral
Church of St Philip is 'a most
subtle example of the elusive
English Baroque'

Below Formerly derelict,
the Brindleyplace
development follows a Terry
Farrell masterplan

'It is an honour for me to be here in Birmingham, the beating heart of England.' MALALA YOUSAFZAI

Basin, the centre of the network; now all beautifully restored, still carrying narrowboats and replete with restaurants and bars.

Brindleyplace's central square is an agreeable open space with well-tended lawns and trees. Named after the eighteenth-century canal engineer, James Brindley, this district used to be a warren of factories but had lain derelict for many years. If you're not into post-modern architecture (the overall master plan was laid out by Terry Farrell), you probably won't warm to these buildings – they seem to lack a sense of time and place – but at least in terms of walkability, dwell time and community space the development is undoubtedly a success.

Next, we sweep over the canal footbridge, through the rather disjointed ICC building and out into the impressive **Centenary Square**, renamed in 1989 to commemorate the centenary of Birmingham achieving city status. Now we are in front of the new **Birmingham Library** (2013), designed by Dutch architect Francine Houben. In a similar way to the Cube, the exterior's interlacing rings are intended to reflect the city's canals and tunnels. 'We see the circle as a motif of the city,' Houben explains. 'The façade recalls the industrial gasometers as well as the history of the jewellery trade here.' The best bit for us is that we can do a 'vertical walk' through the library, ably assisted by a scintillating array of escalators. At the top, we gaze out from the Skyline Viewpoint, across the city and towards the many surrounding hills.

And then we relax for a few minutes in the **City Centre Gardens** (0.8 hectares, 2 acres), hidden away behind the library; attractive, well-planted, old-fashioned gardens that seem to be little known or visited.

Entering Chamberlain Square, the first building that grabs our attention is the 'perfect and aloof' **Birmingham Town Hall** (1834) atop its tall, rusticated podium. It was the first of the monumental town halls that would come to characterise the cities of Victorian England, and also the first significant work of the nineteenth century revival of Roman architecture, a style chosen here in the context of the highly charged radicalism of 1830s Birmingham with its republican associations.

Now we reach the **Cathedral Church of St Philip** (1715) and its churchyard, a swathe of green in the middle of the city; in Alexandra Wedgwood's words, 'a most subtle example of the elusive English Baroque'. In 1884 it was enlarged in anticipation of its becoming a cathedral, which it did in 1905. At this time four stained glass windows were designed by Edward Burne-Jones, made by Morris & Company and installed in the chancel and at the west end.

We love **Hudson's Coffee House** (1900) at 122 Colmore Row, designed in the Arts and Crafts style. Pevsner describes it as 'one of the most original buildings of its date in England'. There are also several good buildings in upper Newhall Street, including the former **Bell Edison Telephone Exchange** (1896) on

'Birmingham, where they made useful things and made them well.' LEE CHILD

the corner of Edmund Street – a gorgeous terracotta building with beautifully decorated metal gates in the archway.

Next, we take a little detour down Edmund Street towards the Bridge of Sighs to reach my favourite Victorian Birmingham building of them all, the **Birmingham School of Art** (1885), the first Municipal School of Art. Its Venetian style and naturalistic decoration are much influenced by John Ruskin's *Stones of Venice*.

Morris and Burne-Jones had originally intended to join the priesthood, but in 1855, returning to Burne-Jones's house in Bennett's Hill after touring the cathedrals of Northern France, they decided instead to pursue careers in the visual arts, Burne-Jones resolving to become a painter and Morris an architect. The following day they discovered a copy of Malory's *Morte d'Arthur* in a Birmingham bookshop, which was to be one of their great inspirational works. They formed a group of fellow believers that became known as the Birmingham Set.

Arts and Crafts practitioners in Britain were critical of the government system of art education which was based on design in the abstract with little teaching of practical craft. This lack of craft training also caused concern in industrial and official circles, and in 1884 a Royal Commission recommended that art education should pay more attention to the suitability of design to the material in which it was to be executed. The first

school to make this change was the Birmingham School of Arts and Crafts, a tradition which it carries on to this day.

Once across the 'concrete collar' of the ring road, we find ourselves in the attractive and unpretentious Jewellery Quarter. **Birmingham's Assay Office** (1773) is still the busiest in the world today, hallmarking around twelve million items a year. The Jewellery Quarter has Europe's greatest concentration of businesses involved in the jewellery trade and produces around half of all the jewellery made in the UK, employing over 6,000 skilled craftsmen; each workshop typically small-scale, employing between five and fifty people. In other words, Birmingham is still doing what it has always done so well, making specialised items in workshops.

The Birmingham and Fazeley Canal, a short stretch of which we take at this point, plunges down here through floodlit archways, undercrofts and narrow tunnels. It is an atmospheric link to the past in the middle of a modern city. In its industrial heyday, this Farmer's Bridge Flight was a hectic place, kept open day and night, and lit by gas during the hours of darkness. There were said to be nearly seventy steam engines and more than 120 wharfs and works along the banks of the canal between here and Aston.

St Paul's Square, which we approach next, was created in the late 1770s; it started out as an elegant and desirable residential location, but by the end of the nineteenth century had largely been taken over

Left The engineers Matthew Boulton and James Watt had their own pews at St Paul's Church

'Key Hill Cemetery is the most interesting place in the world to a Birmingham man.' JOSEPH CHAMBERLAIN

by workshops and factories, with the fronts of some buildings being pulled down to make way for shop fronts or factory entrances. The well-proportioned **St Paul's Church** (1779) was the church of Birmingham's early manufacturers and merchants – the engineers Matthew Boulton and James Watt had their own pews here.

At the top of Vittoria Street, we admire the **Birmingham School of Jewellery** (1890). The Birmingham Jewellers and Silversmiths Association took the lead role in setting up the school, with the aim of promoting 'art and technical education' among apprentice jewellers. Take a look to see if there is an exhibition on: the students' work is often displayed.

The splendid **Chamberlain Iron Clock**, which serves as a landmark for the Jewellery Quarter, was presented to local MP Joseph Chamberlain by his constituents in 1903. The Rose Villa Tavern, just behind it, has fine 1920s tiling and stained glass. After a quick refreshment here, we stroll down through the **Warstone Lane Cemetery** (1847). A major feature is the two tiers of catacombs, whose unhealthy vapours led to the Birmingham Cemeteries Act which required that non-

interred coffins should be sealed with lead or pitch. Among several prominent Birmingham people buried here are John Baskerville, inventor of the eponymous typeface.

We trudge briefly alongside a dual carriageway and quickly escape through a pair of massive stone gateposts into the **Key Hill Cemetery**. This cemetery was set up in 1836 by a group of non-conformist businessmen concerned that free-church ministers were prevented from officiating at burial ceremonies in Church of England churches, and to meet the much-needed requirement for burial space.

We found out more about the cemetery from Margaret, a Friend of Key Hill Cemetery, one of those who had taken on the onerous, perhaps impossible, task of holding back nature; when we met her, she was in the process of unearthing some headstones that had been lost in the undergrowth. Notable burials include John Skirrow Wright, the inventor of the Postal Order; just beyond him, Alfred Bird, inventor of eggless custard; and squeezed between them, Joseph Gillott, a pen maker. Then we move on to the Chamberlain family headstones (just in front of the catacombs, on the left-hand end)

Left The splendid
Chamberlain Iron Clock
serves as a landmark for the
Jewellery Quarter

and see what an extended and established family the Chamberlains had been in Birmingham. Next, we head along the base of the catacombs and see the headstone of scales manufacturer Thomas Avery (hard to say how much it weighed) and then Joseph Tangye, who helped launch Brunel's steamship SS *Great Eastern*.

We finally drag ourselves away from these fascinating histories and exit through the equally imposing gates on the north side; turning up Key Hill Drive, and then through an enclosed passage, at the end of which we are brought back with a jolt into the Jewellery Quarter.

We traverse St Paul's Square again and re-join the canal at Livery Street; heading along it until we reach the Aston Junction, where the Digbeth Branch Canal terminates and meets the Birmingham and Fazeley Canal. The Spaghetti Junction of the nineteenth century, today it is mainly frequented by cyclists and the odd narrowboat.

Eastside City Park (2.7 hectares, 6.8 acres) is an urban park located alongside the Thinktank Birmingham Science Museum, on our way back from the canal to the city centre. Opened in 2012, it was the first new city-centre park in Birmingham created for more than 130 years. A sign hopefully that once again we understand the vital importance of green spaces within cities.

Directly to the south of the park is a space that looks ominously open, ready for 'redevelopment' as the HS2 terminus plonked alongside the new park. The good news is that the Grade I **Curzon Street station** (1838), the original terminus of both the London and Birmingham Railway and the Grand Junction Railway, hangs on doggedly to its site and will be a feature of the new station – a symbol hopefully of how much better Birmingham has become at mixing old and new.

The proposed HS2 terminal is a timely reminder as we approach the end of our walk of how vital transport communications are to the landlocked Birmingham; and that this could once again give it a massive advantage as it battles to remain 'Britain's second city.'

PIT STOPS
- **CAFÉ OPUS AT IKON**, 1 Oozells Street, B1 2HS. Light-flooded, minimal white space.
- **BUREAU BAR**,110 Colmore Row, B3 3AG. Vintage cocktail and deli bar, with roof terrace.
- **JAVA LOUNGE COFFEE HOUSE**, 124 Colmore Row, B3 3SD

QUIRKY SHOPPING
- **THE JEWELLERY QUARTER**: jewellery and art galleries.
- **GREAT WESTERN ARCADE** (B2 5HU) is an ornate relic of Brum's Victorian heyday. Now has some of the city's most unusual shops.

PLACES TO VISIT
- **IKON CONTEMPORARY ART** (B1 2HS), contemporary art venue.
- **BIRMINGHAM MUSEUM & ART GALLERY** (B3 3DH) has the best collection of pre-Raphaelite art in the country.
- **THINK TANK**, Birmingham Science Museum (B4 7XG) is a great family destination.

WHEN TO VISIT
Birmingham Pride (late May), Birmingham International Carnival (Aug 2019 – biennial), St Patrick's Day City Centre Parade (March), Frankfurt Christmas Market (Dec)

Leeds

Leeds is a city of industry and enterprise but also a very human-scaled town – this walk takes you through the old industrial areas, the retail district, the civic centre and the universities.

From being a compact market town in the valley of the River Aire in the sixteenth century, Leeds expanded and absorbed the surrounding villages as the industrial revolution swept all before it. But it didn't expand at the helter-skelter speed of a city like Manchester, and this is reflected in a built environment that sits midway between a solid regional town and a booming city.

Leeds really came of age as a great city in the second half of the nineteenth century. The new Town Hall, admired throughout the Empire and a model for numerous other civic buildings, was opened by Queen Victoria in 1854.

In the 1920s, Leeds also became one of the first cities outside London to start to plan the way it was laid out rather than letting things happen willy-nilly. The Headrow was created as an east-west link between Mabgate and the Town Hall to relieve traffic congestion, to create a 'planned' civic route and get rid of slum housing; and the Outer Ring Road was also started.

Sadly, in common with most UK cities, it suffered much damage from the motor car in the 1960s, especially through the construction of the Inner Ring

WALK DATA

- **DISTANCE:** 10.2 km (6.4 miles)
- **HEIGHT GAIN:** 66 metres
- **WALK TIME:** 2½ hours
- **START & FINISH:** Leeds station (LS1 4DY)
- **TERRAIN:** All on pavements

Road that severed the city centre from the university. But from the 1970s, things started to improve again, thanks to the leadership of John Thorp, City Architect from 1970 to 2010, widely lauded as the man who shaped modern Leeds. His philosophy was to examine and understand what already existed, looking for ways to improve or enhance it rather than sweep things away and bring in the new. He called the exercise 'urban dentistry'.

In 2017 *The Times* voted Leeds as the number one cultural place to live in Britain, and in the same year Lonely Planet ranked it in the Top 10 best places in Europe to visit.

THE WALK

The **New Station** (1869) was built on arches that span the River Aire, Neville Street and Swinegate. Over eighteen million bricks were used during their construction – and the arches underneath became known as the **Dark Arches**. They have a cavernous and eerie feeling about them that takes you back in time – you half expect to bump into a Dickens character with a lantern around the next corner.

We cross the **Hol Beck** stream, which used to take a meandering path across the flood plain but now flows along a rather uninspiring culvert. Its waters were originally believed to have spa properties, but were then instead used to power the many mills that were built around here. On the other side, **Holbeck Urban Village** is a conservation area where many nineteenth-century industrial buildings survive in an unaltered group within the original street pattern.

Tower Works (1919) used to be a factory making steel pins for carding and combing in the textile industry. The design of its three extraction towers was heavily influenced by the owner's love of Italian architecture and art. The largest and most ornate tower is based on Giotto's Campanile in Florence; the smaller after the Torre dei Lamberti in Verona; and a third plain tower represents a Tuscan tower house.

As we head up Marshall Street, so we are confronted by what appears to be an Egyptian temple. This was the office building of the **Temple Works** (1841), built in the style of the Temple of Horus at Edfu by John Marshall who, in common with many other well-to-do gentry of the era, had a fascination for Egyptology and would also have been aware that flax, the source of his wealth, originally came from Egypt. When it was completed, it was one of the largest factories in the world, with two acres of factory floor employing over 2,000 workers and utilising 7,000 steam-powered spindles.

A curious feature of the building is that sheep used to graze on the grass-covered roof with its sixty-five conical skylights. The reason to have grass on the roof was to wick the moisture from the air to help retain

WALK DATA

- **CITY POPULATION:** 751,500 (#4 in UK)
- **ORIGINS:** 5th century AD
- **CITY STATUS:** 1893
- **FAMOUS INHABITANTS:** H.H. Asquith (Prime Minister), Damien Hirst (artist), Helen Fielding (novelist), Marco Pierre White (chef), Ernie Wise (comedian)
- **NOTABLE BUILDERS:** Cuthbert Brodrick (Corn Exchange, Town Hall), Thomas Ambler (St Paul's House, St James's Hall), John Thorp (City Architect, 1970–2010).
- **SCREEN TIME:** One of the earliest films ever made, by Louis Le Prince in 1888, shows Roundhay Gardens and a Leeds Bridge street scene. *Peaky Blinders* TV series (Leeds Town Hall)
- **ICONIC CITYSCAPES:** Leeds Town Hall Clocktower (as part of tour), Sky Lounge (LS1 4BR)

the humidity in the flax mill, thus preventing the linen thread from becoming dried out and unmanageable.

Leeds Bridge (1873) is a rather fine Victorian cast-iron bridge. The east side bears the arms of the Corporation of Leeds (crowned owls and fleece). The western side has the names of civic dignitaries on a plaque. This was the original centre of Leeds and there has been a bridge here since medieval times and before that a ferry.

There has been a church on the site of **Leeds Minster** (St Peter's) since the seventh century, but the one we see today is early Victorian Gothic (1841), and at the time the largest church built in England since St Paul's. More importantly, it was the first great 'town church', intended to minister to the increasingly disillusioned working classes of the Industrial Revolution.

Penny Pocket Park (0.9 hectares, 2.2 acres) was once part of the old graveyard. It had stopped being used for burials by the 1830s as, like most urban churchyards, it was overflowing; a new cemetery was laid out in

LEEDS

Woodhouse Moor

St George's Fields

University of Leeds

Hanover Square

Leeds General Infirmary

Queen Square

The Arcades

St Paul's House, Park Square

The Corn Exchange

Penny Pocket Park

Leeds Town Hall

START

DARK ARCHES

RIVER AIRE

LEEDS & LIVERPOOL CANAL

Temple Works

N E S W

Above left Leeds is justly famous for its splendid shopping arcades

Above right The former Corn Exchange has a Pantheon-style roof

Below The east side of Leeds Bridge bears the arms of the Corporation of Leeds

'It always seems odd to come back to Leeds and to see people having wine with their meal and eating avocado pears. You want something on toast; you don't want an avocado pear. This is Leeds!' ALAN BENNETT

St George's Field, where we walk later. But when the construction of the New Station began in 1866, it became clear that the route to Selby would need to pass through the old graveyard. It was agreed that the railway would be built on a solid embankment, with the gravestones on a slope, which makes for a rather curious sight.

The Calls area, along with neighbouring Clarence Dock, served as docks on the Leeds and Liverpool Canal and the Aire and Calder Navigation throughout the Industrial Revolution and the early twentieth century. Today, many of the old warehouses have been renovated into pubs and restaurants, and if you're feeling like refreshments this is a good place to pause.

Queen's Court is an eighteenth-century house built for wealthy wool merchants; and a bit further along is **Lambert's Yard** (1600), which boasts Leeds' oldest surviving timber frame building.

Then on to one of Leeds' most fabulous and unusual buildings, the **Corn Exchange** (1863), designed by Leeds' favourite architect Cuthbert Brodrick, best known for Leeds Town Hall. He took as his model the Halle au Blé in Paris, built in the 1760s, but we can't help but be reminded of the Royal Albert Hall.

Now we really are in the commercial heart of the city, and next up is **Kirkgate Market**, the largest covered market in Europe. It first opened in 1822 as an open-air market, and between 1850 and 1875 the first covered sections were added. In 1884, it was the founding location of Marks & Spencer which opened here as a penny bazaar.

The 1904 hall is the most ornate of the halls and is situated at the front, the route we take. It has a grand Flemish-style frontage with Art Nouveau details – shop fronts below, offices above and an extravagant skyline of towers, turrets and chimneys. Behind this amazing façade is an even more striking market hall with clustered cast-iron Corinthian columns supporting a central octagon. Somehow, this old-fashioned market has survived the onset of out-of-town malls and is full of life, hosting 800 stalls and typically having more than 100,000 visitors on a Saturday.

The Arcades are one of Leeds' great joys, bustling and busy with shoppers. They were built around 1900 and designed in ebullient style by the theatre architect Frank Matcham. The exteriors are mainly of faïence from the Burmantofts Pottery, and the interiors contain several mosaics and plentiful use of marble. They were built to appeal to the affluent middle-class as a safe and clement place away from the hustle and bustle of the grimy streets. The fashion for arcades spread right across the country during this period.

St John's (1634) is the oldest church in the city, built at a turbulent time when very few churches were constructed. The glory of the church lies in its magnificent Jacobean fittings, particularly the superb carved wooden screen.

Merrion Gardens (0.3 hectares, 0.7 acres) was

Right The Leeds Civic Hall was built in the 1930s as part of a Keynesian make-work scheme

originally laid out as a memorial to Thomas Wade who, in 1530, left a will that stipulated that the money be used to benefit the people of Leeds. Often full of lunch-breakers relaxing in the sunshine, it seems his money was well spent.

Next, we walk past the Leeds Art Gallery and look ahead of us to see the **Leeds Town Hall** (1853), Cuthbert Brodrick's most famous work, and opened in great pomp and ceremony by Queen Victoria. It became a model for civic buildings across Britain and the British Empire.

Millennium Square is one of those 'prairie' squares which has been left 'intentionally blank' so that lots of events, festivals and fairs can take place there; but when there is nothing going on, it looks rather . . . empty. It was Leeds' flagship redevelopment project to mark the year 2000. Just to the south are the pocket-sized **Nelson Mandela Gardens**.

Leeds Civic Hall (1933) is the work of Vincent Harris, best known for his work on the Exeter University campus (see our Exeter walk). This was in the depths of the Great Recession and the building was used as a piece of Keynesian job creation to stimulate the economy. I love the golden owl sculptures, the emblem of Leeds. It's surprising to discover that they were in fact added only in 2000 by **John Thorp**, the much-respected City Architect, based on a pair of originals on the roof.

Before we head to the two universities, we can't resist a short 'green space' diversion to the close-by Georgian **Queen Square**, built between 1806 and 1822, each house originally having access to warehouses and workshops at the rear. Late-nineteenth-century gas lamp posts with fluted shafts complete the scene. It is an architectural oasis in this part of town, but that doesn't detract from its charm and tranquillity.

The university campuses

The impressive **Broadcasting Tower** (2009) on the Leeds Beckett campus is clad in weathering Corten steel, which intentionally makes it look as if it is rusting away (the *Angel of the North* is made of the same material). I love this building.

The University of Leeds campus is, in the words of Maurice Beresford, 'a free open-air museum of architectural and social history'. It comprises a mixture of Georgian, Gothic Revival, Art Deco, Brutalist, Postmodern and eco-buildings, making it one of the most architecturally diverse university campuses anywhere in the country.

In the heart of the campus, **Chancellor's Court** is a little green haven. Its architects likened it to the great Oxbridge quadrangles, but to my mind, it has more life, intimacy and interest. It is beautifully landscaped with trees and plants dotted around the square and two huge rock features.

As we stroll uphill past the Edward Boyle Library, we soon reach the old heart of the university, Alfred Waterhouse's wonderful **Great Hall** of 1894. Then we head left into **St George's Fields** (3.8 hectares,

'People do not realise that many of my works are done in urban places. I was brought up on the edge of Leeds, five miles from the city centre – on one side were fields and on the other, the city.' ANDY GOLDSWORTHY

9.3 acres), which served as Leeds' General Cemetery from 1835, when St John's Churchyard became full. There is an elegant Greek Revival Gatehouse and non-denominational temple. Again, another lovely tranquil spot much used by students.

Woodhouse Moor (26 hectares, 64 acres) is now a park, but it wasn't always so; it was once part of a much larger moor of the same name. High above Leeds, it has been a military rallying point, and Rampart Road (on the north-east side) is named after the ramparts which were once there. During the English Civil War, Parliamentary forces led by Thomas Fairfax massed on Woodhouse Moor before taking Leeds from the Royalists. In the nineteenth century there started to be 'encroachments' upon the moor; parts of the land were being parcelled off for development, and rumours circulated that a substantial section might be given over to the army as an encampment. A grassroots campaign in support of a public park gathered momentum and in 1857 the park was acquired by the council to improve public health in the city. It has often been referred to as 'the lungs of Leeds'. By the end of the nineteenth century, the moor was used for a wide variety of purposes, including sport,

musical concerts and political meetings. The allotments that we pass on our right, incidentally, are survivors from the Second World War, when the park was put to productive wartime use growing vegetables.

We head right up the cobbled **Kendal Lane,** which had been an ancient pre-turnpike road that climbed the hill towards Great Woodhouse Moor. Behind the brick wall on our left is **Claremont House** (1772), from whose grounds Hanover Square was subsequently created.

Continuing along Kendal Lane, we soon spot **Hanover Square** down the slope to our left. First, though, we pass the impressive **Denison Hall** (1786) which was built in just 101 days according to the blue plaque! However, it proved a difficult house to sell as, in the words of the Leeds Guide of 1806, it was 'too large for a man of moderate fortune, and too near the town to be relished by a country gentleman'. In 1823, Hanover Square was created in the extensive gardens of the house with the hall at the north side, in an attempt to bring harmony and make a buck or two. But it was never fully realised, simply because the developers underestimated the reluctance of well-to-do families to live so close to industry (they mostly preferred the leafy Headingley).

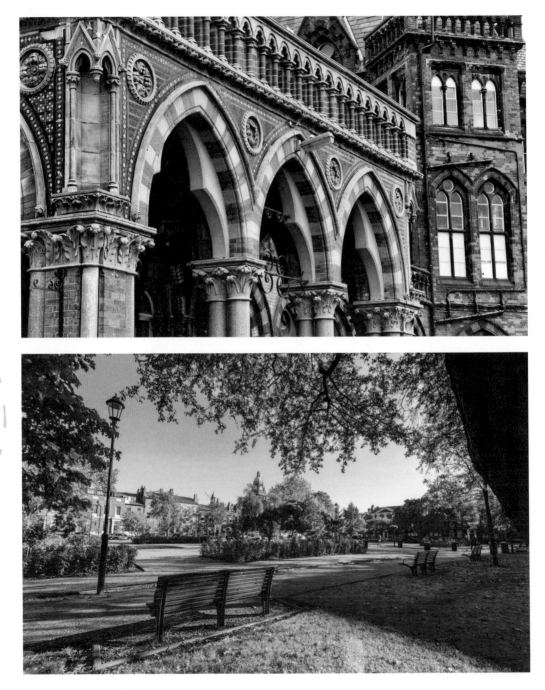

Woodhouse Square was laid out in the 1840s by John Atkinson with a similar intention, but likewise was never fully completed. The sloping central garden became a public park in 1905.

For the last leg of our walk, we cross back over the ring road to be greeted by one of the most scrumptious buildings in Leeds, the old Leeds General Infirmary (1869). And yes, if it conjures up St Pancras station in your mind there is a reason . . . it is by the same architect, George Gilbert Scott, and dates from the same period.

Park Square was laid out in 1788. It is the most attractive piece of green space in the city centre, so we pause and enjoy it. On the south side is St Paul's House (1878), built by Thomas Ambler in an ornate Hispano-Moorish style as a warehouse and cloth cutting works, complete with minarets. So much more appealing than your typical warehouse or factory today.

Bank House (1969) at the junction with King Street is an architecturally adventurous example of the Bank of England's 1960s building program, designed by BDP architects as an inverted ziggurat in grey granite. What appear to be balconies on the first floor are actually remnants of the 1960s plan to connect the whole city via a network of elevated pedestrian skywalks that (fortunately in my opinion) never materialised.

Just on our right at this point is the sumptuous Hotel Metropole (1897), designed in what Pevsner describes as 'undisciplined French Loire taste'. You'll understand what he means when you see it! Inside, giant columns and a bronze-panelled staircase evoke the extravagance of late Victorian Leeds.

City Square was laid out from 1893 in grand style to celebrate the granting of city status. The Old Post Office (1896) was built by Sir Henry Tanner and was Leeds' largest post office and also served as the city's telephone exchange. The Queens Hotel (1930s) has played host to many famous guests including Laurel and Hardy.

Going back through the station, we see perhaps the best bit of it – the stylish 1938 Art Deco North Concourse with wide concrete arch crossbeams.

PIT STOPS
- **OUT OF THE WOODS 1**, 113 Water Lane, LS11 5WD
- **COFFEE 44**, 44 The Calls, LS2 7EW
- **JUST GRAND! VINTAGE TEAROOM**, 8–9 Grand Arcade, LS1 6PG
- **TILED HALL**, Leeds Art Gallery, The Headrow, LS1 3AB
- **FETTLE CAFÉ**, 73 Great George Street, LS1 3BR

QUIRKY SHOPPING
Wander up and down **THE ARCADES**. Thornton's Arcade (LS1 6LB) is especially good with OK Comics and the Village Bookstore, through **KIRKGATE MARKET** (LS2 7HY), also the **CORN EXCHANGE** (LS1 7BR).

PLACES TO VISIT
- **THE HENRY MOORE INSTITUTE**, 74 The Headrow, LS1 3AH. One of the largest sculpture galleries in Europe.
- **LEEDS ART GALLERY**, The Headrow, LS1 3AA
- **LEEDS CITY MUSEUM**, Millennium Square, LS2 8BH for a history of Leeds.

WHEN TO VISIT
Leeds Indie Food Festival (May), Leeds Walking Festival (June), Leeds Carnival (Aug), Leeds Festival (Aug), Leeds International Film Festival (Nov)

Manchester

There is more social and cultural history per square inch of a walk in Manchester than in just about any other city – but we have to rely on the canal to provide our 'greenway'.

Manchester lies in a bowl-shaped land area bordered to the north and east by the Pennines, and to the south by the Cheshire Plain. This low-lying city is on the confluence of three rivers – the Irwell, the Medlock and the Mersey; the latter of which, via the Manchester Ship Canal, gives access to the sea. Its geographic features were highly influential in its early development as the world's first industrial city – its climate, proximity to a seaport, the availability of water power and its nearby coal reserves.

Manchester perhaps more than anywhere else is a product of the Industrial Revolution and is widely regarded as the first modern, industrial city. It is synonymous with warehouses, railway viaducts, cotton mills and canals – remnants of a past when the city principally produced and traded goods. Manchester has minimal Georgian or medieval architecture, but a vast array of nineteenth- and twentieth-century buildings.

Cotton made Manchester and, in Asa Briggs' words, it was the 'shock city of the industrial revolution' – witnessing unplanned urbanisation, a focus on money-making, extremes of wealth and squalor, an exploding population, little civic structure until the mid-nineteenth

WALK DATA

- **DISTANCE:** 8 km (5 miles)
- **HEIGHT GAIN:** 20 metres
- **WALK TIME:** 2 hours
- **START & FINISH:** Manchester Piccadilly station (M1 2PB)
- **TERRAIN:** Pavements throughout

century but at the same time formative social values. It was always perceived as a 'modern city' and full of vitality – qualities which it exhibits just as strongly today.

Manchester was also a bastion of radicalism and non-conformism. It was here in 1819 that the Peterloo Massacre occurred among a large crowd campaigning for better parliamentary representation. And it was the city where Engels met Marx in 1845 and started to write the Communist Manifesto.

Today, Manchester is rated as one of the UK's most creative cities, and this walk makes it evident why, passing by art galleries and eclectic independent shops and food outlets: buzz and creativity fill every corner.

THE WALK

We set out from **Manchester Piccadilly station** (1842) and just before the Dale Street bridge we drop down right to join the Rochdale Canal (1804) at Lock 85. The canal has great charm and intrigue as it passes right through the heart of the city, under buildings on huge concrete stilts, in a part known as the Undercroft. We feel like urban invaders stealing up unannounced on the city. But there are quite a few people who sleep here rough, so you probably don't want to be on your own or walking through in the dark. The nine locks between here and the Bridgewater Basin are known as the 'Rochdale Nine' and they follow in fairly quick succession one after the other.

Coming out of the Undercroft, we find ourselves in the Gay Village quarter. With the decline of the canal, the area became a well-known 'red light' district and also a place for gay men to meet clandestinely. The turning point to putting the area on the map was the opening of Manto in 1990, an openly gay bar with large plate glass windows that declared no-one was trying to hide anymore.

On the south side of the canal we pause a moment in **Sackville Gardens** (0.5 hectares, 1.2 acres), which has a memorial to Alan Turing, sitting on a bench. The cast bronze bench carries the motto 'Founder of Computer Science' as it might appear if encoded by an Enigma machine: 'IEKYF RQMSI ADXUO KVKZC GUBJ' (although arguably it should change every day!). The park was chosen because, according to one pundit, 'It's got the university science buildings where he worked after the war on one side, and all the gay bars on the other.'

The **Beetham Tower** (2006) is a landmark forty-seven-storey mixed-use skyscraper, described as 'the UK's only proper skyscraper outside London'. In a short space of time, it has become an iconic building, featured in the opening titles of several television programmes, including *Coronation Street*.

After Deansgate, we reach Castlefield. History books are often wont to say that the arrival of the Bridgewater Canal here in 1761, linking the Duke of Bridgewater's mines at Worsley to the centre of the city, marked the

WALK DATA

- **CITY POPULATION:** 503,000 (#2 in the UK)
- **ORIGINS:** AD 79, founded by the Romans
- **CITY STATUS:** 1853 – the first new British city for 300 years
- **FAMOUS INHABITANTS:** Norman Foster (architect), Friedrich Engels (political philosopher), Liam and Noel Gallagher (music), L.S. Lowry (artist), Emmeline Pankhurst (suffragette)
- **NOTABLE BUILDERS:** Alfred Waterhouse (Manchester Town Hall), Charles Barry (Manchester Art Gallery), Norman Foster (Hardman Square), Urban Splash (Chips Building)
- **SCREEN TIME:** *The Iron Lady* (Town Hall); *Captain America* (Northern Quarter); *Coronation Street*, *Shameless*, *Queer as Folk* (Gay Village), *The Royle Family*, *Cutting It* (Deansgate) TV series
- **ICONIC CITYSCAPES:** Hilton's Cloud 23 cocktail bar in the Beetham Tower (M3 4LQ)

start of the Industrial Revolution, halving the price of coal and making steam power commercially viable.

We follow the basin round to the gleaming white sickle-shaped **Merchant's Bridge** (1995) that spans the main canal basin opposite Barca Bar. Then we head under the railway lines and take the next right to the Roman Fort of Mamucium, established around AD 79. The fort was sited on a sandstone bluff near the confluence of the Medlock and Irwell rivers in a naturally defensible position.

Up next is the **Museum of Science and Industry**. Among many interesting exhibits, it incorporates the world's first railway station, **Manchester Liverpool Road** (1830). Apparently, the railway was so keen to attract genteel travellers that it offered flat trucks on which private coaches could be loaded, occupants, horses and all.

I like the little park we wander into next – **St John's Gardens** (0.6 hectares, 1.5 acres) – which is one of very few green spaces in the city centre. And even that's really

Above left The Museum of Science & Industry very much merits a visit

Below St Peter's Square was the scene of the 1819 Peterloo Massacre

Above right The John Rylands Library is one of Manchester's great late-Victorian buildings

more by mishap than design, as this was formerly the site of St John's Church (1769), demolished in 1931 after a long period of neglect. Today a stone cross stands in the gardens to commemorate the church and the 22,000 souls that lie buried in the graveyard. Among them is John Owens, founder of Owens' College, the forerunner to the University of Manchester.

We leave the gardens by what was the original gate to the church. Opposite we see St John Street, in which the majority of the houses are listed – it is the only Georgian part of the city that still survives – occupied now by solicitors, accountants and medics.

Walking up Byrom Street, we pass the **Cobden House** (1770s) on our left. This was originally the home of Richard Cobden, prominent entrepreneur, politician and member of the Anti-Corn Law League. It was bought by John Owens in 1851 to fund the establishment of Owens College, which was on this site until 1873 when it moved to a new home on Oxford Road, today the University of Manchester.

Now we enter one of the newest parts of the city, Spinningfields, which was re-developed in the 2000s as a business, retail and residential area. We stroll through **Hardman Square** (0.5 hectares, 1.2 acres), and soon our eyes alight upon one of Manchester's finest modern buildings, the **Manchester Civil Justice Centre** (2007), named one of the 'Best British Buildings of the twenty-first century' by *Blueprint* magazine.

The **John Rylands Library** (1900) is one of Manchester's great late-Victorian neo-Gothic buildings, full of Arts & Crafts touches. It was designed by Basil Champneys, best known for his work designing Oxbridge colleges. Inside, it looks like a cathedral filled with books, and houses one of the world's finest collections of rare books and manuscripts, including a first edition of Chaucer's *Canterbury Tales*. John Ryland was one of the wealthiest and most successful Manchester cotton barons of his era.

We head down the pedestrianised Brazennose Street, past the Lincoln statue, arriving at the grandeur of Albert Square and the iconic **Manchester Town Hall** (1877) looming large in front of us. Designed by Sir Alfred Waterhouse, it's one of the finest examples of Gothic Revival architecture in the world.

Facing St Peter's Square, the **Manchester Central Library** (1934) was designed by Vincent Harris. The form of the building, a columned portico attached to a rotunda-domed structure, is loosely derived from the Pantheon in Rome. It was the successor to the Manchester Free Library (1852), the first ever public lending and reference library in the country. Alongside the library is the grand **Midland Hotel** (1903), designed by Charles Trubshaw in a highly individualistic Edwardian Baroque style. **The Free Trade Hall** (1856) – now the Radisson Blu Hotel – in Peter Street was an important meeting place in the long campaign for the repeal of the Corn Laws.

St Peter's Square was the scene of the 1819 Peterloo Massacre when cavalry charged into a crowd of nearly

'Manchester is in the south of the north of England.
Its spirit has a contrariness in it.' JEANETTE WINTERSON

80,000 that had gathered to demand the reform of parliamentary representation. Fifteen people were killed, and many hundreds injured. On the far side of the square, alongside the tram route, is the **Manchester Art Gallery** (1824), built by Charles Barry in the Greek neoclassical style. The gallery has a good collection of Victorian art, especially the Pre-Raphaelites and Victorian decorative arts.

Piccadilly Gardens (0.8 hectares, 1.9 acres), in many people's eyes the 'heart of the city', started life, like almost all the open space in the city centre, as reclaimed land. It ended up being the largest green space in the city centre, originally looking very much like a traditional city park with flower borders and wooden benches. In 2002, however, it was reconfigured with a water feature and concrete pavilion by Japanese architect Tadao Ando. The pavilion wall is soon to be removed – people never warmed to it and it became known as 'Manchester's Berlin Wall'. While the space works admirably as a place of congregation, market stalls and as a transport hub, I miss the traditional flower borders and it lacks a sense of repose.

Incredible as it might seem walking through it today, in the 1840s the **Northern Quarter** was the centre of one of the most significant economic changes in history, with the Industrial Revolution at full throttle and Manchester taking its place as the world capital of the textile industry. It was the spot where Manchester's first cotton mill was opened by Richard Arkwright in 1783. Within seventy years, there were 108 mills in this central area.

Today the Northern Quarter is a mecca for independent, quirky shops, bars, and cafés . . . and a magnet for alternative and bohemian culture. We take a look round the Richard Goodall Gallery, one of the UK's largest commercial galleries; and further along Oak Street, we discover the Manchester Craft and Design Centre, formerly a Victorian fish and poultry market.

Emerging from the Northern Quarter and crossing the busy Great Ancoats Street, we marvel at the **Daily Express Building** (1939), designed by engineer Sir Owen Williams in Futurist Art Deco style, with horizontal lines and curved corners, clad in a combination of opaque and vitrolite glass. It was considered highly radical at the time and incorporated curtain walling, an emerging technology. Norman Foster admired it very much in his youth and now lists it as one of his top five favourite buildings in the world.

As we head down Cornell Street, so we enter the Ancoats quarter. We are puzzled by the name of a street – Anita Street – which seems out of place with the other street names here. Anita Street, it turns out, was originally called Sanitary Street, part of a project by the Sanitary Committee of the Corporation in the 1890s to improve the quality of housing and hygiene. The 'S' and 'ry' were discretely dumped in the 1960s when 'sanitary' became less a badge of honour and more a taint of municipalism.

Our source of this information was Toni, a talkative local of Italian descent; he also describes to us how, when

Above left The 'Chips' building was inspired by … chips!

Above right The canal system is a big feature of this city, seen here with the iconic Beetham Tower

Below Canal Street is the centre of the Gay Village quarter

he had been born here the area was still known as 'Little Italy' and was full of Italian families, many of whom were in the ice cream trade, which they then dominated in the city. At its peak, the population of Italians in Little Italy was over 2,000.

Ancoats at the height of the Industrial Revolution boasted the biggest concentration of mills anywhere in Europe. **Royal Mill** (1912) is one of many restored mills that collectively comprise the best and most-complete surviving examples of early large-scale factories concentrated in one area. We wave goodbye to Toni on the 'Ponte Vecchio' bridge as he calls it (notice its shape) and then head east along the southern side of the Rochdale Canal.

The New Islington Marina comes up soon on our right, including a new public eco-park called Cotton Field. It consists of a new body of water, a boardwalk, an 'urban beach' and distinctive islands. Extensive planting includes an orchard island, a grove of Scots pines, and wildflowers and reed beds. Just to the south of here is the New Islington Project, developed by Urban Splash, which includes the famous **Chips** (2009) development. Will Alsop, the architect, offered the following honest assessment of his inspiration: 'My inspiration was chips! Three fat ones to be precise, stacked on top of each other.' This building is pure fun.

On our way back along the Ashton Canal we cross the **Store Street Aqueduct** (1798), built by Benjamin Outram on a skew of forty-five degrees across Store Street, and believed to be the first major aqueduct of its kind in Great Britain and the oldest still in use today. We re-join the Rochdale Canal at Piccadilly Basin.

Dale Street Warehouse (1806), on the north side of the Rochdale Canal, is the only stone-built canal warehouse in Manchester, using Pennine Millstone Grit

stone brought down from the moors. It has four shipping arches at ground level that once opened onto the water of the canal, so goods could be loaded and deposited. We walk through the Archway of the Bridgewater Basin and turn left along Dale Street to complete our walk.

PIT STOPS

- **HEY! LITTLE CUPCAKE 2**, Hardman Street, M3 3HF, does the most delicious, quirky cupcakes.
- **NORTH TEA POWER**, 36 Tib Street, M4 1LA. is a friendly coffee shop where freelancers are often found huddled over their laptops.
- **EZRA & GIL**, 20 Hilton Street, M1 1FR. A delightful modern vibe with good light bites.

QUIRKY SHOPPING

The Northern Quarter is one of the best spots in the UK for independent, quirky shopping. Don't miss Affleck's Palace, a multi-storey bazaar for alternative clothing.

PLACES TO VISIT

- **MUSEUM OF SCIENCE & INDUSTRY**, M3 4FP. Industrial history.
- **MANCHESTER ART GALLERY** (M2 3JL) for the Pre-Raphaelites, and Victorian decorative arts.

WHEN TO VISIT

Manchester Day (mid-June); Manchester International Festival (early July–biennial); Manchester Jazz Festival (early Aug), Manchester Pride Festival (Aug Bank Holiday weekend), Manchester Food & Drink Festival (mid-Sept)

Sheffield

This is a simply unbelievable walk that propels you onwards and downwards from the ruggedness of the moors to the heart of Sheffield in six gripping miles of stream-side rambling and culvert hugging.

The city nestles in a natural amphitheatre created by seven hills and the confluence of five rivers: The Don and its four tributaries the Sheaf, Rivelin, Loxley and Porter. Consequently, much of the city is built on hillsides with views into the city centre or out towards the countryside. Nearly two-thirds of Sheffield's entire area is green space, and a third of the city lies within the Peak District National Park. There are more than eighty-eight parks and 170 woodlands and over two million trees, giving Sheffield the highest ratio of trees to people of any city in Europe.

The villages around Sheffield were established as centres of industry and commerce well before the onset of the Industrial Revolution, utilising the fast-flowing rivers and streams that brought water down from the Peak District. The valleys through which these flowed were ideally suited for man-made dams that could be used to power water mills, the remains of several of which we see on this walk. This facilitated Sheffield's move into cutlery and steel production, in which it became pre-eminent in the nineteenth century as a result of Benjamin Huntsman's invention of the crucible technique for making exceptionally high-quality steel,

WALK DATA

- **DISTANCE:** 10 km (6 ¼ Miles)
- **HEIGHT DROP:** 286 metres
- **WALK TIME:** 2½ hours
- **START:** Norfolk Arms, Ringinglow (S11 7TS); reached by taxi from station or Bus 84
- **FINISH:** Sheffield station (S1 2BP)
- **TERRAIN:** Steep initial downhill section, walking boots required

which for decades gave Sheffield the edge over other steel-producing cities.

The city centre lies where these rivers and valleys meet. The city has expanded out along and up the valleys and over the hills between, creating leafy neighbourhoods and suburbs within easy reach of the city centre. Each valley that stretches out from the city centre has its own character, from the densely industrial Don Valley in the north-east, to the green and cosmopolitan residential streets around the Ecclesall Road on the Porter Valley to the south-west.

THE WALK

The moment we get into the taxi at Sheffield station on our way up the hill, we are reminded that we are in a city famous for its music. As we pull away from the rank the light flashes on in the door – 'Red Light Indicates Doors are Secure' – the name of a favourite Arctic Monkeys song.

The incredible thing about Sheffield is how quickly we get out of it, which is even more surprising if you consider it's one of the largest cities in the UK. Within five minutes, we are on the Ringinglow Road and the ancient taxi is labouring up the hill like a shire horse, one minute huffing past Victorian mansions and the very next chugging past sheep and a traditional Peak District Farm, complete with sheepdogs and untidy yard.

We alight at the **Norfolk Arms**, an old coaching inn which is now a popular place for walkers to stay to explore the Peak District National Park on its doorstep. We, however, set out north east along the Fulwood Lane to the head of the Porter Brook Valley.

The Porter Brook derives its name from its brownish colour, similar to the colour of Porter beer, a discolouration obtained as it passes over iron-ore deposits. Like the other rivers in Sheffield, the Porter Brook is ideally suited for providing water power, as the final section falls some 135 metres in a little over 2.5 km. This enabled dams to be constructed reasonably close together, without the outflow from one mill being restricted by the next downstream dam.

By 1740 Sheffield had become the most extensive user of water-power in Britain. Ninety mills had been built, two-thirds of them for grinding. In the Porter Valley alone twenty-one mill dams served nineteen water-wheels, mostly used for grinding corn, operating forge-hammers and rolling mills, grinding knives and the various types of blades that made Sheffield famous.

Nowadays, of course, the Porter Brook's role has changed – it is used to expend energy rather than harness it. During our steady descent, we pass many people walking, jogging or cycling; for the Porter Brook is truly a city escape nowadays, offering the rural idyll of a small, fast-flowing stream in a narrow, verdant valley.

WALK DATA

- **CITY POPULATION:** 552, 698 (#10 in the UK)
- **ORIGINS:** 8th century
- **CITY STATUS:** 1893
- **FAMOUS INHABITANTS:** Malcolm Bradbury (author), Bruce Oldfield (fashion designer), Arctic Monkeys (band), Eddie Izzard (comedian), Michael Palin (comedian), David Blunkett (politician), Amy Johnson (aviator), Jessica Ennis-Hill (athlete)
- **NOTABLE BUILDERS:** J.L. Womersley (City Architect, 1953–64)
- **SCREEN TIME:** *The Full Monty*
- **ICONIC CITYSCAPE:** Ringinglow Moor

The first such spot we came to is **Forge Dam** (1765) which was used for the production of saws. Today the café is a popular spot for Sheffield families walking up the valley or bringing their toddlers to play in the playground here.

Next, we come to the **Shepherd Wheel**, which first started generating power way back in the 1550s, became derelict and was then lovingly restored by the Friends of the Porter Valley, who have reopened it as a working museum. We are left spellbound watching the water feed into the mill wheel, turning the axles, the crown wheel, the pinions, the drums, the belts, the lion shaft, all finally connecting up with the grind stones. The atmosphere today is mellow, with the soft and agreeable rumbling of the wheels; but during its working life there would have been all sorts of health and safety risks, from silicosis to exploding grindstones, making it a very hazardous place to work

We continue down to **Endcliffe Park** (15 hectares, 37 acres), a delightful space opened in 1887 to commemorate Queen Victoria's Golden Jubilee. Near the entrance is a statue of her and midway up the path towards Whiteley Woods is an obelisk also in her honour. The park was laid out by William Goldring, a nationally acclaimed park designer, who was responsible for work on nearly

START

The Norfolk Arms

Porter Brook Valley

SHEFFIELD

Forge Dam

Shepherd Wheel

Endcliffe Park

PORTER BROOK

Sheffield Botanical Gardens

Sharrow Mills

Sheffield General Cemetery

RIVER SHEAF

Cutting Edge Water Feature

FINISH

W N S E

'Sheffield is the greenest city in the EU, by a long chalk. We've got two and a half million trees, 250 parks and wetlands and a third of the city is in the Peak District.' RICHARD HAWLEY

700 different garden landscape projects across England and was in charge of the Herbaceous Department at the Royal Botanic Gardens in Kew.

From the Ecclesall Roundabout onwards into the city, the character of the Porter Brook changes substantially as it plays second fiddle to the urban landscape. It becomes confined and increasingly culverted as it heads towards the city centre. If you enjoy topographical detective work, you will relish the search for it.

The 1830s saw a wave of philanthropic activity in this part of Sheffield, as newly wealthy non-conformist industrialists sought to make their mark on the rapidly expanding city. Outside the conservative, Anglican, land-owning establishment, these non-conformists were cementing their positions in society. One of the most notable was the Wilson family of Sharrow Mills, just along the road from here. They had bought more land in the valley than they needed for their business and sold some of it to help create the Botanical Gardens and the General Cemetery.

The **Sheffield Botanical Gardens** (7.7 hectares, 19 acres) was opened in 1836. Designed by Robert Marnock, in the Gardenesque style, the site now has fifteen different garden areas featuring collections of plants from all over the world, and impressive curvilinear glass pavilions.

Leaving by the south-east (Thompson Road) exit, we can just glimpse Sharrow Mills at the end of Snuff Mill Lane (no access), which has been producing snuff since the 1730s and is still in operation today! And perhaps most amazingly, a descendant of the founding Wilson is still running it (seven generations later).

Next, we enter the **Sheffield General Cemetery** (5.5 hectares, 13.6 acres) through the somewhat dilapidated Egyptian-style gatehouse which lies directly over the Porter Brook, giving the crossing of this boundary a more mythological feel.

The cemetery was also opened in 1836, in what was then countryside. The graveyards in the city centre were overflowing and there was an urgent need to find more space. The cemetery was intended to be a place where people could be buried in a way that reflected their earthly wealth and status, and it became established as the principal burial ground in Victorian Sheffield, containing 87,000 graves.

But it was also intended as a place for the living. It has sweeping vistas and inspiring architecture – the grand

Left The Corbusier-inspired
Park Hill estate, the
Victorian station and the
Cutting Edge water feature

'The best thing about Sheffield music is that it's DIY,
it's participatory, it's democratic, anyone can put a gig on.'
PETE GREEN

scheme celebrated designer Robert Marnock's attitudes towards life. The cemetery was one of the first in Britain to promote this type of landscape, with the explicit purpose of creating an uplifting outlook, in which people could contemplate the beauty and tranquillity of their surroundings.

The cemetery is the resting place of many important figures in Sheffield history such as Mark Firth, the steel manufacturer, and Samuel Holberry, the Chartist. It was closed for burials in 1978 and is now a local nature reserve.

We get three significant final glimpses of the brook as it becomes more culverted, modified and neglected. To the citizens of Sheffield, the Porter Brook is a hidden, forgotten stream, hard to recognise from its natural beginnings in the countryside (where we were only a couple of hours earlier), seemingly devoid of life and interest, a place that attracts rubbish and pollution. It is only really noticed when it floods occasionally.

Our last sightings: as we pass down Mary Street, just to the left of the road, with a view across a deserted car park and a derelict cutlery factory. Then going under the road in Matilda Street, and finally just alongside the car park on the south side of the station, before it finally enters a culvert.

How many people have stood on Platform 5 of the station, not realising that Sheffield's Porter Brook joins with the flow of the River Sheaf in the darkness below, in a culvert called the Megatron. The station is elevated above the water on stone Victorian pillars, and the culvert

is so large and impressive that it has featured on a list of most impressive caves in the world.

And so, our journey ends at the *Cutting Edge* water feature at the station entrance – the flow of which, at least in my mind, is that of the Porter Brook which passes so close by. What a totally satisfactory completion of our journey.

PIT STOPS

- **FORGE DAM CAFÉ**, S10 4GN. For over eighty years, a well-loved spot for walkers and cyclists.
- **THELMA'S CAFÉ**, 345 Sharrow Vale Road, S11 8ZG. Original, fun and friendly.
- **ENDCLIFFE PARK CAFÉ**, The Old Pavilion, S11 7AB. A favourite with families.

QUIRKY SHOPPING

Sharrow Vale Road (S11 8ZG) is full of good independents and occasionally a Sunday market.

PLACES TO VISIT

Shepherd Wheel, open Sat & Sun only, run by volunteers, free admission. A great insight into early industrialisation.

WHEN TO VISIT

Endcliffe Park Duck Race (April), Music in the Botanical Gardens (July)

CAPITAL CITY

Whilst the London Loop (240 km, 150 miles) and the Capital Ring (120 km, 75 miles) are both multi-day adventures, the **London Inner Circle** can be done (just!) in a day. The idea behind it is to enable you to get 'under the skin' of the capital in potentially one long summer's day walk, about 25 miles in total. Or you can break it down into its four stages and dwell more along the way.

The London Loop is sometimes called the 'walkers' M25' because of its route around the edge of the capital. One layer in, the Capital Ring takes a circular path not far away from the North and South Circular Routes. The London Inner Circle, by contrast, takes a much more central route, with the City as its pivot and making use of old waterways: the canals (Regent's Canal, Lee Navigation, Grand Junction), conduits (The New River), rivers (Lea, Thames) and 'hidden' rivers (Walbrook, Fleet, Tyburn, Westbourne) of the capital. Around two-thirds of the route is close to water – although sometimes you wouldn't know it, as it's a few metres below ground!

The route we have designed was driven by a determination to take you through as much green space as possible – be it parks, squares, churchyards, waterways, dockyards, terraces or even a sky garden. Thrown in too are the next best things to quiet, green spaces – medieval passages, alleyways and mews.

One of my favourite recent initiatives is the campaign to make London the world's first National Park City: 'a city where people and nature are better connected; a city that is rich with wildlife and every child benefits from exploring outdoors'. London has a world-beating 3,000 parks, 13,000 species of wildlife and 47 per cent of its surface area is green spaces; and in the last generation things have got so much better with major regeneration projects and environmental improvements.

Olympic
Stadium

The Gherkin

Tower
Bridge

e Shard

I. King's Cross to Olympic Park

It's hard to imagine a walk anywhere that more epitomises the transformation of English cities, passing as it does through two massive and successful urban regeneration zones, King's Cross and the Olympic Park.

A key strand of this walk is its interplay with so many of the historic supply routes into the city from the north as resources were moved first by river, packhorse and drovers and then by canal, rail and road.

Agricultural produce has been shipped in along the River Lea since the twelfth century. And from the sixteenth century, cattle and sheep were being driven along the drovers' route through London Fields down to Smithfield Market. In the early nineteenth century, the Regent's Canal was dug on an east-west axis to give access to the city via the Thames and onwards to the Grand Union. Finally, the railway arrived into King's Cross, taking much of the business of the other modes of transport; until, in turn, its freight business was eroded by road hauliers, whom we hear all too easily as we pass under the A12 East Cross route. Oh, and the New River Conduit which has channelled fresh water into the city via Islington since the early seventeenth century. Many of these supply routes, as they have become superseded, have been repurposed as leisure and cultural amenities.

Another key strand of this walk is the writers who have used this area as the backdrop for their bipedal wanderings. First, George Orwell in the 1930s, who

WALK DATA

- **DISTANCE:** 10.5 km (6.5 miles); add 1.5 km (1 mile) for the Hoxton loop
- **HEIGHT GAIN:** 25 metres
- **WALK TIME:** 3 hours; or 3½ hours with Hoxton loop
- **START:** King's Cross station (N1 9AL)
- **END OF THIS STAGE:** Monier Road Bridge (E3 2ND)
- **TRANSPORT IF STOPPING HERE:** Stratford International station (E15 2LZ)
- **TERRAIN:** All pavement or canal path

wrote in *Down and Out in Paris and London* about his experiences of staying overnight in the casual ward of a workhouse in the East End, close to where we walk. Then, by Iain Sinclair, a London Fields resident, who writes so vividly about walking as a way of experiencing and understanding a city in its unadorned and unrehearsed state. And by Will Self, who walked along the River Lea to Epping Forest from his home. 'You don't know London,' he wrote, 'until you've physically walked around it and out of it.' Agree with that.

THE WALK

Coming out of the gloriously refurbished and enhanced King's Cross station, we enter that highly unusual thing, a brand-new postcode – N1C – coined for this major area of regeneration around King's Cross, comprising a mix of offices, houses and leisure. For an urban rambler, one of the best bits about the scheme is the sheer number of new urban green spaces that have been created, covering 40 per cent of the total area.

Designed by Edward Gruning, the **German Gymnasium** (1865), between King's Cross and St Pancras stations, was the first purpose-built gymnasium in England. The National Olympian Association held the indoor events of the first Olympic Games here in 1866. These games continued annually at the German Gymnasium until the White City Games in 1908. Long forgotten sports were practised here, including Indian club swinging and broadsword practice.

We admire **One Pancras Square** (2014) in front of us, designed by David Chipperfield. It is wrapped in columns faced in a sleeve of moulded cast iron in a basket weave pattern, intended to symbolise the industrial heritage of both the railways and the gas holders. I'm getting to like this building.

With lawned areas and seating beneath mature trees, **Pancras Square** is both a green route from the stations to the canal and a place to pause and relax. Water cascades through the space in a series of stepped terraces flowing towards the view of the St Pancras Clock Tower. Someone took the trouble to line up the view in Capability Brown style, and it really works.

The Goods Yard complex (1852) comprises the Granary Building, the Train Assembly Shed, and the Transit Sheds, which have been well converted by Thomas Heatherwick into retail space. The Granary Building was mainly used to store Lincolnshire wheat for London's bakers. Today, it is a creative warehouse, home to Central Saint Martin's Art College. In front is Granary Square, where barges used to unload their goods. Its aquatic history has been worked into the new design, which is animated with over 1,000

WALK DATA

- **FAMOUS ISLINGTON INHABITANTS:** Douglas Adams (writer), Sir Walter Raleigh (explorer), George Orwell (writer), Tony Blair (Prime Minister)
- **FAMOUS HACKNEY INHABITANTS:** Alfred Hitchcock (film director), Michael Caine (actor), Iain Sinclair (writer), the Kray twins (gangsters), Dick Turpin (highwayman)
- **SCREEN TIME: ISLINGTON:** *The Other Man* and *Fever Pitch* (Camden Passage), *Just Ask for Diamond* (The Screen on the Green) **HACKNEY:** *Luther* (TV series), *Eastern Promises* and *Odd Man Out* (Broadway Market), *Buster* (Regent's Canal), *Pride* (Victoria Park)
- **ICONIC CITYSCAPES:** East side of Victoria Park; high ground in Olympic Park

choreographed fountains.

In 1812, the Regent's Canal Company was formed to cut a new canal from the Grand Junction Canal's Paddington Arm to Limehouse, where a dock was built at the junction with the Thames. The architect John Nash oversaw its construction, describing the result as 'barges moving through an urban landscape'.

We pass **Battlebridge Basin** on the other bank, which used to be a major unloading point for cargo. In 1856, the Swiss-born Carlo Gatti had started importing ice into London and built himself a large storage unit here, now home to the London Canal Museum. Huge stacks of ice were cut from Norwegian fjords and shipped to the Limehouse Canal Basin and thence on barges to here, from where it was distributed to hotels and bars.

The Islington Tunnel comes into view, at which point we take the overland route through the heart of Islington, as the barge horses would have had to do. The barges consequently had to be 'legged' through the tunnel, men lying on their backs and propelling the barge forwards with their feet on the tunnel roof. In 1826 the tunnel was upgraded with a steam tug

Above left Duncan Terrace Gardens used to be the route of the New River Conduit

Above right Battlebridge Basin was a major unloading point for cargo

Below Head for Hackney City Farm if you have kids in tow

'Hackney gets a bit of a bad rap, but it's the only place I've ever lived that felt like a community. I know my neighbours.' SHARON HORGAN

attached to a continuous chain on the canal bed which would heave barges through. That saved a lot of legwork.

Our route runs directly above the tunnel initially, going through **Culpeper Community Garden** (0.5 hectares, 1.2 acres), a green space that serves both as a city park and as an environmental community project. It is a locally-run project where people from all walks of life come together to appreciate and enhance their environment. The garden contains sixty-five plots for local people without gardens, as well as communal areas and a playground. Created in 1982 from a derelict bomb site, it is one of the oldest community gardens in London and is a fabulous example of just what regeneration is possible with impassioned residents.

Islington Green is not an old village green like others in London, but rather a surviving patch of common land that was carved out of old manorial wasteland, where local farmers and tenants had free grazing rights. The original land was far more extensive but was largely built over in the nineteenth century. At the southern end of the green is a statue of Sir Hugh Myddelton, designer of the New River that supplied so much of London's water from the seventeenth century onwards

– it still supplies a tenth of the city's drinking water. The route of the New River ran along **Duncan Terrace Gardens**, which we walk through next, having strolled down Camden Passage, famous for its antiques.

We re-join the canal at Duncan Street, sticking to the north side and heading east once again, heading past the Kingsland Basin and eventually reaching Broadway Market.

Hoxton loop

We leave the canal at New North Road Bridge and head south-east through Shoreditch Park. This route takes us past Hoxton Market, the Hoxton Trust Community Garden, Hoxton Street (full of indie shops) and then to the exquisite **Geffrye Museum** (1714), set in the former almshouses of the Ironmongers' Company. We explore the museum's walled herb garden and period gardens which show how domestic gardens have changed over the past four centuries. Then we take a look round **St Mary's Secret Garden** (a community project) and **Haggerston Park** (6 hectares, 15 acres). At the south end is the **Hackney City Farm**, which was set up to bring a farm experience to urban families.

Above The drinking fountain was erected by Baroness Angela Burdett-Coutts

Below Broadway Market is open every Saturday, with shops, bars and restaurants open through the week

Back on the main route

Broadway Market is a bustling shopping street full of quirky independent shops and inviting cafés. It has been home to market traders since the 1890s and still has a thriving market on a Saturday with a range of deli food products, arts and crafts and fashion.

London Fields (12.7 hectares, 31.3 acres) was first recorded in 1540, when it was common ground used by drovers to pasture their livestock before their final stop at Slaughter Street in Brick Lane or East Smithfield. Today it is home to a wildflower meadow and a woodland section with rustic furniture made out of fallen branches. A great place to escape on a hot day.

It's now a short run along the canal to **Victoria Park** (86 hectares, 213 acres), London's first public park and today a beautifully managed space, one of my favourite London parks. It was opened in 1845 after a local MP presented Queen Victoria with a petition of 30,000 signatures, campaigning for a park to allow the working classes to escape from the grime of city life and experience some fresh air and green spaces.

Walking through the park today is an absolute pleasure. It is beautifully maintained and there is so much to do and look at. The lakes are a fantastic feature, and there are several interesting structures: the ornate Bonner gates on the west side, the Dogs of Alcibiades guarding them, the bandstand and the drinking fountain erected by Baroness Angela Burdett-Coutts in 1862 to bring fresh water to the local populace. And on the east side of the park, there

are two pedestrian shelters, originally located on the old London Bridge which was demolished and replaced in 1831. They look very out of place but are delightfully quirky. And there's the Model Boating Lake, home to the oldest model boat club in the world, the Victoria Model Steam Boat Club founded in 1904 and still holding regular Sunday regattas.

As we approach the eastern end of the park, so we get our first glimpse of the Olympic Stadium, looking like a flying saucer landed in the middle of the urban landscape. It takes our breath away when we first see it, instantly bringing back memories of that great Olympic summer of 2012. There are also impressive views back to central London from here.

We cross over the footbridge onto **Fish Island**, once an industrial enclave but now something of an artistic hot spot – it has around 600 studios, one of the highest densities of fine artists, designers and artisans in Europe. It is bounded by water on two sides, but that really doesn't feel sufficient for it to be called an island. In fact, the real reason is in the street names – five are named after freshwater fish – Smeed Road, Dace Road, Monier Road, Bream Road and Roach Road – whilst the other three are full of water imagery: Beachy Road (self-explanatory), Wyke Road (an old term for a safe landing place) and Stour Road (an East Anglian river). These names were conjured up by the Gas Light and Coke Company back in 1865 when they bought up the land to develop it – no doubt one of their employees was a keen fisherman. So much more inventive than some of the

Above left The Copper Box, known as 'the box that rocks' during the 2012 Olympics

Above right The Geffrye Museum is under refurbishment until 2020 but the garden remains open

Below The Velodrome, 'like a Pringle crisp on a bed of spinach'

modern street names that dullen British suburbs today, the sprinklings of herbs and spices and the like.

Opposite Monier Road is the Monier Road Bridge that spans the River Lee Navigation Channel into the Olympic Park; and to its left, there is a nineteenth century chimney, the letters on it referring to the MK Carlton Shoe Company that used to have their factory here. If you are finishing at this stage, The Timber Lodge Café is a good end point – go left along the Lee Navigation once over this bridge. If you are continuing on to Stage II, then turn right once over the bridge heading towards The Old Ford Locks.

Route to Timber Lodge Café

Throughout the centuries there has been conflicting pressure on the resources of the River Lea: as a major source of fresh water for Londoners to drink, via the New River extraction; as a power source for mill owners; and as a navigation channel for the barges bringing in materials and produce from the countryside. Navigation was markedly improved in the eighteenth century when the Lee Navigation Channel and the Limehouse Cut were dug, enabling barges to avoid the tight bends in the river.

We come off the Lee Navigation at the **Copper Box Arena**, a world-class sports venue that became known during the London 2012 Games as the 'box that rocks'; it works visually in its own modernist way, with the copper coating ageing beautifully.

The **Queen Elizabeth Olympic Park** (227 hectares, 560 acres) is a delightful space. One or two design critics have sniffed at it but to me it has a modern quality not present in other English parks, which typically have a very Victorian feel about them (nothing wrong with that). This park feels modern, open, forward-looking, Scandinavian even – and above all it has oodles of space!

Soon we are admiring the **Velodrome**, another stunning building which enhances the overall look and feel of the park, its concave form resting lightly on its landscaping, 'like a Pringle crisp on a bed of spinach' as someone so perceptively observed. The Timber Lodge Café beckons.

PIT STOPS

- **TOWPATH CAFÉ**, 42 De Beauvoir Crescent, N1 5SB. Highly recommended for its ambience, quirkiness and interesting food.
- **CAFÉ VILLA D'AVERSA**, 15 Broadway Market, E8 4PH. We loved this café; bustling with convivial conversations.
- **COUNTER CAFÉ**, 7 Roach Road, E3 2PA. A great vibe and an unbeatable view of the Olympic Stadium.
- **UNITY KITCHEN TIMBER LODGE CAFÉ**, 1 Honour Lea Avenue, Queen Elizabeth Olympic Park, E20 1DY.

QUIRKY SHOPPING

- **CAMDEN PASSAGE** (N1 8EA); not as many antiques as there used to be, but lots of boutique shops and interesting finds.
- **BROADWAY MARKET** (E8 4QJ) is every Saturday; the area is full of quirky shops and services.

PLACES TO VISIT

- **LONDON CANAL MUSEUM** (N1 9RT)
- **QUEEN ELIZABETH OLYMPIC PARK**, (E20 2ST), one of the largest urban parks created in Western Europe for more than 150 years.

WHEN TO VISIT

Victoria Park Model Steam Boat Festival (first Sunday in July)

II. Olympic Park to Tower Hill

This second stage of the walk takes us through the heart of the old London Docks to the City, both keys to London's wealth.

The River Lea has been a vital artery for Londoners for the last two millennia, provisioning the city with fresh water and having the mantle of 'service shaft' to the city forced upon it, looking after its sewage, solid waste, electricity & gas, and general provisioning needs.

It is very much 'boundary' territory, a no man's land between boroughs (it's the dividing line between Tower Hamlets and Newham), the 'ugly sister' of the Thames that is seldom seen; relegated to a purely supporting role but, with the massive impetus of the Olympic regeneration, now re-discovered as a natural green space with unlimited potential as a place to live and flourish.

Almost the whole of our walk is alongside water – part natural, part created, all used to provision London and to help make Britain the greatest trading nation on earth in the nineteenth century.

And, after several stutters and delays, that industrial heritage is being transformed in front of our eyes as a haven of waterfront apartments, green spaces and leisure activities; starting in the early 1980s closest to the city at St Katharine Docks, then the Limehouse Basin, then the London Docks, moving steadily outwards with a major shot in the arm from the Olympic regeneration. As we walk south from the Olympic Park near the start of the walk, we feel at times as if we are in the midst of a new city emerging from the rubble of a wasteland. More than almost any other urban ramble, this makes us realise the huge potential to redevelop brown field sites.

And as our walk concludes, so our vista of central London suddenly opens up, with glorious views of Tower Bridge and beyond from the Riverside Memorial Gardens, giving us a jolt of energy and excitement as we gaze upon one of the greatest cities in the world.

WALK DATA

- **DISTANCE:** 9.3 km (5.8 miles); add 1.5km (0.9 miles) for Abbey Mills loop
- **HEIGHT GAIN:** 10 metres
- **WALK TIME:** 2¾ hours (add 20 mins for loop)
- **START:** Monier Road Bridge (E3 2ND)
- **END OF THIS STAGE:** Tower of London (EC3N 4AB)
- **TRANSPORT IF STOPPING HERE:** Tower Hill Tube station (EC3N 4DJ)
- **TERRAIN:** Canal side path and pavements throughout

THE WALK

The Olympic Stadium is on our left as we set out, a happy reminder of the halcyon summer of 2012 and now West Ham Football Club's home. We soon reach the Old Ford Lock, which marks the end of the Hackney Cut, a channel built in the eighteenth century to cut off a large loop in the river to ease navigation.

Stay on the river to head straight to Three Mills. If you have the time though, take the Abbey Mills loop, turning left up onto the embankment to join the Greenway.

Abbey Mills loop

We speculate as we climb onto the embankment that this must have been some Anglo-Saxon defensive wall, like Offa's Dyke, protecting the good folk of London from the wild men of Essex; but the truth turns out to be more prosaic. Its acronym is NOSE, standing for the Northern Outfall Sewage Embankment (1858), a key component of Victorian engineer Sir Joseph William Bazalgette's famous London sewers. It runs from Wick Lane in Hackney to Beckton sewage treatment works south of Barking by the River Thames. Below our feet are four 9-inch pipes containing the biggest sewage flow in Britain. Just thought you should know.

Shortly before the View Tube Café, which offers excellent views of the Olympic Park, we clamber down off the Greenway along Marshgate Lane, left after the bridge over the Bow Back Rivers and then re-join the Greenway heading south-east.

Now, what's this coming up on our right? It looks like a town hall that has lost its town, a piece of Venetian Gothic splendour which has popped up out of nowhere. It turns out to be the splendidly over-the-top **Abbey Mills Pumping Station** (1868), a part of Bazalgette's grand scheme, aptly described as a 'cathedral of sewage'. Two Moorish-styled chimneys – unused since steam power had been replaced by electric motors in 1933 – were demolished in 1941, as it was feared that a bomb strike from German bombs might topple them onto the pumping station. Next to it, we

WALK DATA

- **FAMOUS LIMEHOUSE INHABITANTS:** Christopher Huffam (Charles Dickens' godfather), Sir Ian McKellen (actor), Matthew Parris (journalist), Steven Berkoff (actor), Captain James Cook (seafarer)
- **NOTABLE BUILDERS:** The London Docklands Development Corporation (LDDC), Thomas Telford (St Katharine Docks)
- **SCREEN TIME:** *Big Breakfast* and *Breaking and Entering* (Old Ford Lock); *The Sweeney* (old London Docks); *The Long Good Friday* (St Katharine Docks); *An American Werewolf in London*, *The World Is Not Enough*, *Harry Potter and the Order of the Phoenix*, *Sherlock Holmes* (Tower Bridge)
- **ICONIC CITYSCAPES:** River Thames entrance to Limehouse Basin, Hermitage Riverside Memorial Garden

spot its much more functional replacement. We then follow a path alongside the Channelsea River to reach Three Mills Green.

End of Abbey Mills loop

The **Three Mills** are former working tidal mills. There have been mills here since the twelfth century and they supplied flour to city bakers for several hundred years. From the seventeenth century onwards, output switched to grain for gin. The site had a completely new lease of life in the 1980s as a recording studio and has become one of London's most important film and TV studios.

Navigating from the River Lea to the River Thames using nature's intended route necessitates traversing Bow Creek, a winding tidal waterway not best suited to inland vessels. Consequently, the River Lea Act 1766 authorised the construction of the Limehouse Cut, a straight section linking the River Lea at Bromley-by-Bow to the Thames at Limehouse, saving considerable time and trouble. It's London's oldest canal.

Heading along it, we spot Spratt's Works on the

left bank. A century ago this was the largest dog food factory in the world. James Spratt set up his business in 1860 and soon his PR outfit declared the business to be 'a howling success'. Barges would deliver fish heads for processing into pet food. After the business closed in 1969 (gone to the dogs?), the warehouses were left derelict for some years until they were redeveloped in the late 1980s as residential apartments.

Further up on our right we spot a massive cathedral-like building, standing back about 200 metres from the canal. A real mishmash of architectural styles (Art Deco, Perpendicular Gothic, neo-Georgian, Art Nouveau) but nonetheless impactful and imposing, **The Mission** (1924) was built as a hostel for sailors who'd arrived in the nearby Limehouse Basin and needed a bed.

St Anne's Limehouse (1730) is a classic church designed by Nicholas Hawksmoor, one of several Queen Anne churches built to serve the needs of the rapidly expanding population of the day. Queen Anne decreed that as the new church was close to the river it would be a convenient place for sea captains to register vital events taking place at sea. Therefore, she gave the church the right to display the Royal Navy's flag, the White Ensign.

Ropemakers' Fields (1.2 hectares, 2.9 acres) was formerly the site of rope making in Limehouse, where rope for marine anchors, rigging and mining was made for many centuries. Samuel Pepys refers to a visit to the rope-yard in 1664. Limehouse became famous for the quality of rope it produced for nautical use.

The Limehouse Basin (1820) was used by seagoing vessels and lighters to offload cargoes to canal barges, for onward transport along the canal. By the mid-nineteenth century, the dock and canal were a huge commercial success. To the east of the canal entrance, behind a viaduct arch, is the **Accumulator Tower** (1852), built to provide hydraulic power for cranes and winches in the basin. It was the first of its kind in the country.

Charles Dickens' godfather Christopher Huffam lived and ran his sail making and chandlery business from a substantial house in Newell Street, just on the south side of the basin. Huffam adored his godson, declaring the boy a prodigy, tipping him half a crown on his birthday and encouraging him to dance and perform comic songs upon the kitchen table – and also, it is said, upon the bar at The Grapes. In the company of his godfather, Dickens first explored Shadwell and Limehouse, engendering a lasting fascination with these teeming waterside regions that he returned to throughout his writing life.

As we head west along the Thames Path, we pass through the **King Edward Memorial Park** (3.3. hectares, 8.2 acres). It was opened in 1922 by George V and Queen Mary with the following dedication: 'In grateful memory of King Edward VII. This park is dedicated to the use and enjoyment of the people of

'The English Channel narrowed to a ditch, as poets and painters travelled in both directions', IAIN SINCLAIR

East London for ever.' Still working as intended nearly a century later.

Shadwell Basin is the only significant body of water surviving today from the London Docks, which extended west from here but were in-filled in the 1970s as a prelude to redevelopment. It is now a maritime square of 2.8 hectares used for recreational purposes – and surrounded on three sides by a (dull) Postmodernist waterside housing development.

The London Docks occupied a total area of about 12 hectares (30 acres), consisting of Western and Eastern docks linked by the short Tobacco Dock. The Western Dock was connected to the Thames by Hermitage Basin to the south-west and Wapping Basin to the south. The Eastern Dock connected to the Thames via the Shadwell Basin to the east. The docks specialised in high-value luxury commodities such as ivory, spices, coffee and cocoa as well as wine and wool, for which elegant warehouses and wine cellars were constructed. One drawback was that the system was never connected to the railway network.

As early as the start of the twentieth century the docks were becoming outdated, as steam power meant ships were built too large to fit into them. Cargoes were unloaded downriver and then ferried by barge to warehouses in Wapping. This system was uneconomic and inefficient and one of the main reasons that the docks in Wapping were the first to close in the late 1960s. After more than a decade of inaction, the area

was finally redeveloped in the early 1980s and now comprises over 1,000 private properties.

Tobacco Dock (1811) was originally a store for imported tobacco. At its north entrance is a bronze sculpture of a boy standing in front of a tiger. In the late 1800s, wild animal trader Charles Jamrach owned the world's largest exotic pet store, which was nearby. The statue commemorates an incident where a Bengal tiger escaped into the street and carried off a small boy, who had approached and tried to pet the animal having never seen such a big cat before. The boy escaped unhurt after Jamrach gave chase and prised open the animal's jaw with his bare hands.

The Ornamental Canal is a pleasant route to take, more interesting in my view than the Thames Path, which does not run along the waterfront at this point. The canal was created from the 'edge' of the huge Western Dock and is, in contrast to the Limehouse Cut, probably London's newest canal, although I suppose purists would argue that it's not a canal at all. The wall on its south side is the original dock side and is full of interesting regalia – metal hooks, rings, depth marks and metal ladders recessed into the stonework.

The Hermitage entrance used to be the westernmost entrance to the London Docks but was too small to admit large modern ships and was closed in 1909. The **Hermitage Riverside Memorial Gardens** (0.4 hectares, 1 acre) has a monument to those killed during the Blitz. There is also an interesting dove sculpture by Wendy

Taylor, which overlooks the park. The view from here is simply stunning.

St Katharine Docks (1828) was designed by engineer Thomas Telford and was his only major project in London. Most of the original warehouses around the western basin were demolished and replaced by modern commercial buildings in the early 1970s. The development has often been cited as a model example of successful urban redevelopment, but the architecture doesn't set the heart beating.

In the second half of the nineteenth century, increased commercial development in the East End of London led to a requirement for a new river crossing downstream of London Bridge. A traditional fixed bridge at street level could not be built because it would cut off access by sailing ships to the port facilities in the Pool of London, between London Bridge and the Tower of London, so a bascule bridge was the solution. Tower Bridge opened in 1894 and has been loved by all ever since. The bascules are still raised around 1,000 times a year. They are only raised to an angle sufficient for the vessel to safely pass under the bridge, except in the case of a vessel with the Monarch on board, in which case they are raised fully no matter the size of the vessel.

Our final point is the **Tower of London** (from 1066), steeped in history but almost always heaving with tourists too; so, you may just want to skirt by along the embankment, enjoying the architecture. The White Tower, which gives the entire castle its name, was built by William the Conqueror in 1078 and was a resented symbol of oppression, inflicted upon London by the new ruling elite. The castle was used as a prison from 1100 until 1952 (the Kray twins were among the last prisoners here), although that was not its primary purpose. A grand palace early in its history, it served as a royal residence. There were several phases of expansion, mainly under Richard the Lionheart, Henry III, and Edward I in the twelfth and thirteenth centuries. The general layout established by the late thirteenth century remains despite later activity on the site.

And this is where the second leg of our walk finishes. If you are stopping here, walk up to Tower Hill tube; if you are continuing on to Stage III, then stay on the Thames Path.

PIT STOPS

- **THE VIEW TUBE**, The Greenway, E15 2PJ. Quirky, great view over Olympic Park.
- **PROSPECT OF WHITBY**, 57 Wapping Wall, E1W 3SH. Henry VIII used to drink and eat here, great balcony overlooking the Thames.
- **WHITE MULBERRIES**, St Katharine Docks, E1W 1AT. An independent café, great cakes.

QUIRKY SHOPPING

St Katharine Docks

PLACES TO VISIT

- **TOWER OF LONDON**, if you absolutely, positively need to see the Crown Jewels.
- **TOWER BRIDGE** – explore its structure, enjoy spectacular views and experience the glass floor, exhibitions and magnificent Victorian Engine Rooms.

WHEN TO VISIT

Limehouse Festival (July), Shadwell Basin Paddle-Fest (Sept), St Katharine Docks Classic Boat Festival (Sept)

III. Tower Hill to Lancaster Gate

This walk takes us past London's major seats of power
- the city, the church, the government and the monarchy,
with the river linking them all together.

As we make our way from east to west, so we go through four major seats of power. First, the City of London, centre of London's mercantile activity since Roman times and still the beating heart of our finance industry, with a medieval street pattern that has persisted despite the Great Fire and the massive rise skywards in the last generation. Second, past two of the country's most iconic churches, St Paul's Cathedral and Westminster Abbey, bastions of our religious heritage and scene of many of the coronations, weddings and famous funerals in our history. Third, on to the seats of government power, past the former Greater London Council building to the Houses of Parliament and Whitehall. And then, finally, into the Royal Parks and the orbit of the monarchy, passing three palaces – Buckingham Palace, St James's Palace and Kensington Palace.

Geographically, our whole walk is traversing the slope that steadily comes down to the Thames from the north, crossing four 'hidden' tributaries of the Thames that have their sources in Islington or the heights of Hampstead.

Our first river is the River Walbrook, passing by the

WALK DATA

- **DISTANCE:** 9.6 km (6 miles)
- **HEIGHT GAIN:** 19 metres
- **WALK TIME:** 2½ hours
- **START:** Tower of London (EC3N 4AB)
- **END OF THIS STAGE:** Lancaster Gate Tube station (W2 2UE)
- **TERRAIN:** All on pavements

Bank of England at 11 metres of elevation; next is the River Fleet, at an elevation of 7 metres just to the west of St Paul's, which Wren modified into a canal from here to the Thames; then down to sea level as we cross the Thames; then back up to Green Park and the River Tyburn at 12 metres; and finally climbing to the River Westbourne in Ladbroke Grove at 19 metres. We will find evidence of all four rivers on our walk.

You could go on this walk a dozen times and there would still be more to discover, it is so rich in history and interest.

THE WALK

We are almost immediately able to break free from the crowd as we head down Lower Thames Street and around the front of The Customs House (1813–17) and the old Billingsgate (1875).

We peep inside **St Magnus the Martyr Church**, the first of many Wren churches on our route. After the Great Fire of London in 1666, Christopher Wren was instructed to design and rebuild fifty-one churches in the city. He was later knighted and would become the architect who, more than any other, left his mark on the city.

Nearly half of these churches still survive today, thirteen in their original form, and eleven substantially altered or rebuilt. Eight were lost to the Blitz, nine were demolished to make way for other buildings or street widening and ten were demolished as a result of the Union of Benefices Act (1860) that reduced the number of churches in line with the sharp decline in the City of London population during that period.

The **Monument** (1677) to the Great Fire of London stands close to where the fire started in Pudding Lane. We look up and see a flaming gilded urn, symbolising the fire itself. Climb the steps inside for panoramic views of London.

The **Sky Garden** at the top of the 'Walkie Talkie' (20 Fenchurch Street) claims to be London's highest public park, but since opening, there have been debates about whether it can be described as a 'park', and whether it is truly 'public' given you need to book ahead. Personally I love it, yet another addition to the tourist possibilities that the capital offers. And because the building sits somewhat on its own, views are spectacular in pretty much all directions.

Leadenhall Market (1881) is an indulgent delight, with its ornate roof structure and cobbles. Originally a meat, game and poultry market, it stands on what was the centre of Roman London.

And now we take the advice of none other than Dr Johnson, who in 1763 declared that 'if you wish to have a just notion of the magnitude of this city, you

WALK DATA

- **NOTABLE BUILDERS:** Sir Christopher Wren (St Paul's Cathedral), Sir Horace Jones (Tower Bridge, Leadenhall Market), the Gilbert Scotts: George – Foreign & Commonwealth Office, Albert Memorial; Giles – Bankside Power Station, Waterloo Bridge, County Hall.
- **SCREEN TIME:** *Harry Potter and the Philosopher's Stone* (Leadenhall Market), *101 Dalmatians* (St James's Park), *The Ipcress File* and *Johnny English* (Hyde Park)
- **ICONIC CITYSCAPES:** Monument, Sky Garden, New Change Place, Tate Modern

must not be satisfied with seeing its great streets and squares, but must survey its innumerable little lanes and courts.' For the next ten minutes or so we do just that, finding ourselves happily in that state of nearly-being-lost-but-not-quite, exploring myriad alleys, courtyards and passages between here and the Bank of England.

The **George and Vulture Tavern**, which has its entrance in Castle Court, boasts a history dating back to the twelfth century. Chaucer is said to have frequented it and Dick Whittington used to call in when he got bored with council meetings. Dickens referred to it in *The Pickwick Papers* when Mr Pickwick and Sam Weller dined there; fittingly it is now the headquarters of the City Pickwick Club. Originally, the tavern was merely named the George but when the Great Fire swept through these alleys it devoured everything in its path and left the George as a shell of charred embers. A 'fire refugee' wine merchant from George Yard, with his pet vulture, negotiated with the landlord for part-use of the George, and at some point, was given equal billing in the name.

The origins of the Stock Exchange can be traced back to the coffee houses of **Change Alley** which we explore next. The coffee house formed the seventeenth-century hub of daily life (and there we were, thinking they didn't really exist until Starbucks); they were where the news was gathered and distributed; and

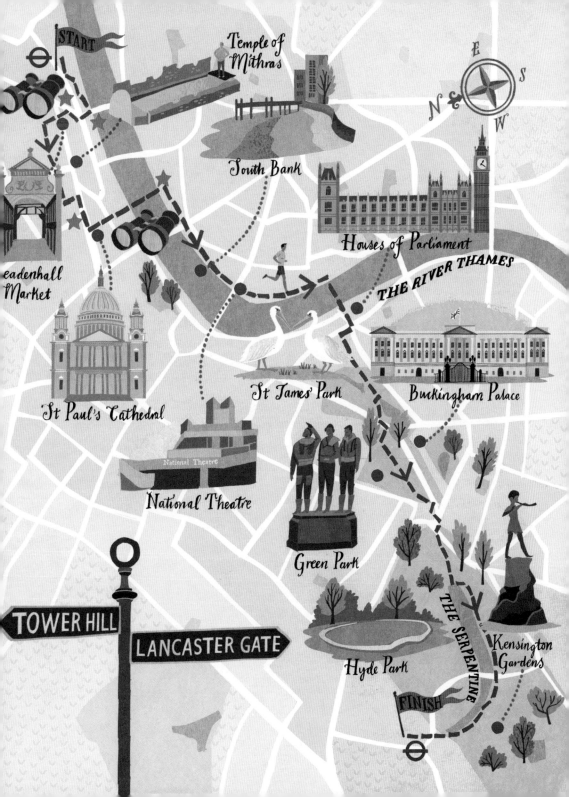

Above left The Monument to the Great Fire stands close to where the fire started in Pudding Lane

Above right Rooms at Ye Olde Watling were used as an office during the building of St Paul's Cathedral

Below Leadenhall Market, originally a meat and poultry market, stands on what was the centre of Roman London

were the main places for the exchange of gossip. Here a businessman could meet his client and discuss a deal in relative comfort and warmth over a coffee. By the eighteenth century, it was estimated that there were over 3,000 coffee houses in London (we don't seem to have caught up yet – TripAdvisor only lists 2,819 in London today).

Popping out finally onto Cornhill, we feel like rabbits popping out of their hole into bright daylight. Across the way stands the former Royal Exchange, founded in the sixteenth century by the merchant Thomas Gresham to act as a centre of commerce for the City. The present building was designed by William Tite in the 1840s. The site was occupied by Lloyd's insurance market for nearly 150 years till it moved to its famous Richards Rogers-designed Lloyds Building (1986).

Just beyond the Mansion House (1739–52), **1 Poultry** (1997) steams into view, designed by James Stirling. It's that rare thing for me, a piece of postmodern architecture that I like! It stands out from the surrounding buildings because of its polychromatic colour and yet it fits in well all the same. Its exterior is clad in stripes of pink and yellow limestone, and its two long façades are characterised by the layering of angular and curved forms, with an ancient Egyptian tomb-like opening that takes visitors into the heart of the building. 'It's the most important piece of postmodern design in the UK,' according to Catherine Croft, Director of the Twentieth Century Society.

The Romans built the **Temple of Mithras** (third century AD) on the east bank of the River Walbrook, which is now an underground river. It has been fully restored as part of the construction of the impressive and eco-friendly Bloomberg Office (2017). A new retail arcade cuts through this development, with several restaurants along its way; and a pair of sculpted fountains pay tribute to the Walbrook flowing underneath.

On the corner of Bow Lane and Watling Street is one of London's oldest pubs, **Ye Old Watling**. Rebuilt after the Great Fire by Sir Christopher Wren, utilising old ships' timbers, the upstairs rooms were used as a drawing office during the building of St Paul's Cathedral, whilst downstairs provided refreshment for Wren's workmen during the lengthy construction of the cathedral, which took fort years in all.

Above left St Paul's Cathedral dome, described by Pevsner as 'one of the most perfect in the world'

Above right The National Theatre comes top of Brutalist aficionados' lists

Below The Tate Modern, transformed from generating power to championing art

'Alongside the Thames flowed imperturbably on. So it would flow until the Embankments crumbled and Westminster became once more an island in a marsh' JOHN WYNDHAM

Today's Watling Street runs along the line of the ancient Watling Street, which connected Canterbury with the City, crossing the Thames over the Roman London Bridge, then heading up to St Albans and eventually to the Welsh Borders. There is a very undistinguished shopping centre on the right here, called One New Change. It has one great virtue, though: we ride up the glass elevator to the top and enjoy one of the best views of St Paul's for free.

Wren's most celebrated work, of course, is **St Paul's Cathedral** (1708), designed in the English Baroque style and built after the destruction of the previous cathedral by the Great Fire. Its dome dominated the skyline for 300 years, the tallest structure in London until well into the twentieth century, described by Pevsner as 'one of the most perfect in the world'.

Heading down the pedestrian route to the Thames from here, we cross the **Millennium Bridge** (2000), which for a while became known as the 'Wobbly Bridge'. The natural sway motion of people walking caused small sideways oscillations in the bridge, which in turn caused people on the bridge to sway in step, increasing the amplitude of the bridge oscillations and continually reinforcing the effect. A wonderful demonstration of the power of urban rambling! It took two years to sort it out.

The **Tate Modern** (1947 and 2000) used to be the Bankside Power Station, designed by Sir Giles Gilbert Scott, and was re-purposed as the home for the new Tate Modern by Herzog & de Meuron architects. More recently, the impressive Tate Modern Switch House has been added at the back of the site, 'the bricks draped like chainmail over a muscular concrete cage', as the *Guardian* neatly puts it. Cracking building, though not so popular with the penthouse apartments it overlooks.

It took a while for people to appreciate the brutalist **National Theatre** (1976), but it has become a familiar and much-loved building, changing the rules of theatre spaces for ever. It is the embodiment of architect Denys Lasdun's philosophy of 'architecture as urban landscape'. In the dusk, it looks like a range of foothills, with many different valleys, ridges and corries giving it interest and 'ways in', with lights playing on the different spaces and angles in myriad ways.

In 1951, Britain's cities still showed the scars of the war. With the aim of promoting the feeling of recovery, the **Festival of Britain** opened in the early summer of 1951, celebrating British industry, arts and science, and inspiring the thought of a better Britain, 'a tonic to the nation'. It was also the centenary of the landmark 1851 Great Exhibition, which had been such a high point for British influence and ingenuity. The main site of the Festival was constructed here on the South Bank which, over the following thirty years has developed into the popular arts complex we enjoy today.

It's hard to know what to add about a building as iconic as the **Houses of Parliament**. To me, it epitomises 'Empire Victorian' architecture and is also a symbol of how we muddle along as a nation – no fundamental

'It came to me that Hyde Park has never belonged to London - that it has always been, in spirit, a stretch of countryside; and that it links the Londons of all periods together most magically - by remaining forever unchanged at the heart of an ever-changing town.' DODIE SMITH

restoration has been carried out on the building since the war, when it was damaged by bombs, and the country is now faced with a repair bill of at least £4 billion; furthermore, MPs and Lords will have to find somewhere else to carry out their work for at least six years.

The four sides of **Parliament Square** reflect the different powers of the country: legislature to the east (the Houses of Parliament), executive offices to the north (Whitehall), the judiciary to the west (the Supreme Court), and the Church to the south (Westminster Abbey). With the fifth influence – the leaders and the populace in the square itself – both those who have shaped history in the eleven statues, including Churchill's; and the 'vox populi' in the shape of campaigners and demonstrators. This is the stage of British life and history.

The **Foreign & Commonwealth Office** (1868) occupies a building on the right of King Charles Street, which we walk along next. It originally provided premises for four separate government departments: the Foreign Office, the India Office, the Colonial Office and the Home Office. It was designed by George Gilbert Scott, the most prodigious architect of his age. His works spanned the empire, from New Zealand to Newfoundland. In England alone, he designed 800 buildings and oversaw hundreds more restorations, including eighteen of the twenty-six medieval cathedrals.

And then we enter **St James' Park** (23 hectares, 57 acres), and for the rest of the walk we are in the embrace of green spaces. This area was originally a swampy wasteland, often flooded by the River Tyburn on its way to the Thames. The Royal Court was based at the Palace of Westminster, and in 1536 Henry VIII decided to create a deer park here, putting a fence around it and building a hunting lodge that later became St James's Palace.

Green Park (19 hectares, 47 acres) had been a burial ground for lepers, but was taken over by Charles II and enclosed. He built an ice house there to supply him with ice for cooling drinks in summer. In 1820, John Nash landscaped the park, in roughly the form we see today. It remains a personal favourite of mine, despite its simplicity, consisting almost entirely of mature trees and no flower beds.

Hyde Park (142 hectares, 350 acres) is London's

Above The distinctive
zig-zag roof of the listed
Serpentine Bar and Kitchen

Below Rummaging for
books under the Waterloo
Bridge on the South Bank

most impressive space. It was originally created in 1536 by Henry VIII for hunting, and it remained a private hunting ground until James I permitted limited access to gentlefolk, appointing a ranger to take charge. In 1637 the park was opened to the public.

One of the most famous events to take place in the park was the **Great Exhibition** of 1851. The Crystal Palace was constructed on the south side of the park, designed by Joseph Paxton. It was prefabricated, assembled on site, and used large quantities of iron and glass – a high-tech building 150 years ahead of its time, admired by Le Corbusier no less. Six million people visited the Great Exhibition, and the event made a healthy financial surplus that was used to fund the creation of the Victoria and Albert Museum, the Science Museum and the Natural History Museum.

We now find ourselves on the Diana, Princess of Wales Memorial Walk. We savour the aromas in the pretty **Rose Garden,** and then walk along the south side of the Serpentine, memorably used as the venue for the swimming portion of the triathlon and for the marathon swimming events at the 2012 London Olympic Games.

The **Princess of Wales Memorial Fountain** (2004), has become a star London attraction, successful in every way. It's beautiful to watch the water gliding and gurgling along the Cornish granite and to watch children and adults alike enraptured by it as they paddle and splash.

Kensington Gardens (111 hectares, 270 acres) is technically everything to the west of the Serpentine Bridge, although it feels like a continuation of the park and you will hardly notice. The author J.M. Barrie lived close to Kensington Gardens and published his first Peter Pan story in 1902, using the park for inspiration. In his Peter Pan tale 'The Little White Bird', Peter flies out of his nursery and lands beside the Long Water. The **Peter Pan Statue** (1912) is located at this exact spot.

The exquisite **Italian Gardens** (1860s) were created as a gift from Prince Albert to Queen Victoria, based on gardens he had previously created at Osborne House on the Isle of Wight. What a tranquil spot to finish this leg of the walk.

PIT STOPS

- **SKY GARDEN CAFÉ**, 1 Sky Garden Walk, EC3M 8AF. Book in advance
- **TATE MODERN CAFÉ**, Level 1, Bankside, SE1 9TG. Great views.
- **THE SERPENTINE BAR & KITCHEN**, Hyde Park, W2 2UH. 1960s listed building.
- **THE ITALIAN GARDEN CAFÉ**, W2 2UE

QUIRKY SHOPPING

- **LEADENHALL MARKET** (EC3V 1LT)
- **BOW LANE** (EC4M 9EB) Shoe shops, food and drink.
- **SOUTHBANK CENTRE BOOK MARKET** – browse for second-hand books under Waterloo Bridge.

PLACES TO VISIT

- **THE MONUMENT**, Fish Street Hill, EC3R 8AH. Climb to the top for a great view.
- **TEMPLE OF MITHRAS**, Bloomberg, 12 Walbrook, EC4N 8AA
- **TATE MODERN**, Bankside, SE1 9TG

WHEN TO VISIT

British Summer Time Hyde Park (July – music, comedy acts, film)

IV. Lancaster Gate to King's Cross

This final stage of the London Inner Circle takes us through Little Venice and along a charming stretch of the Regent's Canal, passing through two more of London's finest open spaces, Regent's Park and Primrose Hill.

This stage of the walk is a story about the evolution of transport and communication, and the way in which regeneration takes place once a particular stage of transport or communication technology has been superseded.

So, we start in a mews, symbol of the coach and horse age, morphing in the 1960s to trendy places for people to live, but still with a country feel about them with their back-to-front gardens spilling onto the cobbles.

Then to Paddington Basin, which at the start of the nineteenth century became the hub of 'goods inwards' to central London, bringing building materials and coal along the canal from the Midlands; now, completely regenerated with offices, apartments, restaurants and quirky bridges.

Next, under the Westway, that concrete memorial to the motor car, crashing through London in the 1960s, intended to relieve congestion and kick-start a new age of modernism. The thumping noise and ugliness are still there, reminding us of just how horrible most UK cities were in the 1970s.

Then, passing through the elegant Regent's Park, which used to be a royal hunting ground but was 'regenerated' as a smart place for Georgians to hang out and promenade in; allowing wild animals back, but strictly in captivity.

WALK DATA

- **DISTANCE:** 10 km (6.25 miles)
- **HEIGHT GAIN:** 40 metres
- **WALK TIME:** 2½ hours
- **START:** Lancaster Gate Tube station (W2 2UE)
- **END:** King's Cross station (N1C 4TB)
- **TERRAIN:** Pavements and paths all the way; steep climb to Primrose Hill

And towards the end of the walk, observing redundant railway yards transformed into seats of learning (The British Library, the Francis Crick Institute) or up-market shopping arcades (Coal Drops Yard). Even an old gas works which has become a circular garden.

And finally, the headquarters of Google alongside King's Cross, laying down the information superhighway in what used to be just a railway siding, and supplying the mapping with which all our walks are driven – for which many thanks – first the Ordnance Survey and now Google have transformed our sense of place and our enjoyment of the outdoors.

THE WALK

Starting out from Lancaster Gate, we head along Bathurst Mews. Mews used to be the 'service conduits' for the grand townhouses, the place where the horses, carriages and staff were housed whilst their masters were staying in London. We imagined that the stables had long gone in favour of bijoux conversions for folk looking for a more 'individualistic' lifestyle, a trend begun back in the 1960s – think Michael Caine's Charlie Croker in *The Italian Job* and Twiggy posing in front of a Mini. But not Bathurst Mews, which incredibly still has two stable yards that are very much still alive and kicking: grooming and tacking up their ponies ready to take groups around Hyde Park at whatever speed their skill allows.

Norfolk Square was laid out in the 1840s on the site of the former Upper South Reservoir of the Grand Junction Canal Company. The garden was originally provided for the private use of the residents of the square. They had their own constable who patrolled daily and acted as gateman. The ladies of the houses would take afternoon tea in the gardens, served by their maids in the shade of the trees.

Paddington station (1854) was designed by Brunel, who is commemorated by a statue on the concourse, although much of the architectural detailing was by his associate Matthew Wyatt. It opened in 1854 and is regarded as one of the country's finest stations architecturally, albeit the station is all but invisible from the outside. Pop in to admire it.

We appreciate the Art Deco **GWR Paddington Building** up London Street just before we turn right down Winsland Mews. It dates back to the mid-1930s and has many Art Deco features, including a row of shell-like protrusions which contain the lights that illuminate the sign.

On the outer wall of **St Mary's Paddington Hospital** there is a plaque commemorating the discovery of penicillin by Alexander Fleming in this wing in 1928. The tiny laboratory has been restored and is open to the public.

The Paddington Basin (1801) was the terminus of the Grand Junction Canal before the Regent's Park arm was constructed a decade or so later. The site was chosen because of its position on the New Road which led to the east, providing for onward transport into the city. The basin has been completely redeveloped in the last few years. As we go through the arch, we encounter the **Floating Pocket Park**, the first of its kind in London, floating on pontoons, with lawns, raised borders, seating areas and a separate wildlife island to encourage waterfowl.

If unusual bridges are your thing, then the basin is the place to come, as we cross two. the **Fan Bridge** (2014) gracefully splays as it rises, whilst the **Rolling Bridge** (2004), conceived by Thomas Heatherwick, curls itself up into a ball like a shy caterpillar. Both bridges 'perform' on Wednesdays and Fridays at twelve noon (fan first, then rolling) and Saturday afternoons at 2 p.m.; so the next time you're in the area, go and catch the show.

Sheldon Square, forming the major part of Paddington Central, is an impressive recently created space with a grass amphitheatre that features live music in summer. Perhaps inevitably, in the rush to get it open, most of the concessions have been given to chains, making it a little impersonal.

WALK DATA
- **FAMOUS INHABITANTS:** Alan Turing (Paddington), Nancy Mitford, Richard Branson (Little Venice); H.G. Wells (Regent's Park); Jude Law, Kate Moss, Noel Gallagher (Primrose Hill)
- **NOTABLE BUILDERS:** John Nash (Regent's Canal, Regent's Park)
- **SCREEN TIME:** *Scandal* (Bathurst Mews); *Jason Bourne* (Paddington Basin); *Georgy Girl, A Fish Called Wanda* (Little Venice); *Brief Encounter* (Regent's Park); *An American Werewolf in London, Withnail and I, About a Boy* (Regent's Park Zoo); *Bridget Jones: The Edge of Reason* (Primrose Hill)
- **ICONIC CITYSCAPE:** Primrose Hill

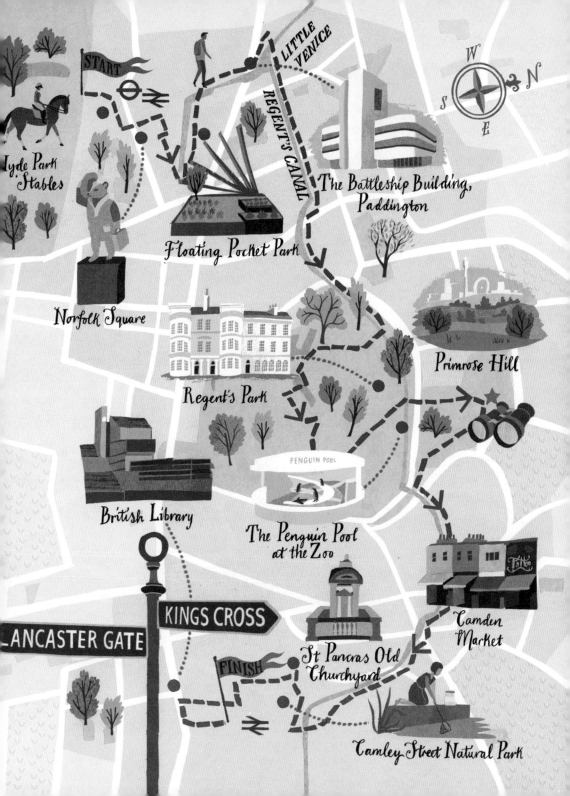

'I have conversed with the spiritual sun. I saw him on Primrose Hill.'

WILLIAM BLAKE

So, what is to be said about the **Westway**? Well. All that was bad about 1960s planning really. The road was constructed to relieve congestion at Shepherd's Bush. It followed existing railway lines, but also involved the clearance of many homes adjacent to the railway, particularly in the area west of Westbourne Park, where roads were unceremoniously truncated or demolished to make way for the concrete structures.

Oddly, though, the Westway seems to have inspired creative thinking, cropping up in the songs of the Clash and Blur and featured on the front cover of the Jam's *This Is the Modern World*. But its most famous outing was the dystopian vision of author J.G. Ballard in the 1974 novel *Concrete Island*, in which an architect is marooned Crusoe-like on a triangular strip of motorway intersection when his car plunges off the exit road after a tyre blowout.

The Battleship Building (1969) was originally designed as a British Rail maintenance depot. It is in the 'Streamline Moderne' style, a style that emphasises curving forms, long horizontal lines and nautical elements. It won the Concrete Society's 'Building of the Year' in 1969 (an accolade to be proud of presumably; it's still there on the side of the building) and was listed Grade II* in 1994.

In sharp contrast to the Westway, we admire the visual appeal of **Little Venice**, where the Paddington Spur meets the Grand Union and the Regent's Canal, a haven of genteel tranquillity. But it was not always thus. In its bustling heyday, it would have had a very industrial feel to it, with the movement of food and materials, especially coal, making it an undesirable place to take the air.

The next section of the canal after Lisson Grove is much broader, so that commercial barges could load and unload at the Great Central Railway Goods Yard on the southern bank. The **Canal House on Lisson Grove** (1906) is the only house that straddles the canal, built for the manager of the Regent's Canal. The Lisson Grove Moorings are an entrancing spot. Because of the canal being broader, the boats are moored end on which means there is quite a community as communication between boats is much easier. And the residents have cultivated the towpath into a sort of linear garden, with deck chairs, trellises, roses and even a garden gnome.

Charlbert Street Bridge across the Regent's Canal is designed for both aesthetic and practical purposes. Its gracious curves belie the fact that it was also designed to accommodate the course of the Tyburn River. There is an iron tube through the crown of the bridge. The only visible evidence today of the footbridge's real purpose is an inspection hatch that we walk over on our way into the park.

The Regent's Park (166 hectares, 410 acres) was first formed when Henry VIII appropriated the land, and it has been Crown property ever since. It was set aside as a hunting park until 1649, when it was let out in smallholdings for hay and dairy produce. When the leases expired in 1811, the Prince Regent commissioned architect John Nash to create a masterplan for the area,

Above left The leaves starting to fall on Primrose Hill

Above right Gasholder Park, an ingenious repurposing of redundant technology

Below Camden and its Market still offer ethnic food, flowing drapes and exotic incense

which he did in the Picturesque tradition, with slopes, tree planting and natural-looking lakes fed by two streams. The park was first opened to the public in 1835, initially for only two days a week. We head south into the park, following the route of one of these streams, the Tyburn, to the boating lake, passing the Open-Air Theatre (1932) to Queen Mary's Rose Gardens.

We now loop back up, roughly along the line of the other stream that feeds into the boating lake, a tributary to the Tyburn, skirting around the southern perimeter of the world's oldest scientific zoo, opened in 1828. London Zoo was established by Sir Stamford Raffles (a statesman) and Sir Humphry Davy (a prominent scientist) and was originally intended to be used as a collection for study. It was not opened to the public until 1847. The zoo has always prided itself on appointing leading architects to design its buildings – consequently, it has ten listed structures, perhaps the best known being the Penguin Pool and the Snowdon Aviary.

Like Regent's Park, **Primrose Hill** (83 hectares, 206 acres), was once part of a great chase appropriated by Henry VIII. In 1842 an Act of Parliament secured the land as public open space. At the top of the hill is one of thirteen protected vistas in London, almost all of which involve sight lines towards St Paul's Cathedral. The view from here is quite magnificent.

Back on the canal, we come to the **Interchange Warehouse** (1856), which facilitated the transfer of goods from canal to train. The dock was bridged over with heavy girders supporting the railway tracks and platforms of a railway goods shed, and the barges and narrowboats below were accessed through trapdoors in the platforms.

Camden Market has been an institution for as long as I can remember, and it seems to have changed little – still lots of ethnic food, flowing drapes and exotic incense. How reassuring. A temporary market was first established here in 1974 and today it is one of the most popular visitor destinations in London, attracting 100,000 people each weekend.

MTV Studios (1982) used to be the offices of TV-AM, designed by Terry Farrell. Jonathan Glancey described it as 'one of the most obviously spectacular architect-designed interiors completed in recent years and one of the high points of Postmodernism'. We admire the egg cups on the roof.

When the canal was used for commercial purposes, living by its side would have been considered undesirable. But today, canalside properties have a premium of up to 30 per cent versus their immediate neighbours. One particularly notable run of properties is **Grand Union Walk** (1988), designed by Nicholas Grimshaw and comprising ten high-tech houses, in that rare thing, a modern terrace, bringing an industrial aesthetic to a residential setting. If they remind you slightly of the sides of an old London bus, this is not as daft as it seems – that was the panelling they used.

We relax in **Gasholder Park**, originally constructed in the 1850s as part of the Pancras Gasworks. When

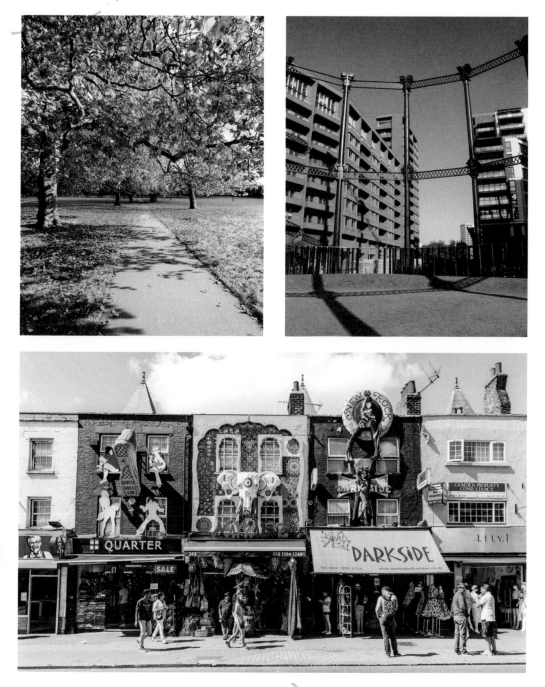

Above St Pancras in its fully restored glory; thank you John Betjeman for helping save it

Below The British Library, not yet come of age and already Grade I listed

the King's Cross redevelopment began, the cast-iron structure was dismantled piece by piece, restored and moved to its new home here, on the north of the canal. The circular lawn inside makes a charming green space.

Then, we delight in the immaculately kept Pancras Lock, with its lock keeper's garden. Here we cross the new Somers Town footbridge to reach the tiny **Camley Street Natural Park** (0.8 hectares, 2 acres), created from an old coal yard in 1984 and the first artificially created park in the country to gain statutory designation as a local nature reserve.

We discover so much of interest in **St Pancras Gardens**, including the extravagant Burdett-Coutts memorial sundial, the Hardy tree encircled by tombstones, and the famous memorial to Sir John Soane's wife, the design of which inspired the classic K2 Gilbert Scott red telephone box. The church here is one of the oldest in London, dating back to the seventh century.

Walking south past the **Francis Crick Institute** (2016), we get a good view of the **British Library** (1999), one of my favourite buildings. Such a beautiful place, a subtle blend of classicism and modernity, matching the brickwork of the neighbouring St Pancras. Designed by architect Sir Colin St John Wilson, it was the largest UK public building to be built in the twentieth century and is already Grade I listed.

And, finally, **St Pancras station** (1868), a wondrous piece of Victorian Gothic Revival architecture designed by George Gilbert Scott; and the train shed, completed in 1868 by William Henry Barlow, the largest single-span structure built up to that time. I have loved St Pancras ever since I was a child. To think it nearly got knocked down . . . Thank you, John Betjeman, for helping save it.

Back to where we started, Battle Bridge Place, an ancient crossing of the Fleet River and the scene of a fierce battle between Boudica and the Romans; today, it is metres away from the European headquarters of Google.

PIT STOPS

- **WATERSIDE CAFÉ**, Browning Pool – you will not get a better spot than this.
- **CAFÉ LAVILLE**, 453 Edgware Road, W2 1TH, built over the western entrance to the Maida Hill Tunnel
- **THE HUB** is in the middle of Regent's Park's busy playing fields.

QUIRKY SHOPPING

- **REGENT'S PARK ROAD**, Primrose Hill (NW1 8XP). The epitome of the 'indie' high street.
- **CAMDEN MARKET** (NW1 8NH). The biggest and the original. Over 1,000 shops and stalls selling fashion, music, art and food.
- **COAL DROPS YARD** (N1C 4AB), with a focus on fashion, craft and culture.

PLACES TO VISIT

- **ALEXANDER FLEMING MUSEUM** (W2 1NY)
- **THE REGENT'S PARK BOATING LAKE**
- **LONDON ZOO**, Regent's Park
- **CAMLEY STREET NATURAL PARK** (N1C 4PW). A beautiful backwater of green amid the clamour of regeneration.

WHEN TO VISIT

Canalway Cavalcade Festival, Little Venice (early May), Regent's Park Open Air Theatre (May–Sept), Primrose Hill Summer Festival (May)

An A-Z of familiar features

Alleyways

We venture down many intriguing passages and alleyways on our walks, but little could we have imagined how many different names there are for essentially the same thing.

In Brighton they are called 'twittens', in Nottingham 'twitchells', in Newcastle 'chares', in Manchester 'ginnels', in Plymouth 'opes', in Liverpool 'jiggers', in Shrewsbury 'shuts', in Darlington 'wynds', in Leicester 'gitties', in the north-west 'snickets'.

The oldest-sounding one of them all – York's 'snickelways' – is in fact the newest, coined in 1983 as a portmanteau of the words 'snicket', 'ginnel' and 'alleyway'.

Bandstands

These were an integral part of the municipal parks movement, designed to alleviate the life of the working class in industrial cities. Victorian worthies believed that good music would free the mind of urban griminess and humanise the industrial landscape.

An incredible 1,200 bandstands were built between the 1860s and World War II, and in their heyday, they were key to the social fabric of a city, often attracting crowds of thousands to musical concerts.

Many survive and have been restored, remaining one of the great glories of our parks' heritage. Perhaps the most notable ones we pass are:

- The Birdcage, Brighton Esplanade (1883)
- Lincoln Arboretum bandstand (1872)
- Leazes Park bandstand, Newcastle (1875)

Cathedrals: does a city have to have one?

There are fifty-one cities in England, but how did they achieve their status? These are the 'rules':

1. In the sixteenth century, a town was recognised as a city by the English Crown if it had a diocesan cathedral within its limits – sometimes they could be small places, e.g. St David's, Wells and Ely.

2. A long-awaited resumption of creating dioceses began in 1836. Accordingly, Ripon, Manchester, Truro, St Albans, Liverpool, Newcastle upon Tyne and Wakefield all gained city status by the 1880s.

3. The link with Anglican dioceses was broken in 1889, when Birmingham successfully petitioned for city status on the grounds of its large population and history of good local government. Leeds, Sheffield, Bradford, Kingston upon Hull and Nottingham followed suit.

4. In 1907, the Home Office and Edward VII agreed on a policy for future applicants with three criteria: a) a minimum population of 300,000; b) a 'local metropolitan character'; c) a good record of local government. This is roughly how towns have been awarded city status ever since, but there still seem to be plenty of disputes, jealousies and definitional 'grey areas'.

5. Some places add the word 'city' to their name without official approval, e.g. Letchworth Garden City (no cathedral, population 34,000).

Dustbins

Not sure what the solution is to this, but many a beautiful street is ruined by bins permanently parked in front gardens, or worse still, on the pavement out front.

Englishness

You'll experience a lot of this on our walks – tea rooms, park benches, bedding plants, blue plaques . . .

Friends of Parks groups

Friends groups enable residents to take a lead role in the development, care and ownership of parks and green spaces. They have made a significant difference to the quality of parks, from the appearance of railings and eradication of litter and dog fouling to facilities and events. Hats off to them.

Graffiti, or street art

Frowned upon when it arrived in the 1970s from New York, graffiti is now often revered as a sign of the cultural vibrancy of a city. Favourites include:

- Bristol – Banksy street art and the Nelson Street See No Evil festival
- Manchester Northern Quarter
- Sheffield – old buildings on Mary Street
- London – Ben Eine's bright colourful letters

Hidden rivers

Before there were cities, the landscape was created by hills and rivers, which, as the cities expanded from their core, became inconveniences rather than desirable natural features. Hills, of course, are still fairly easy to notice on foot but hidden rivers are harder to find. The clues tend to be subtle – maybe a twisting road that is still following the line of an old river, a boundary between two districts, the reference to a 'brook' or a 'bourne' in a street name, or a lake in a park naturally fed.

Ice cream

The indulgence of choice in a park on a hot summer's day.

With the invention of an ice cream machine in 1843 and the widespread availability of ice for the first time, ice cream became a treat for ordinary Victorians. Italy continued to lead Europe in ice creamery, and Italian immigrants to the UK brought tradition and expertise – Manchester's Ancoats, the centre of the Italian ice cream trade until recently, is the best example of this.

Another notable place on our walks is Carlo Gatti's Ice Store, now the London Canal Museum, on the Regent's Canal just east of King's Cross.

Jubilees

These always seem to be an excuse for opening something.

Queen Victoria's Golden Jubilee (1887) and Diamond Jubilee (1897) were celebrated with the opening of several parks and the construction of statues and memorials.

Likewise, Elizabeth II's Silver Jubilee (1977), Golden Jubilee (2002) and Diamond Jubilee (2012) were celebrated in many gardens, bridges and plaques.

Kick-abouts

I have seldom walked through a park without kicking (or mis-kicking) a ball back to a group of would-be footballing stars. And, of course, we walk through the park where it is claimed that football was invented, Parker's Piece in Cambridge.

Love locks

These are padlocks that sweethearts fasten to a bridge to symbolise their unbreakable love. Typically, they scratch their initials on the lock and throw the key away. The trend began on the Pont des Arts in Paris at the start of the Millennium; many British city bridges have now been 'infested'. Councils usually see them as a problem rather than adornment, much like the early days of graffiti. In my experience, they add a story to a plain bridge but they can detract from a beautiful one.

My favourite is Newcastle's High Level Bridge, adding emotional warmth to a bridge that is otherwise rather forbidding, and telling a thousand stories of connectedness, which, after all, is the essence of the bridge itself.

Manhole covers

My uncle used to photograph manhole covers, as, I believe, does Jeremy Corbyn.

What manhole covers are useful for on our walks is dating or giving provenance to a street, not least those of Thomas Crapper (1836–1910), the Victorian purveyor of sanitary ware, or George Jennings, the unitary engineer who introduced the flush toilet to London at the Great Exhibition of 1851.

'Naked' streets

The 'shared space' or 'naked street' concept is the belief that breaking down the barriers between motorist and pedestrian through the removal of kerbs, barriers, lane markings, lights and signs could make the motorist more aware of their surroundings and reduce pedestrian injuries.

The most notable exponent of this concept was Hans Monderman (1945–2008), a Dutch road traffic engineer and innovator. He was known for boldly walking out onto his naked streets, turning his back on the moving traffic and walking to the other side to show that drivers would not run him over.

Brighton has a good example of a 'naked street', Bold Street by the Brighton Pavilion. London's best-known example is Exhibition Road.

Oddities

- The DNA helix symbol above a door in Portugal Street, Cambridge, where Francis Crick, the co-discoverer of DNA, lived in the 1950s.
- Word on the Water floating bookshop on the Regent's Canal at King's Cross.
- The pyramid-shaped William MacKenzie tomb in Liverpool; apparently he was a keen gambler and left instructions that he should be entombed above ground within the pyramid, sitting upright at a card table and clutching a winning hand.

Pavements and pedways

Raised pavements for pedestrians, separated from the carriageway by kerbs, have existed since before Roman times, but they only became widespread in our towns and cities in the nineteenth century, as a means of avoiding the muck in the road and to provide 'safe haven' from carriages.

Their safety role was enshrined in law in the 1835 Highways Act, which made it an offence to 'wilfully ride upon any footpath or causeway by the side of any road made or set apart for the use or accommodation of foot-passengers'.

Queen Victoria

Oh my, it is hard to go on a walk and not see a statue of Queen Victoria – Manchester, Leeds, Liverpool and Sheffield to name but a few . . . there are more than sixty-five altogether in prominent places in English cities!

Red telephone boxes

The iconic red telephone box was the creation of Sir Giles Gilbert Scott. Its shape was apparently inspired by the dome of Sir John Soane's mausoleum in St Pancras Old Churchyard, which we pass on London Inner Circle IV.

The K6 style is the most common, however you will do well to spot an earlier K2 model (Liverpool, by the Town Hall).

Silver balls

Just about every Millennium Square we walk through has large silver balls adorning it, which has certainly been good for the manufacturers of these shiny spheres.

Traffic lights

Parliament Square featured the world's first road traffic signal in 1868 to improve carriage flow. It looked like any railway signal of the time, with waving semaphore arms and red-green lamps, operated by gas, for night use. Tragically, it exploded, killing a policeman. The accident discouraged further development until the era of the internal combustion engine. Modern traffic lights are an American invention. Red-green systems were installed in Cleveland in 1914, and the first lights of this type to appear in Britain were in London in 1925, on the junction between St James's Street and Piccadilly.

Underpasses

They NEVER work. The first reinforced concrete underpass was the Norwood Underpass in 1912. They were part of the 1960s attempt to reduce traffic accidents by separating pedestrians and cars. They are notoriously hard to keep clean and even the safest feel, well, unsafe.

Verges

A green verge along a street can make so much difference to its overall appeal and sense of verdancy . . . if a car hasn't gone and parked on it.

In the words of 'urban guerrilla' Richard Reynolds: 'Let's fight the filth with forks and flowers.'

War memorials

Almost 500 in various forms, the war memorials erected to the Anglo-Boer War (1899–1902) represent the first ever mass raising of war memorials in this country. There are lots to be found in the parks we walk through because they often date from the same period.

The wave of war-memorial building after World War I resulted in thousands of monuments. Sir Edwin Lutyens was the most outstanding designer to work in this field. Scattered across England, in city squares and public parks, are his forty-four memorials to the Great War, including these ones:

- Exeter, Cathedral Square
- Cooper Street, Manchester
- War Memorial Garden Terrace, Norwich
- Station Rise and War Memorial Gardens, York

X-ings

Good road crossings are so important for pedestrians. I like the new initiative of showing you how many seconds are left before it turns red.

The longest rail crossing on our walk is the six-track Exeter St David's; in a nice touch, walkers are let through on a different (and more frequent) flow than cars.

Yellow bridges

Bristol has several of these for some reason (perhaps yellow was a favourite colour of the chief bridge engineer), two of which we cross on our walk – one is even called the Banana Bridge.

Zebra crossings

The first Belisha beacons were erected in London following the Road Traffic Act of 1934, and were then rolled out nationally. They were named after Leslie Hore-Belisha, the Minister of Transport, who added beacons to existing pedestrian crossings – at the time these were marked by metal studs in the road surface. Crossings were later painted in black and white stripes, thus becoming known as zebra crossings.

Picture credits

All photos © Nicholas Rudd-Jones, except the following:

p4 © Troika / Alamy Stock Photo | p7 top © Trinity Mirror / Mirrorpix / Alamy Stock Photo | p10 © Masami Kihara/Shutterstock | p13 bottom © travellight/ Shutterstock | p14 bottom © Harry Green/Shutterstock | p17 bottom © AC Manley/Shutterstock, bottom © ExFlow/Shutterstock | p18 top left © spatuletail/ Shutterstock | p20 © Borna_Mirahmadian/Shutterstock | p25 top left © chrisdorney/Shutterstock, top right © Robert Proctor / Alamy Stock Photo, bottom © KPrice/Shutterstock | p26 top left © creativeoneuk/Shutterstock, below © Alastair Wallace/Shutterstock | p28-29 © David Reilly/Shutterstock | p30 © BIG STOCK | p34 bottom © BIG STOCK | p37 top left © travellight/Shutterstock, top right © Alexey Lobanov/Shutterstock | p38 top © Alexey Lobanov/ Shutterstock | p40 © jremes84/Shutterstock | p45 top left © D K Grove/Shutterstock, top right © Nella/Shutterstock | p66 © Serg Zastavkin/Shutterstock | p48 © BIG STOCK | p52 bottom © BIG STOCK | p55 © BMA/Shutterstock | p62 top right © Alastair Wallace/Shutterstock | p65 top left © D K Grove/Shutterstock, top right © Nella/Shutterstock | p66 © Serg Zastavkin/Shutterstock | p68-69 © Mark Bassett / Alamy Stock Photo | p70 © PlusONE/Shutterstock | p77 top right © lullabi/Shutterstock | p75 top right © lullabi/Shutterstock | p78 top right © Thomas Smith / Alamy Stock Photo | p80 © Caron Badkin/Shutterstock | p84 © Paul Cowan/Shutterstock | p87 below © Chris Hawker/ Shutterstock | p88 top left © Monkey Business Images/Shutterstock, top right © Andrei Nekrassov/Shutterstock, bottom BIG STOCK? | p90-91 © Clare Louise Jackson/Shutterstock | p92 © Joe Dunckley/Shutterstock | p99 © Claudio Divizia/Shutterstock | p101 top left © pjhpix/Shutterstock, top right © Christian Mueller/Shutterstock, bottom © pjhpix/Shutterstock | p102 © Claudio Divizia/Shutterstock | p104 © HeroToZero/Shutterstock | p108 © D S O Media/Shutterstock | p111 top © Kevin George/Shutterstock, bottom © chrisdorney/Shutterstock | p112 top left © Alastair Wallace/Shutterstock, top right © Lighttraveler/Shutterstock, bottom © S-F/Shutterstock | p114 top left © Caron Badkin/Shutterstock, bottom © Tupungato/Shutterstock | p116 © Milosz Maslanka/Shutterstock | p120 top left © Alastair Wallace/Shutterstock, top right © Marcel Brekelmans/Shutterstock, bottom © BIG STOCK | p123 © Dave Head/Shutterstock | p124 top left © Iordanis/Shutterstock, top right © Paul J Martin/Shutterstock, bottom © Harry Green/Shutterstock | p126 © Graeme Peacock / Alamy Stock Photo | p128 © Jim Gibson / Alamy Stock Photo | p133 © Lee Pengelly / Alamy Stock Photo | p134 top left © Helen Hotson/ Shutterstock, bottom © Paul J Martin/Shutterstock | p137 © Lee Morriss/Shutterstock | p138 top left © Peter Titmuss/Shutterstock, bottom © Paul J Martin/ Shutterstock | p140-141 © antb/Shutterstock | p142 © JeniFoto/Shutterstock | p147 top left © chrisdorney/Shutterstock, top right © Anna Jastrzebska/ Shutterstock, bottom © 1000 Words/Shutterstock | p148 © Georgethefourth/Shutterstock | p150 top © Justin Black/Shutterstock, bottom © tviolet/ Shutterstock | p156 top Jeff Morgan 16 / Alamy Stock Photo, bottom © Bobo Ling/Shutterstock | p160 top left © Philip Reeve, top right © Elena Rostunova/ Shutterstock, bottom © NigelSpiers/Shutterstock | p162-163 © Peter Cripps/Shutterstock | p164 © Tupungato/Shutterstock | p168 top left © Jason Wells/ Shutterstock | p171 top © Alastair Wallace/Shutterstock, bottom © Tupungato/Shutterstock | p172 © Tupungato/Shutterstock | p174 © Jacek Wojnarowski/ Shutterstock | p180 top left © PoohFotoz/Shutterstock , top right © A G Baxter/Shutterstock, bottom © philip openshaw/Shutterstock | p183 © Daniel Heighton/Shutterstock | p186 top © Tupungato/Shutterstock, bottom © Shahid Khan/Shutterstock | p188 © jeafish Ping/Shutterstock | p193 top left © jeafish Ping/Shutterstock, top right © Alastair Wallace/Shutterstock, bottom © Moomusician/Shutterstock | p194 top © Alastair Wallace/Shutterstock, bottom © Alastair Wallace/Shutterstock | p196 top right © Electric Egg/Shutterstock, bottom © BIG STOCK | p198 © Darren Galpin / Alamy Stock Photo | p202 top © Jeanette Teare/Shutterstock | p204 © Shahid Khan/Shutterstock | p206-207 © Bikeworldtravel/Shutterstock | p210 © Eugene Regis/Shutterstock | p214 bottom © Benjamin Brading/Shutterstock | p217 bottom © DrimaFilm/Shutterstock | p218 top right © chrisdorney/Shutterstock, bottom © Ron Ellis/ Shutterstock | p225 top left © Kiev.Victor/Shutterstock , top right © Kiev.Victor/Shutterstock, bottom © IR Stone/Shutterstock | p226 © kawrou/Shutterstock | p228 top © Zoltan Gabor, bottom © donsimon/Shutterstock | p230 © Stephen Finn/Shutterstock | p234 top left © Alexey Fedorenko/Shutterstock, bottom © Kiev.Victor/Shutterstock | p237 top left © Anthony Shaw Photography/Shutterstock, top right © Ron Ellis/Shutterstock, bottom © Claudio Divizia/Shutterstock | p238 © Valerija Polakovska/Shutterstock | p240 top © IR Stone/Shutterstock | p242 © lazyllama/Shutterstock | p246 © Balakate/Shutterstock | p249 top left © Neil Lang/Shutterstock, top right © Peter Moulton/Shutterstock, bottom © Valdis Skudre/Shutterstock | p250 top © Christophe Cappelli/Shutterstock

Acknowledgements

Dedication: To my Uncle Alan, who was an ardent urban rambler long before the term was coined
Urbanrambles.org website: Annie Britton (Scottish cities)
Helpful advice: John Hudson, Historic England; Tony Morris, Oxford; Joan Rudd-Jones, topography
Regular walking companions: Oliver Quick, Peter Raffan, David & Sam Rudd-Jones, Mark Sutcliffe

Urban Rambles
© 2018 Quarto Publishing plc.
Text © Nicholas Rudd-Jones, 2018
Photographs as listed above
Cover & interior illustration © Sara Mulvanny / agencyrush.com
Design: Sarah Allberrey

First published in 2018 by Frances Lincoln, an imprint of
The Quarto Group. The Old Brewery, 6 Blundell Street,
London N7 9BH, United Kingdom www.QuartoKnows.com

A catalogue record for this book is available from the British Library.

ISBN 978-0-7112-3974-6
Printed and bound in China
9 8 7 6 5 4 3 2

Brimming with creative inspiration, how-to projects
and useful information to enrich your everyday life,
Quarto Knows is a favourite destination for those
pursuing their interests and passions. Visit our site
and dig deeper with our books into your area of
interest: Quarto Creates, Quarto Cooks, Quarto
Homes, Quarto Lives, Quarto Drives, Quarto
Explores, Quarto Gifts, or Quarto Kids.

MIX
Paper from
responsible sources
FSC® C017606
www.fsc.org